IMAGES
of America

ONTARIO

JoAnn Meaker

ARCADIA
PUBLISHING

ISBN 978-0-7385-5034-3

Published by Arcadia Publishing
Charleston, South Carolina

Printed in the United States of America

Library of Congress Catalog Card Number: 2007922176

For all general information contact Arcadia Publishing at:
Telephone 843-853-2070
Fax 843-853-0044
E-mail sales@arcadiapublishing.com
For customer service and orders:
Toll-Free 1-888-313-2665

Visit us on the Internet at www.arcadiapublishing.com

To all those who have guided me in learning our town's history.

IMAGES
of America

ONTARIO

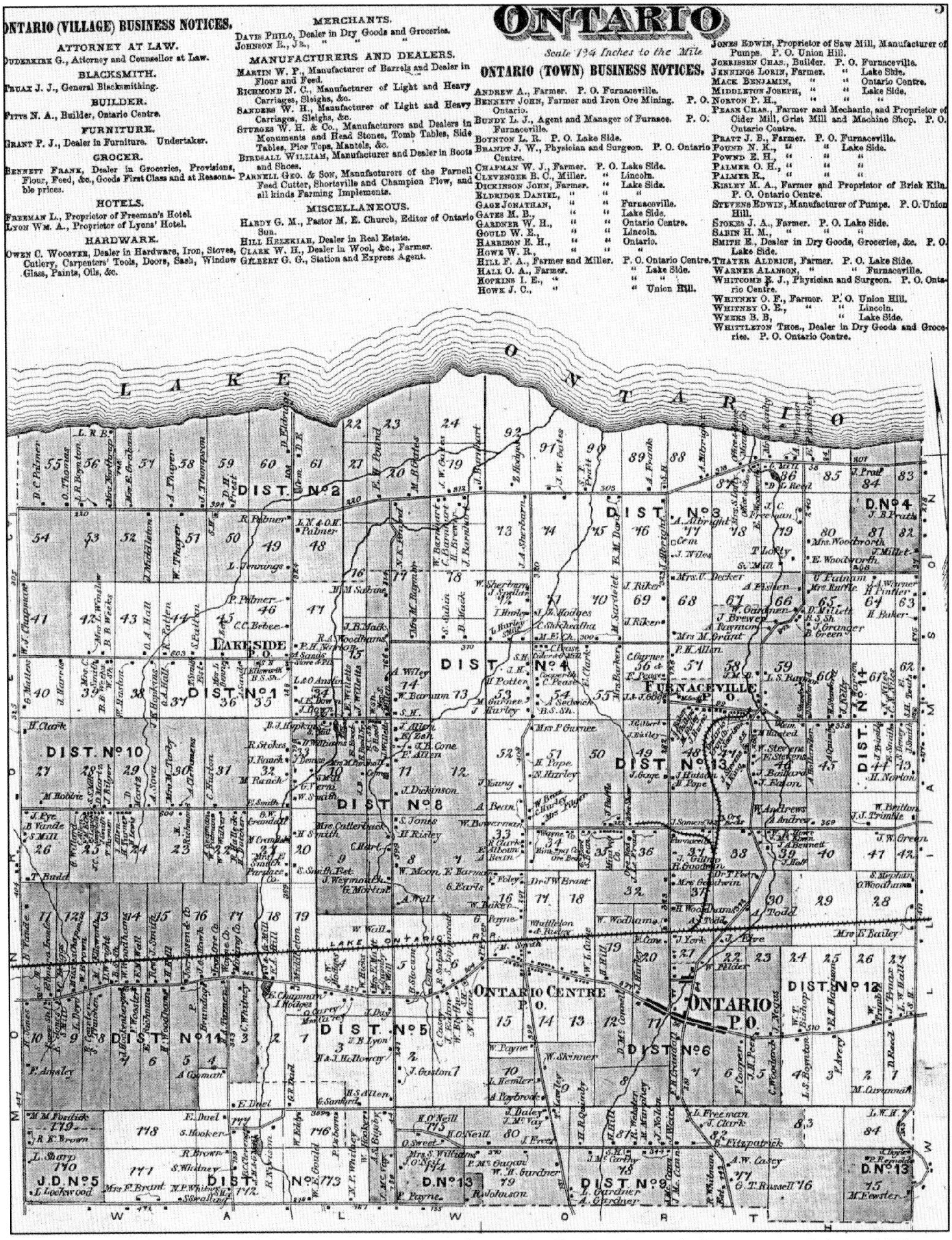

This map of the town of Ontario was taken from D. G. Beer's and Company *Atlas of Wayne County New York, 1874*. The town is bordered by Lake Ontario to the north, Williamson to the east, Webster to the west, and Walworth to the south.

On the cover: This photograph, taken in 1900, is looking east at the corner of Main Street and Furnace/Walworth Road. The first building on the left is the Owen Tin Shop, followed by the residence of T. J. Peer. Main Street was paved in 1912. (Courtesy of Liz Albright.)

Contents

ACKNOWLEDGMENTS

This book would not have been possible without the foundation of work that was done by prior town historians Frank Pratt (1930) and Mabelle Davis (1952–1955). A special note of appreciation goes to Augusta Trimble, Ontario town historian from 1956 to 1969 and to Virginia Scully Hill, Ontario town historian from 1970 to 1998. Through their efforts, the townspeople contributed photographs and their memories.

I am also deeply indebted to Liz Albright, the current Ontario town historian, whose assistance with historic details and encouragement were invaluable.

The photographs selected for this book come from the archives of the Town of Ontario Historical and Landmark Preservation Society and from the collection of the town historian. Many of the photographs were taken by photographer Norman Harris, who donated them to the historian's office and to the historical society. Other photographs were donated by Marian Wulfert and Helen Bowles from their personal collection of family photographs.

I would like to thank my editor, Pam O'Neil, for her enthusiastic support of this project.

Finally I would like to thank my husband, Norman, whose continuous love and support enables me to complete projects such as this. Little did he know that day 10 years ago, when he took me on a walk through the nature trails of Ginna Station, that we would come across the manor house there and my enthusiasm for knowing the town's history would come alive.

INTRODUCTION

Towns draw their history from many contributing factors—people, places, and events. In addition to all of these, Ontario has one more—water! In all forms, water has helped contribute to the town's past, from the ice ages of 10,000 years ago, to the Great Lake on its northern boundary, to the small streams that cross the landscape.

The last glacier covered New York State to a depth of about a mile. This slow-moving layer of ice gouged and smoothed the landscape, leaving behind a variety of glacial evidence. Stretching 150 miles from Sodus to Niagara Falls is evidence of Lake Ontario's previous southern shore, once known as Alluvial Way, now called Ridge Road. This road, also known as the longest Main Street in New York State, began as a Native American trail. During the War of 1812, it was improved with bridges, making it suitable for a military highway. After the war, the state approved $5,000 to make it a passable wagon road. By 1825, stagecoach routes were established, and in the early 1900s, a trolley rolled down the street.

The glacier left behind soil that was enriched, making it suitable for farming. The ground provided some surprises with the discovery of iron ore. Lake Ontario modified the climate, helping with the growing season for the fruit grown here. All of which led to the development of both agriculture and industry within the town.

Found in the fields and along the lakeshore are small stones, called cobblestones. Rounded by the action of the glacier moving across the landscape, these were used by masons to build uniquely designed cobblestone houses. Ninety percent of cobblestone houses are located within a 60-mile radius of Rochester and were built between 1825 and 1860. There are 12 such houses in Ontario.

As the glacier retreated northward, the land rebounded upward about 250 feet, draining the land into Lake Ontario. In Ontario, Bear Creek, Deer Creek, and Davis Creek flow north into the lake. It was along these creeks that many settlers built their mills.

Before the first settlers could arrive, however, ownership of the land had to be settled. Both Massachusetts and New York claimed the land in western New York. It was not until 1788 that Massachusetts agreed to sell about six million acres of land to Oliver Phelps and Nathaniel Gorham. The other issue of ownership had to be resolved with the Iroquois Nation, which also claimed this region. Phelps and Gorham met with representatives of the Six Nations at Buffalo Creek in July 1788, and an agreement was made for 2.6 million acres. The area from Lake Ontario to the Pennsylvania border and from Pre-Emption Line west to the Genesee River became known as the Phelps and Gorham Purchase. Ontario is known as Township 13 and 14 in the Third Range containing 19,171 acres, about 10 miles north to south and six miles east to west.

The first of the settlers was Freeman Hopkins, who arrived with his family in the spring of 1806 from New England. He built a log cabin on the lakeshore and the town's first sawmill. Ontario, still a part of Williamson at the time, separated on March 27, 1807, and was then called Freetown. The following year, on February 12, 1808, the town's name was changed to Ontario. It originally included Walworth, which separated from Ontario on April 20, 1829.

Other early settlers are credited with being "the first" in Ontario. Peter Thatcher, who arrived in 1807, was the first blacksmith and built his log shop near his home in 1811. Also in 1807, Daniel Inman purchased 400 acres where Ontario Village now stands. He built a steam sawmill and the town's first tavern. He was also the first postmaster in town. Dr. William Greenwood was the first physician in the village, arriving in 1811 and practicing until his death in 1829. William Middleton purchased 300 acres of land on the lakeshore in 1810 and became the first hatter. Nathan Hallock was the first tailor. The first gristmill was built in 1825 by Henry Barnhart. After Walworth separated from Ontario, John Stolph was the first clerk of the township. The first store was opened in 1830 by Henry S. Gilbert. The first schoolhouse was a log structure built around 1816 on the lake road. The first church, the Methodist Episcopal church, was organized in 1812. Its first meetings were held at the home of Zebedee Hodges.

Smaller hamlets developed within the town—most of them postal centers of their time. Ontario Village lies on Ridge Road and was originally settled in 1807 by Daniel Inman. Ontario Center is situated on Ridge Road about a mile west of Ontario Village. Union Hill straddles the border of the town with Webster. Fruitland was about two miles west of Ontario Center. Lakeside was two and a half miles north of Fruitland. Furnaceville, situated near the lake, took its name from the blast furnace that operated there from 1825 to 1887. New Boston was a hamlet on the lakeshore. These last four no longer exist.

Industries developed quickly in the town, even before agriculture. In an area that was so densely wooded, the land needed to be cleared in order to farm. Sawmills, blacksmithing, and the making of pearl ash, potash, and charcoal all developed due to the abundance of trees. Bricks were made in the area, with several local homes and a church built using these bricks.

In 1810, Noah Fuller was hunting in the area along the lakeshore and found two salt springs. After securing the title, he sold the rights to Stimson and Schanks and salt was manufactured for several years, until it became no longer profitable.

In 1811, a Mr. Knickerbocker discovered a bed of iron ore while digging a well near the center of town. Several years later Samuel Smith constructed a forge and began manufacturing iron at a rate of 400 pounds per year. Soon after two more forges were built. In 1825, Henry S. Gilbert built the first furnace at Furnaceville and generated three to four tons daily. By 1870 the Ontario Iron Company was organized. It had two blast furnaces and two blooming tubes and generated 20 tons per day. By 1890, the ore was getting more and more difficult to mine and the Mesabi Range was discovered in Minnesota. Gradually the mining stopped, the furnace was shut down. Now the only evidence of this once-bustling industry are the water-filled ore beds of the town's Casey Park and some bright red soil along Kenyon Road.

In the late 1960s, a more modern industry came to Ontario. The Ginna Nuclear Power Plant, built by Rochester Gas and Electric and nestled within an apple orchard on the old Smoky Point Farm, began operation in 1969.

Ontario continues to be a town with a rural feel, a mix of open land, farming, and industry—a balance between apples and atoms—a community of good neighbors. As we celebrate the town's bicentennial, through these pages of historic photographs, we glance into the past preserved for the future.

One

Founding Families

Many of the first families to arrive in Ontario came by wagon bringing very little with them. They had to contend with Native Americans, bears and wolves, and illnesses of fever and malaria. As they settled into their new homes, they established farms and businesses. Their stories of hardship, of the trials of building homes, and of creating new lives are captured here.

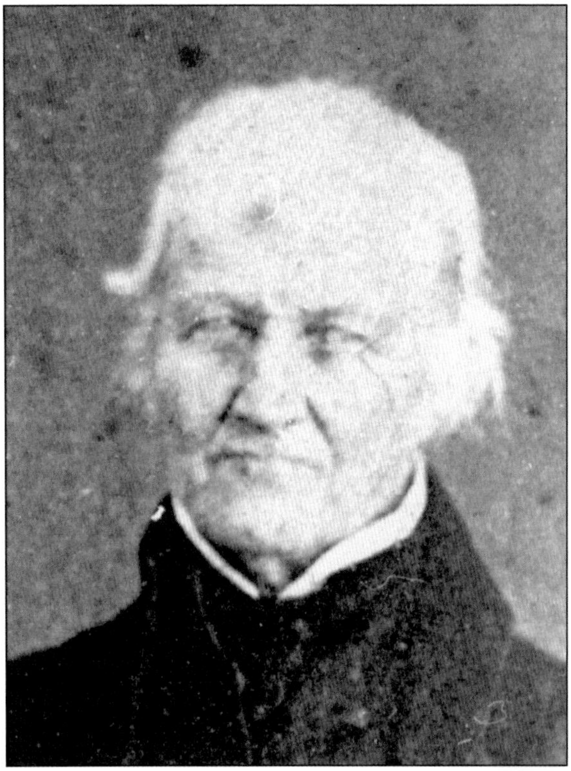

Freeman Hopkins came to Ontario with his family in the spring of 1806 and is noted as the first settler of Ontario. Hopkins was a Quaker (also known as the Society of Friends). Because this religion has a testimony against participation in wars, Hopkins left the area during the War of 1812 and returned when the war ended.

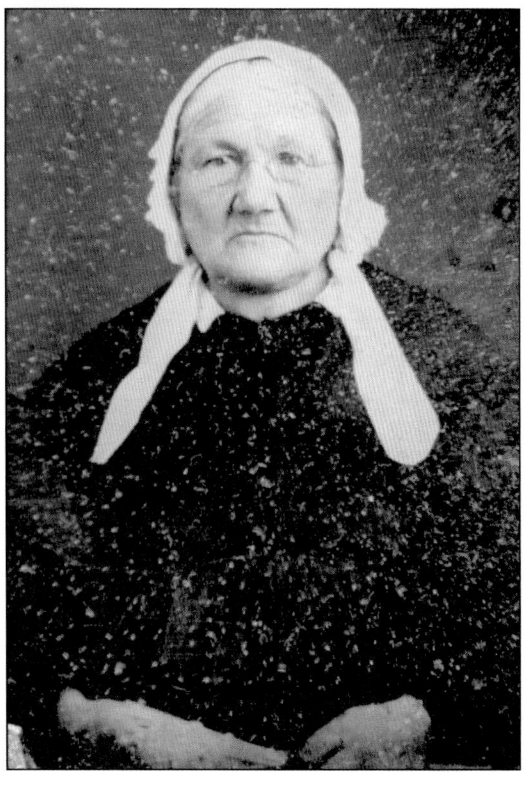

Martha was the wife of Freeman Hopkins. Their children were Alonzo, Melissa, Emma, Julia, Enos, Lucy, Mary, Hannah, Charles Patterson, Mark, and Harriet.

This letter was written by Ira and Emma Shutt from Mount Washington. Dated May 29, 1837, it was sent to Freeman and Martha with news of Charles Patterson, Martha's father. In part it says, "Brother and Sister Hopkins. Duty binds me to write a few lines to you to let you know of our welfare here. I must unfold a tale which you have perhaps long expected to hear. We are worn down with sorrow and afflictions and hope you will sympathize with us when these lines bring you the tiding that Father is no more."

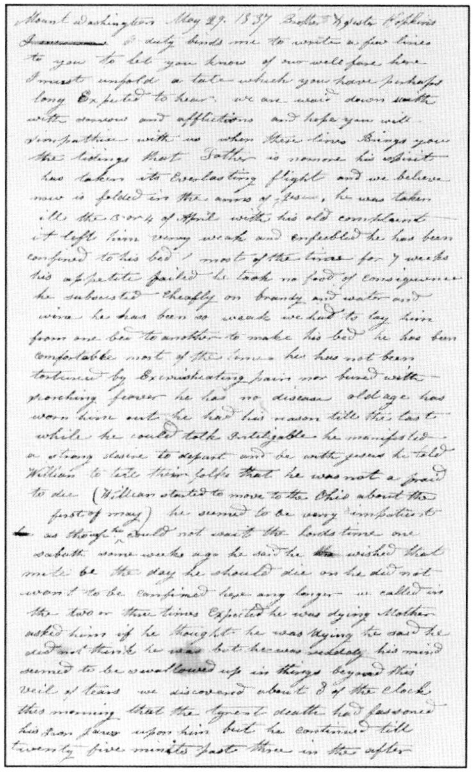

Mount Washington May 29. 1837 Brother & Sister Hopkins
[illegible] duty binds me to write a few lines
to you to let you know of our welfare here
I must unfold a tale which you have perhaps
long Expected to hear we are worn down with
with sorrow and afflictions and hope you will
sympathise with us when these lines Brings you
the tidings that Father is no more his spirit
has taken its Everlasting flight and we believe
now is folded in the arms of Jesus, he was taken
ill the 3 or 4 of April with his old complaint
it left him very weak and enfeebled he has been
confined to his bed most of the time for 7 weeks
his appetite failed he took no food of consequence
he subsisted chiefly on brandy and water and
wine he has been so weak we had to lay him
from one bed to another to make his bed he has been
comfortable most of the time he has not been
tortured by Excruciating pain nor burned with
scorching fever he had no disease old age has
worn him out he had his reason till the last
while he could talk intelligable he manifested
a strong desire to depart and be with Jesus he told
William to tell their folks that he was not afraid
to die (William started to move to the Ohio about the
first of may) he seemed to be very impatient
as though he could not wait the lords time one
sabbath some weeks ago he said he wished that
might be the day he should die as he did not
want to be confined here any longer we called in
the two or three times Expected he was dying Mother
asked him if he thought he was dying he said he
did not think he was but he was [illegible] his mind
seemed to be swallowed up in things beyond this
veil of tears we discovered about 8 of the clock
this morning that the tyrant death had fastened
his [illegible] upon him but he continued till
twenty five minits past three in the after

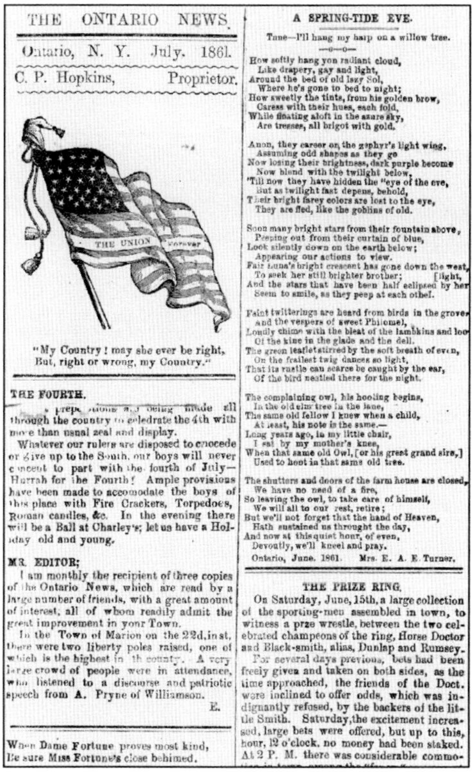

THE ONTARIO NEWS.

Ontario, N. Y. July. 1861.

C. P. Hopkins, Proprietor.

"My Country! may she ever be right,
But, right or wrong, my Country."

THE FOURTH.

[illegible] preparations are being made all through the country to celedrate the 4th with more than usual zeal and display.

Whatever our rulers are disposed to concede or give up to the South, our boys will never consent to part with the fourth of July—Hurrah for the Fourth! Ample provisions have been made to accomodate the boys of this place with Fire Crackers, Torpedoes, Roman candles, &c. In the evening there will be a Ball at Charley's; let us have a Holiday old and young.

MR. EDITOR;

I am monthly the recipient of three copies of the Ontario News, which are read by a large number of friends, with a great amount of interest, all of whom readily admit the great improvement in your Town.

In the Town of Marion on the 22d, inst, there were two liberty poles raised, one of which is the highest in th county. A very large crowd of people were in attendance, who listened to a discourse and patriotic speech from A. Pryne of Williamson.

E.

When Dame Fortune proves most kind,
Be sure Miss Fortune's close behimed.

A SPRING-TIDE EVE.

Tune—I'll hang my harp on a willow tree.

—o—o—

How softly hang yon radiant cloud,
Like drapery, gay and light,
Around the bed of old lazy Sol,
Where he's gone to bed to night;
How sweetly the tints, from his golden brow,
Caress with their hues, each fold,
While floating aloft in the azure sky,
Are tresses, all brigot with gold.

Anon, they career on the zephyr's light wing,
Assuming odd shapes as they go
Now losing their brightness, dark purple become
Now blend with the twilight below,
'Till now they have hidden the "eye of the eve,
But as twilight fast depens, behold,
Their bright farey colors are lost to the eye,
They are fled, like the goblins of old.

Soon many bright stars from their fountain above,
Peeping out from their curtain of blue,
Look silently down on the earth below;
Appearing our actions to view.
Fair Luna's bright crescent has gone down the west,
To seek her still brighter brother; [light,
And the stars that have been half eclipsed by her
Seem to smile, as they peep at each othel.

Faint twitterings are heard from birds in the grove
and the vespers of sweet Philomel,
Loudly chime with the bleat of the lambkins and low
Of the kine in the glade and the dell.
The green leaflet stirred by the soft breath of even,
On the frailest twig dances so light,
That its rustle can scarce be caught by the ear,
Of the bird nestled there for the night.

The complaining owl, his hooting begins,
In the old elm tree in the lane,
The same old fellow I knew when a child,
At least, his note is the same.—
Long years ago, in my little chair,
I sat by my mother's knee,
When that same old Owl, [or his great grand sire,]
Used to hoot in that same old tree.

The shutters and doors of the farm house are closed,
We have no need of a fire,
So leaving the owl, to take care of himself,
We will all to our rest, retire;
But we'll not forget that the hand of Heaven,
Hath sustained us throught the day,
And now at this quiet hour, of even,
Devoutly, we'll kneel and pray.

Ontario, June. 1861. Mrs. E. A. E. Turner.

THE PRIZE RING.

On Saturday, June, 15th, a large collection of the sporting-men assembled in town, to witness a prze wrestle, between the two celebrated champeons of the ring, Horse Doctor and Black-smith, alias, Dunlap and Rumsey.

For several days previous, bets had been freely given and taken on both sides, as the time approached, the friends of the Doct. were inclined to offer odds, which was indignantly refused, by the backers of the little Smith. Saturday, the excitement increased, large bets were offered, but up to this, hour, 12 o'clock, no money had been staked. At 2 P. M. there was considerable commo-

The *Ontario News* was published by Charles Patterson Hopkins, son of Freeman. The article "The Prize Ring" announced, "On Saturday, June 15th, a large collection of the sporting men assembled in town to witness a prize wrestle, between the two celebrated champions of the ring, Horse Doctor and Blacksmith, alias Dunlap and Rumsey."

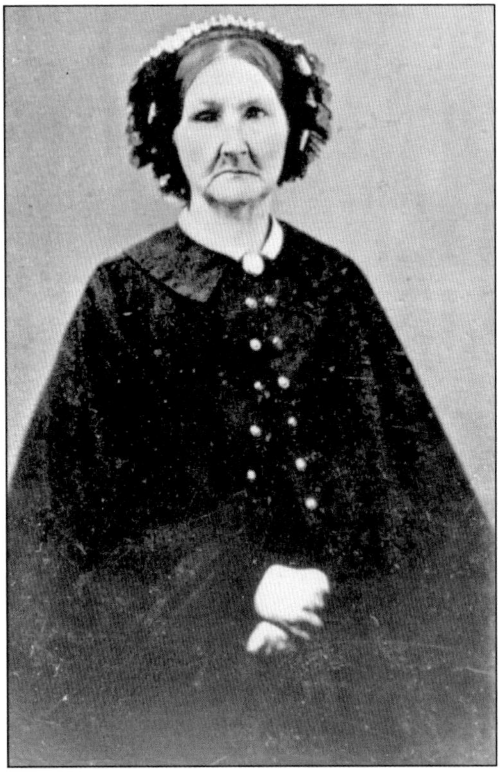

Melissa Hopkins, daughter of Freeman and Martha Hopkins, is known as the first child born in Ontario. She was born on May 7, 1806.

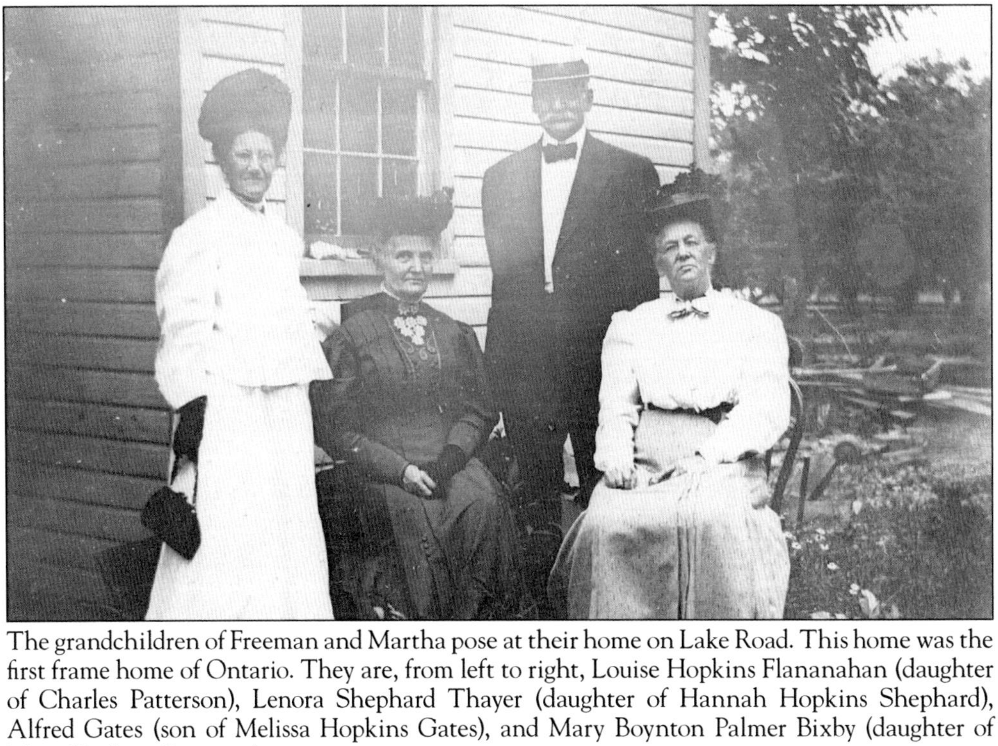

The grandchildren of Freeman and Martha pose at their home on Lake Road. This home was the first frame home of Ontario. They are, from left to right, Louise Hopkins Flananahan (daughter of Charles Patterson), Lenora Shephard Thayer (daughter of Hannah Hopkins Shephard), Alfred Gates (son of Melissa Hopkins Gates), and Mary Boynton Palmer Bixby (daughter of Mary Hopkins Boynton).

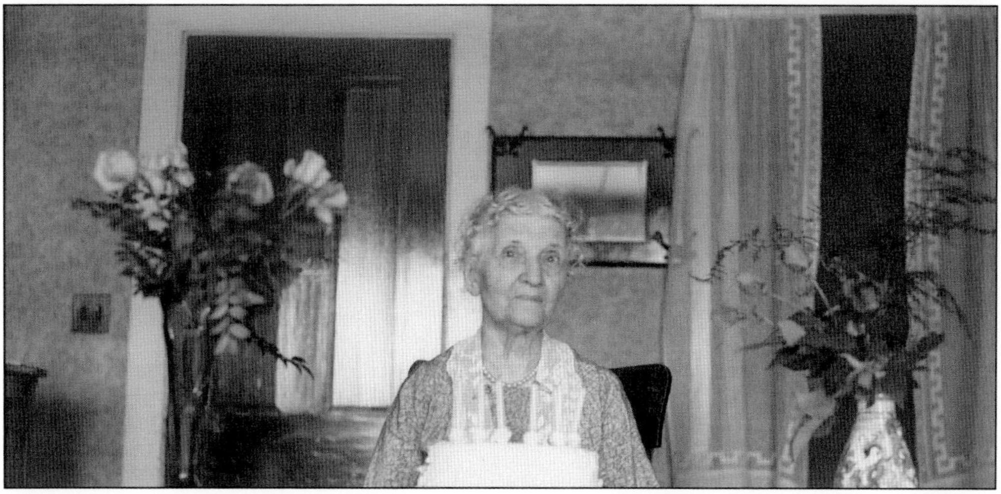

This photograph was taken in 1936. It shows Lenora Shephard Thayer (wife of William Thayer) celebrating her 87th birthday. Unfortunately, it was her last. She was a granddaughter of Freeman Hopkins.

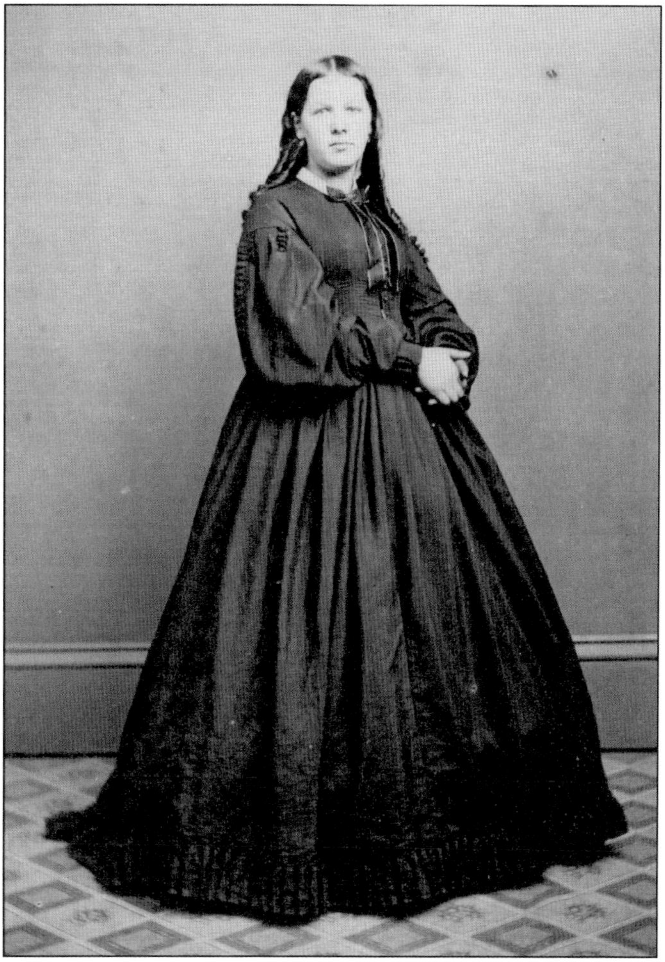

Mary Boynton Palmer Bixby was the daughter of Lorenzo Boynton and Mary Hopkins. She married Oliver Hazard Palmer in 1864. He was a general in the Civil War. Together they bought a 200-acre farm on Lakeside Road.

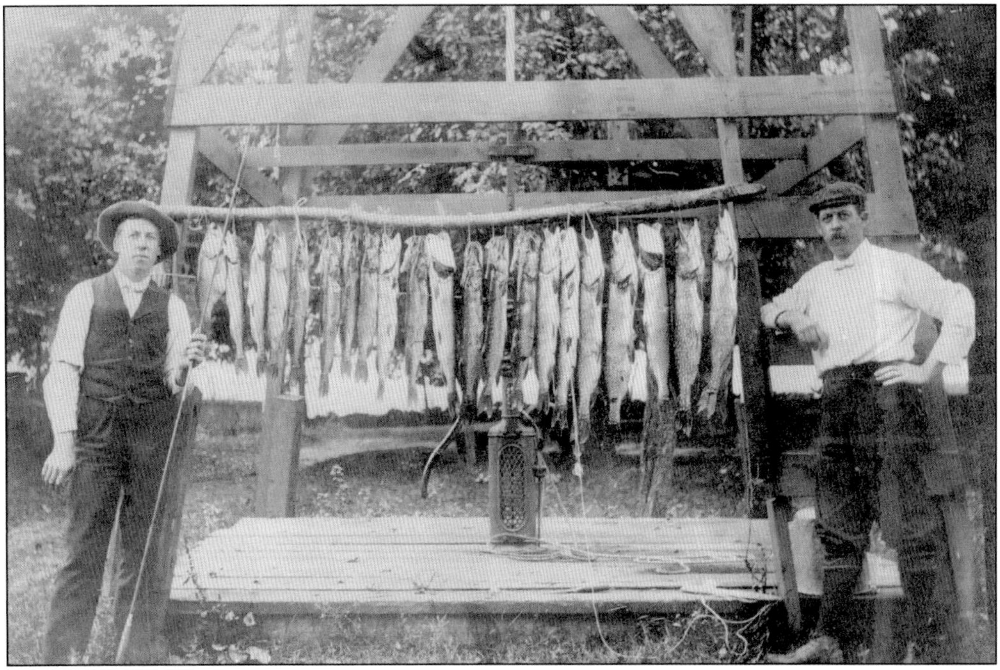

Byron Wilbur Palmer (left) and Dr. John Boynton Palmer are sons of Mary Boynton Palmer Bixby. They are showing off the results of their fishing from Lake Ontario. The fish are hanging on an old windmill on Lakeside Road.

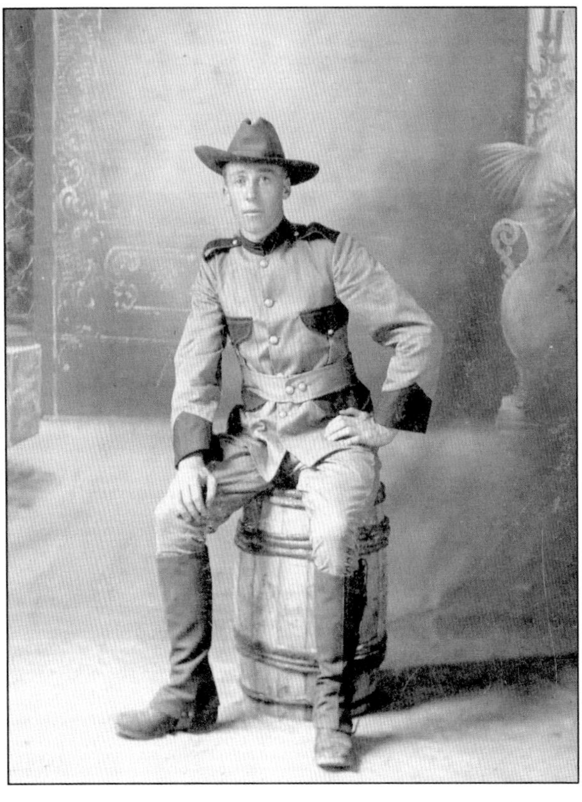

Byron enlisted in the Spanish-American War in 1898. He was a member of the Battery A Light Horse Artillery. He was stationed in Cuba and was honorably discharged. He then continued his college education and became a dentist.

Oscar Palmer was born in Ontario on May 5, 1844. He was a teacher, a store owner in Lakeside, and then a fruit farmer. He was also a soldier in the Civil War in the 8th New York Cavalry, from 1864 to the end of the war. He fought in Sheridan's division under Gen. George Armstrong Custer and was wounded at Five Forks. His uniform, complete with a bullet hole, is on display at the Meeting House at Heritage Square Museum.

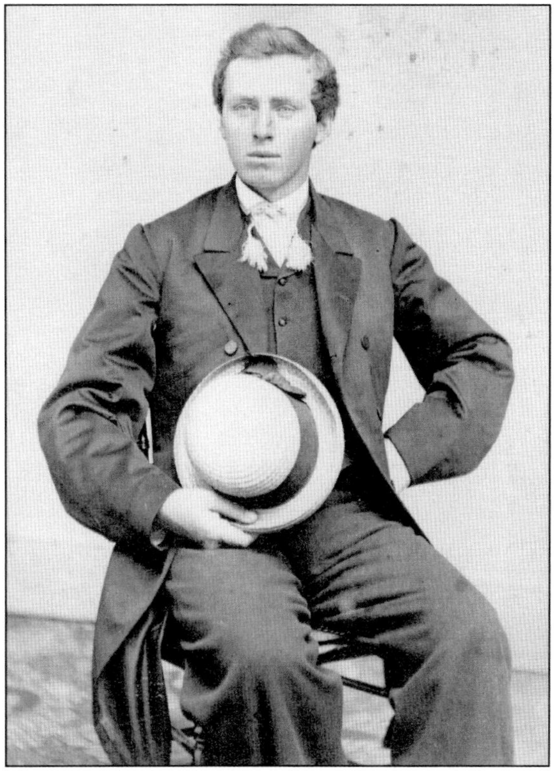

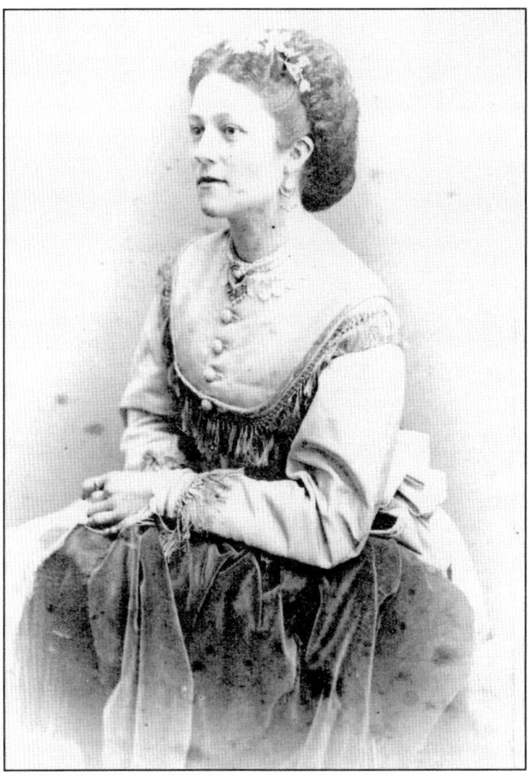

Amelia "Millie" Botsford Palmer was from Webster and was the wife of Oscar. They were married sometime between 1868 and 1870.

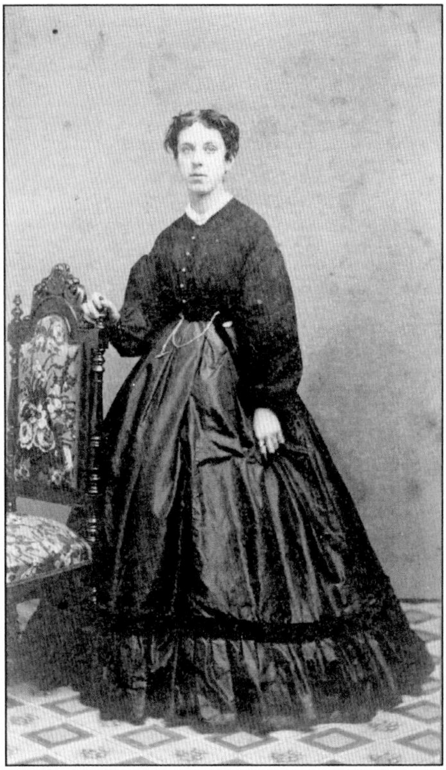

Addie Palmer contracted pneumonia while attending school in Rochester. She died in 1865 at the age of 18.

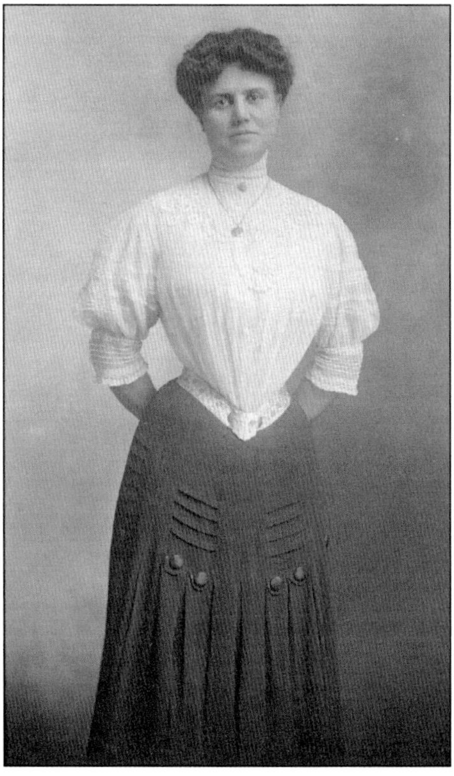

Florence Pease Underhill is the daughter of C. Wesley Pease and Alma Giberson, granddaughter of Charles W. Pease and great-granddaughter of Abel Pease. Abel arrived in Ontario in 1834. He purchased 50 acres and built a log cabin. In 1839, he and his son Charles built the first frame house between Ridge Road and the lake. Charles helped his son Franklin invent the Pease power slicer, root and apple cutters, and apple corers. Franklin started the F. B. Pease Company in 1895. It still exists in Henrietta. The apple slicer can be seen on display in the apple dry house at Heritage Square Museum. Florence worked in the bank, helping children start accounts. She also wrote poetry, which was set to music written by her husband, Leon Underhill.

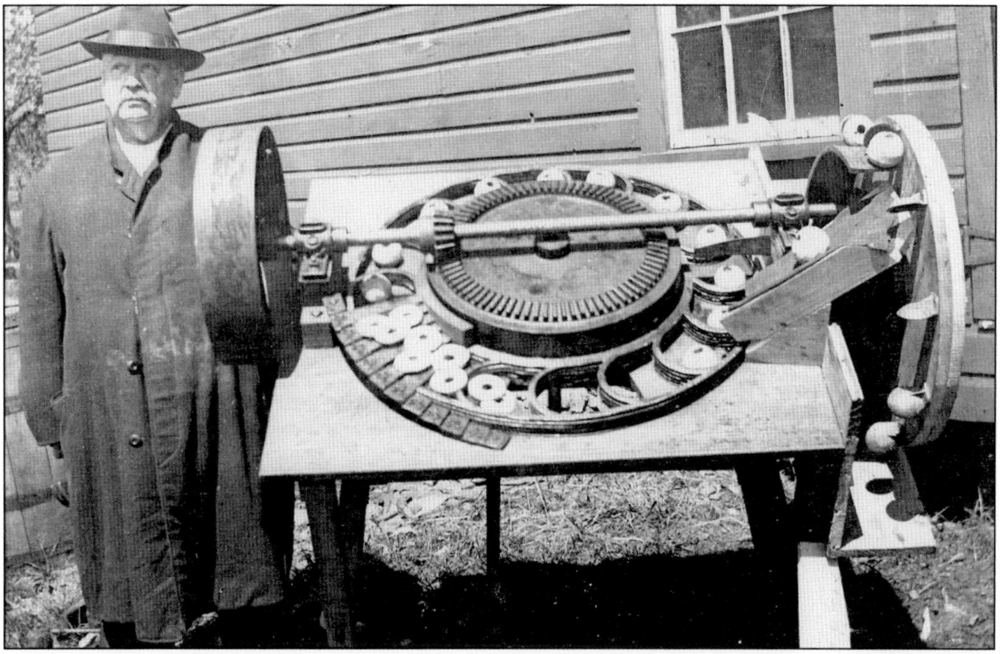

The daughter of Charles Pease, Celinda married Isaac Hurley. On December 18, 1891, Hurley purchased Edwin Church's patent rights for an apple slicer invention. Hurley went on to invent other improvements and received a patent for "Motors" on December 9, 1913, and a patent for "Holders" on June 9, 1916.

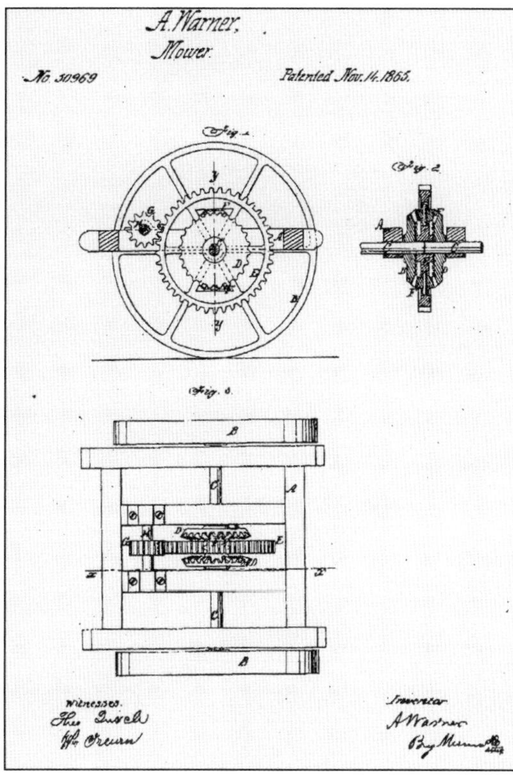

Alanson Warner was also a noted inventor of Ontario. This diagram of a differential, an improvement in gearing for harvesters, is taken from his patent application dated November 14, 1865. The differential is a device that allows one wheel to turn faster than the other. Alanson sold his patent for only $16.

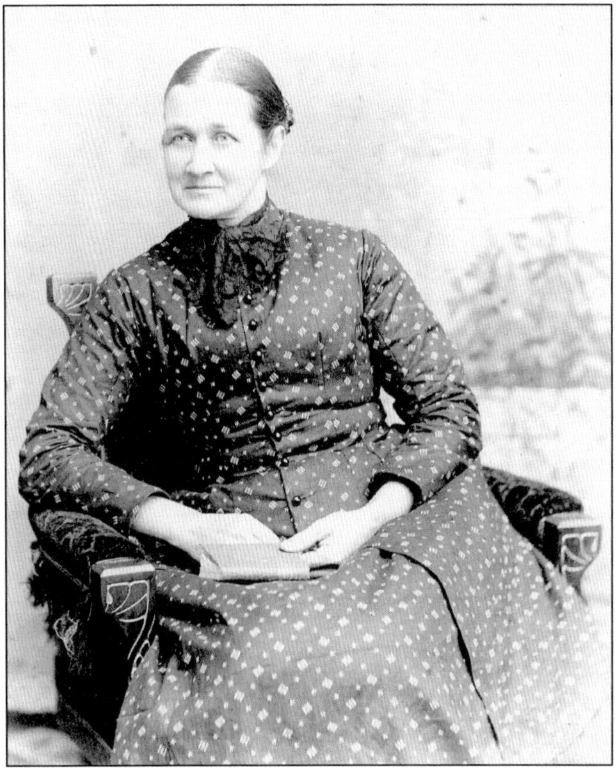

Fannie Woodhams, a native of England, married James E. Eaton in 1851. They bought land on Furnace Road and had a family of 12 children. Five of the children died at an early age, but the others survived so that today there are over 30 family names that can trace their ancestry to these two people.

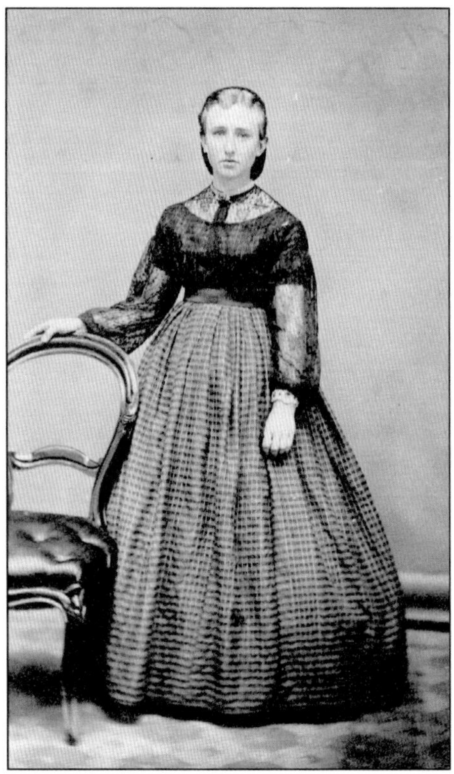

This photograph of Nettie Miller was taken in 1864. She is wearing clothing typical to the period. Skirts were very wide and oval in shape. The bodices had sleeves that were off the shoulder. In 1864, crinolines were shaped so that most of the fullness was in the back.

Dr. John Selden Brandt was born in Ontario on February 15, 1856. He was the son of J. W. Brandt, who was a surgeon in the Civil War. He married Katherine Maher and was an Ontario physician for over 50 years. He was also Ontario's town supervisor for seven years. He died at the age of 75 in 1931.

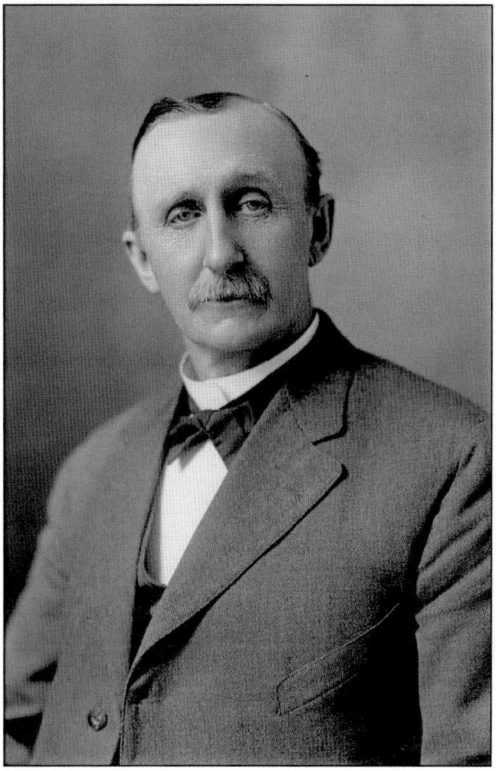

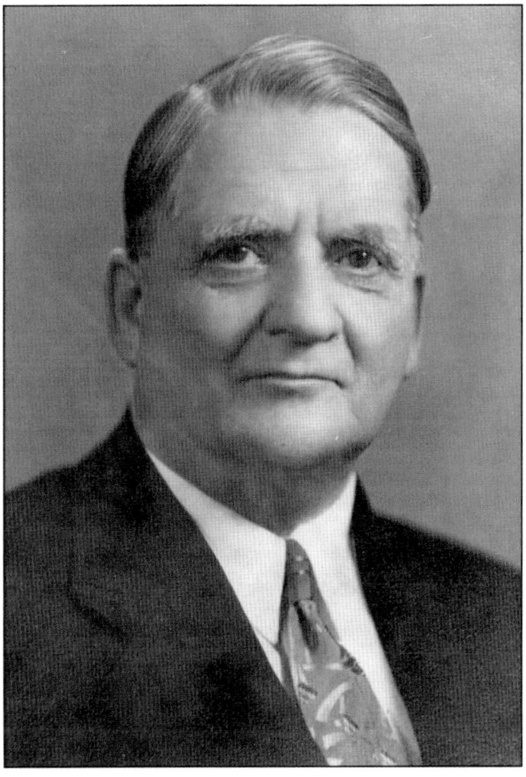

Dr. Floyd C. Thompson was born in Williamson and graduated from the Ontario High School as a member of the first graduating class in June 1897. He taught school for several years and then went to the Homeopathic College in Cleveland. He built a home on Mill Street (now Knickerbocker Road) and began his practice in 1905. It would take him five hours to make the round trip to visit his Williamson patients.

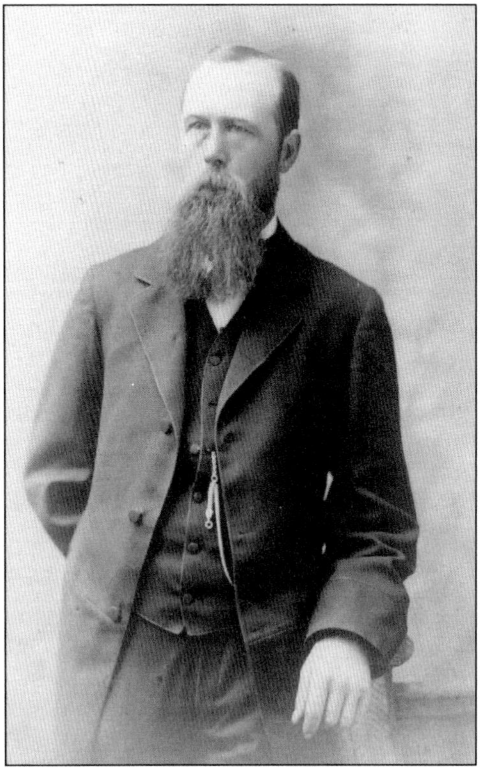

John Henry Albright was born in 1846 and married Joanna Johnson in 1874. He owned a 250-acre farm and was the first farmer in the area to propagate Niagara grapes. He had one child, Johnson Stanley, who was a prominent attorney both locally and in Rochester. Johnson Stanley married Zella Clark. They had one son, James K., who was also an attorney. James K. married Barbara, and they had three children. Their son Johnson and their granddaughter Christine are lawyers today.

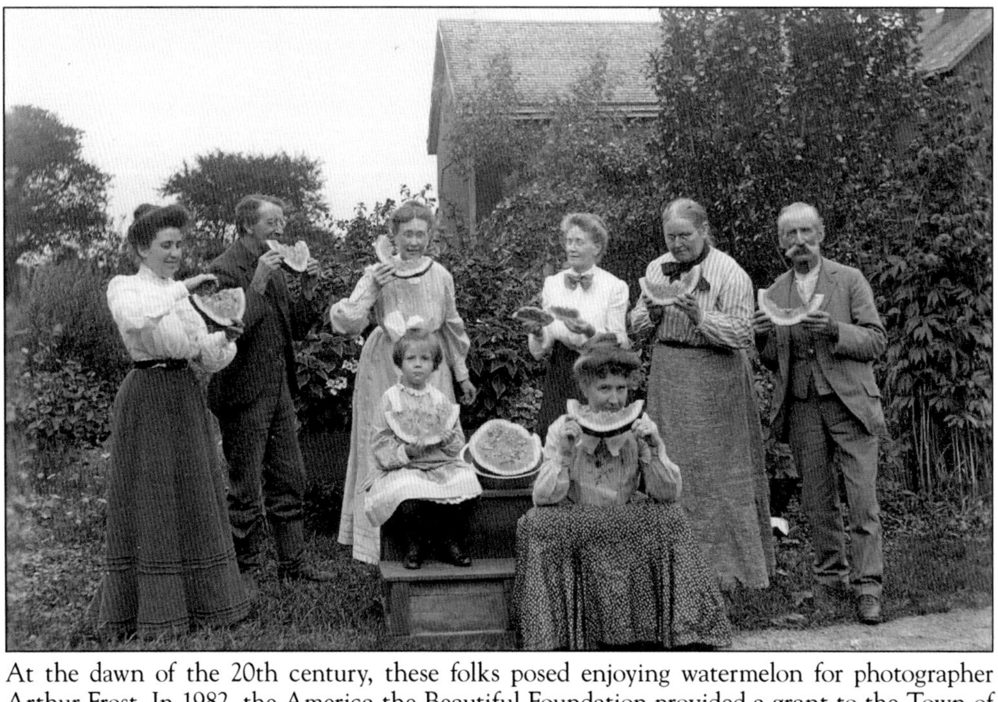

At the dawn of the 20th century, these folks posed enjoying watermelon for photographer Arthur Frost. In 1982, the America the Beautiful Foundation provided a grant to the Town of Ontario Historical and Landmark Preservation Society to produce a slide documentary from Frost's glass plate negatives.

Two

FARMING THE LAND

Farms, both large and small, were found all around the town in its early history. Many new residents came to start farms, or bought existing ones. Farming included the growing of fruits and vegetables and the raising of dairy cattle and other animals. Even though many of these farms are no longer being worked today, the remaining barns and smaller outbuildings remind one of the past.

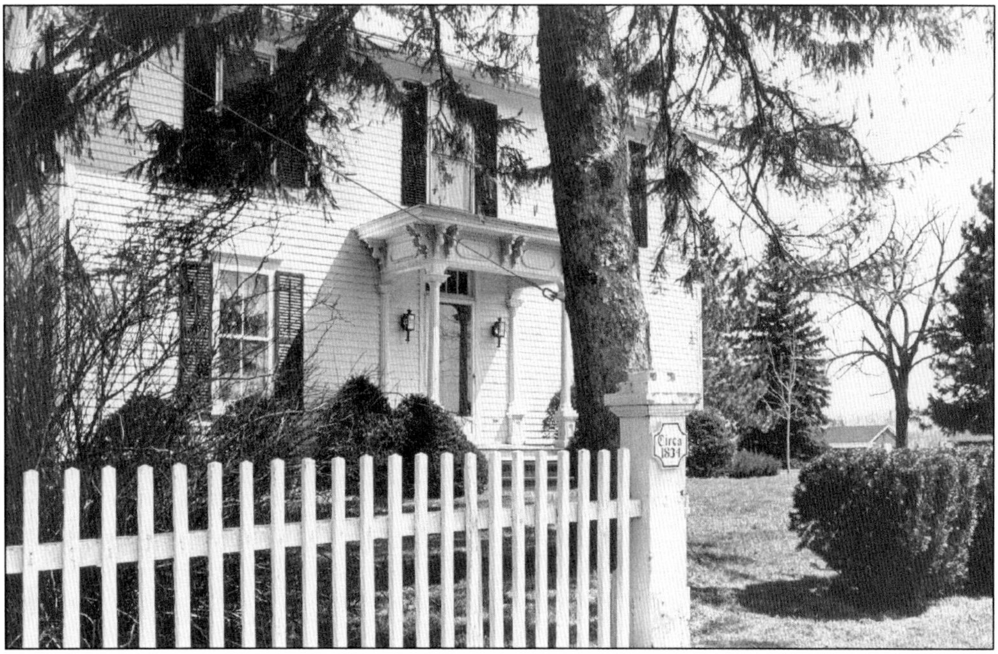

Shown above and below is the Pease Homestead, located at 1568 Brick Church Road. Abel Pease came to Ontario in 1834 and purchased a 50-acre farm for $800. Early maps show that this farm had a steam sawmill and that there was a cider mill as well. Pease and his son Charles built a log cabin as their first house. They built this Italianate-style frame home in 1839. It was the first frame home to be built between Ridge Road and Lake Ontario. It was modernized in 1874. In the dining room there is a sculptured ceiling medallion made for the Pease family by a traveling artist as payment for staying overnight. The handrail and balusters for the open staircase were made by Charles. Pease built an informal post office box in his house so his neighbors would not have to travel to the nearest post offices, which were at Lakeside and Ontario Center.

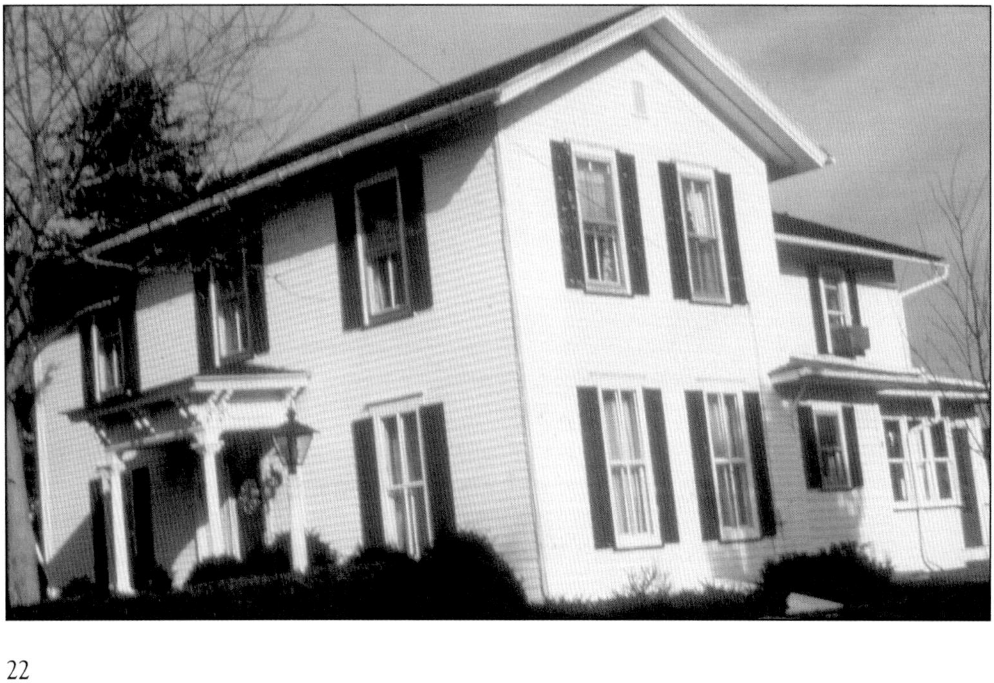

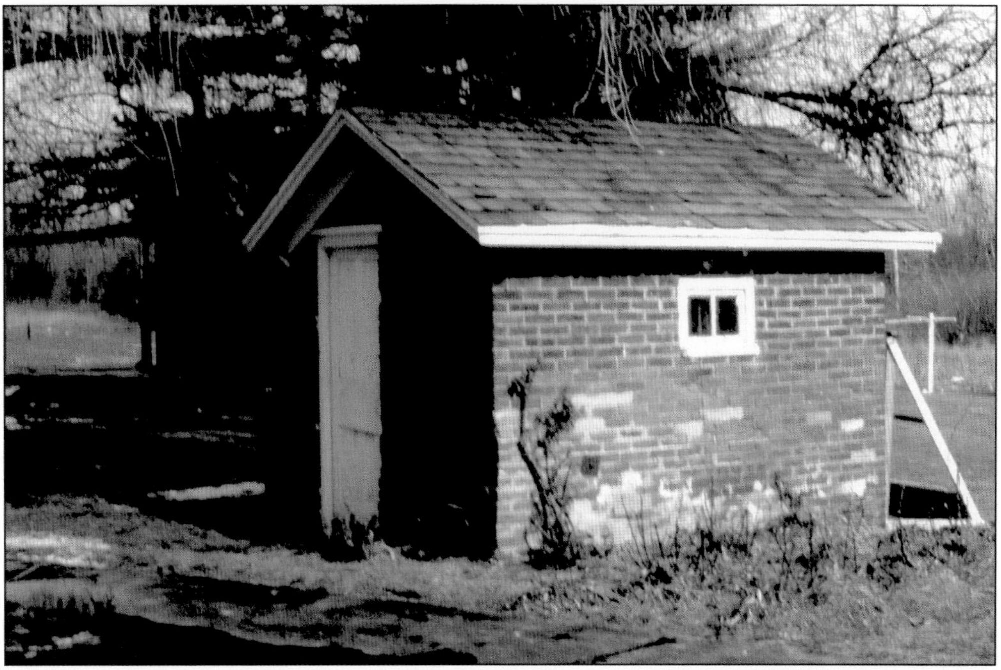

The smokehouse was used to smoke butchered meat. It was made of brick from local clay deposits. Smoking meat involved hanging the meat so no two pieces touched. A fire was built that maintained the ideal temperature of 80 to 90 degrees Fahrenheit. It usually took two days to smoke the meat. A ham could be kept for six months by smoking it.

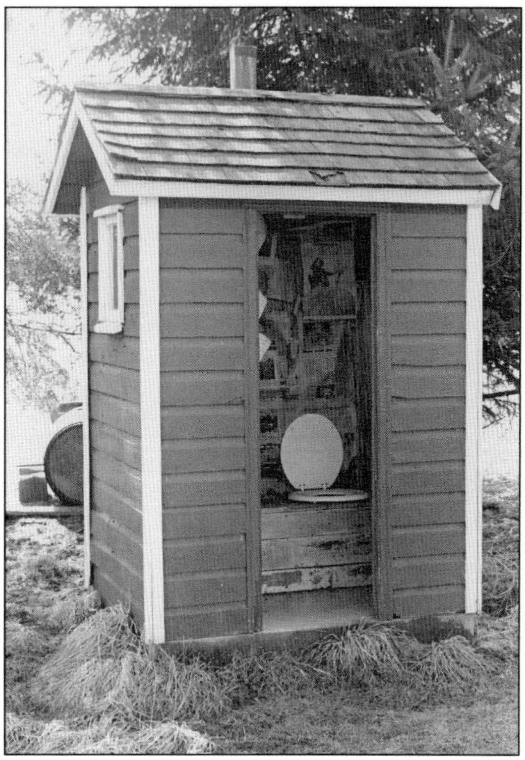

An outhouse was essential in early days since there was no indoor plumbing. Usually these consisted of a hole in the ground covered by a bench with a seat in it. There was no toilet paper at the time. Crumbled up paper, sometimes pages torn from an old catalog, or leaves were used instead. This outhouse is at the Pease farm.

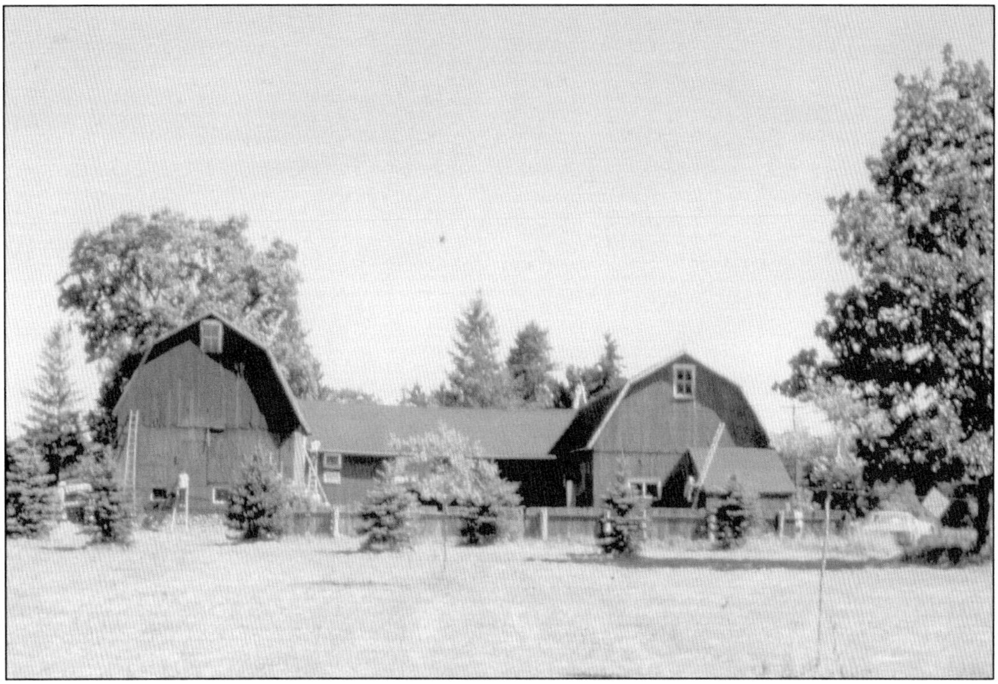

The unusual double barns at the Pease farm housed not only animals and their feed but important farm equipment as well.

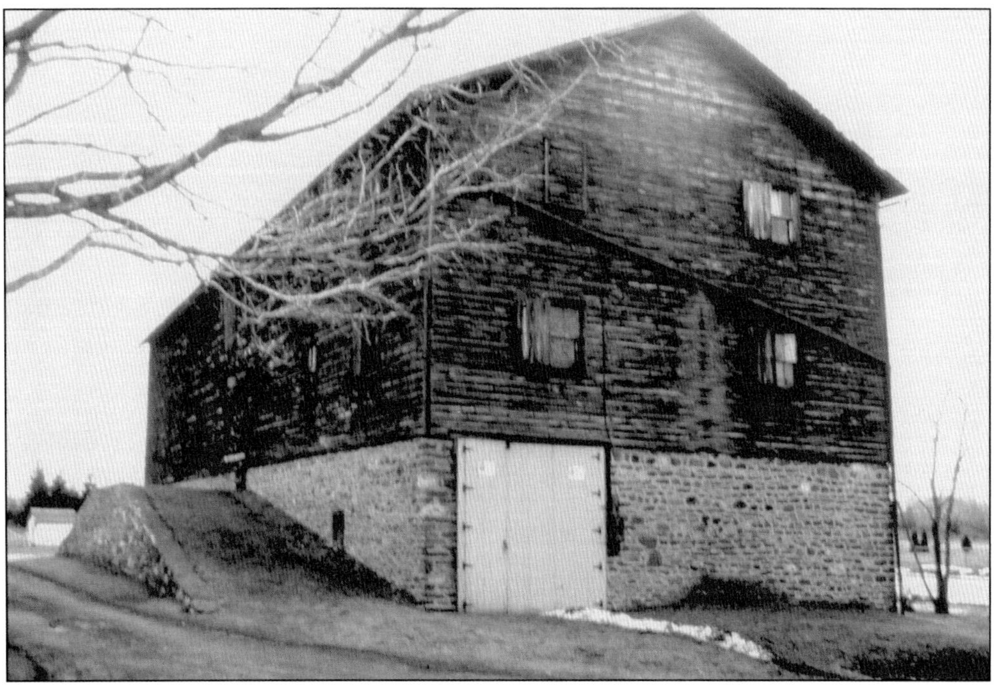

Barns played an important role in early Ontario, as they continue to today. This early barn in northwest Ontario had a gable roof, shuttered windows, and a rubble foundation. It also had an unusual two-way stone ramp.

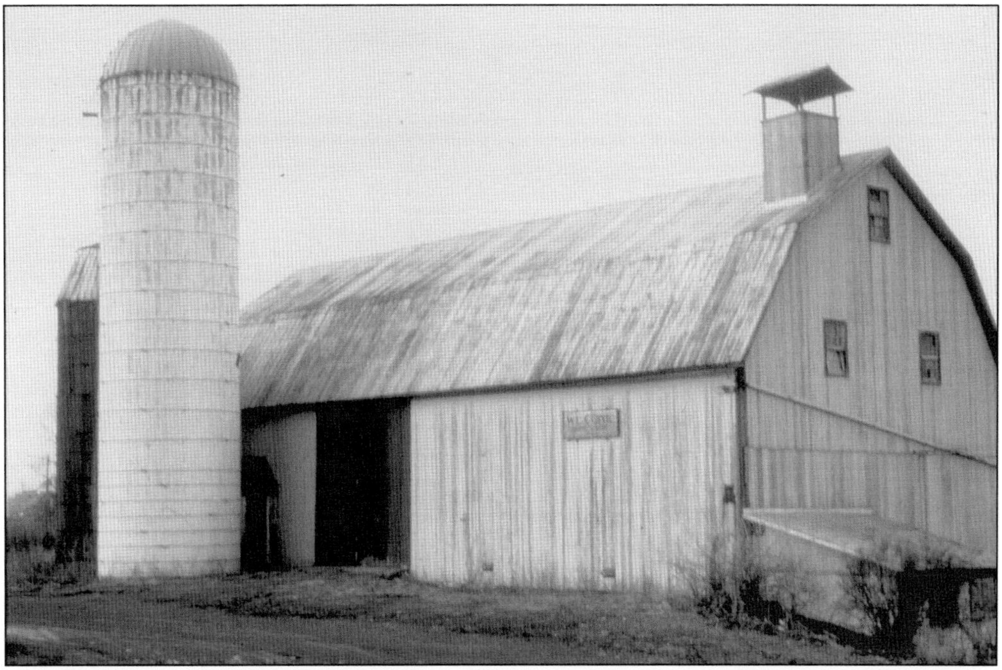

The Cone barn is located on Ridge Road near the original Cone homestead. Styles of architecture for these barns could vary quite a bit. This one has a gambrel roof. Walter L. Cone purchased this 100-acre farm in 1835. Later some of the land was sold for the building of three canning factories, and some for the building of the new Route 104.

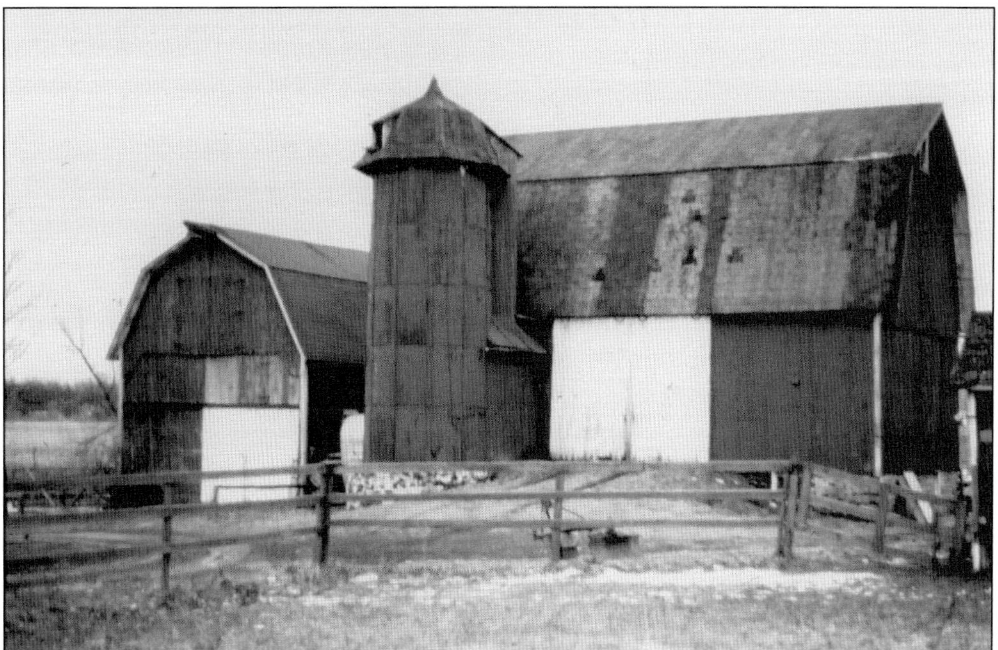

This barn is on Ridge Road. Most early barns and silos were used to preserve corn and other summer crops as silage for winter feed. Sometimes neighbors would gather together for a barn raising—the men building the barn and the women supplying the food.

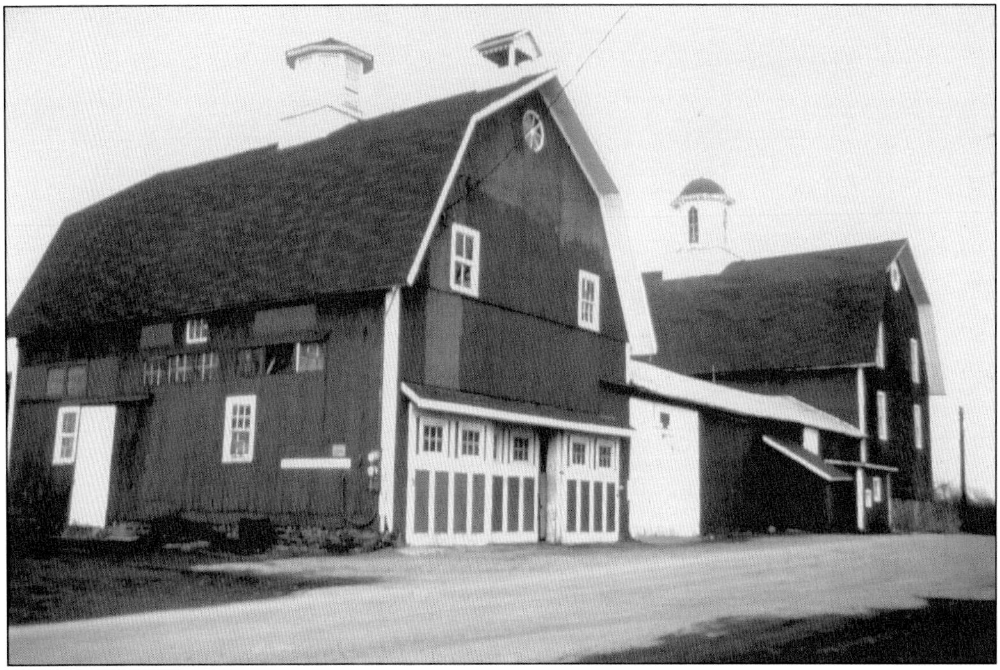

The Wooster barn had three distinctive cupolas, one of which had a bell used to call workers in from the field.

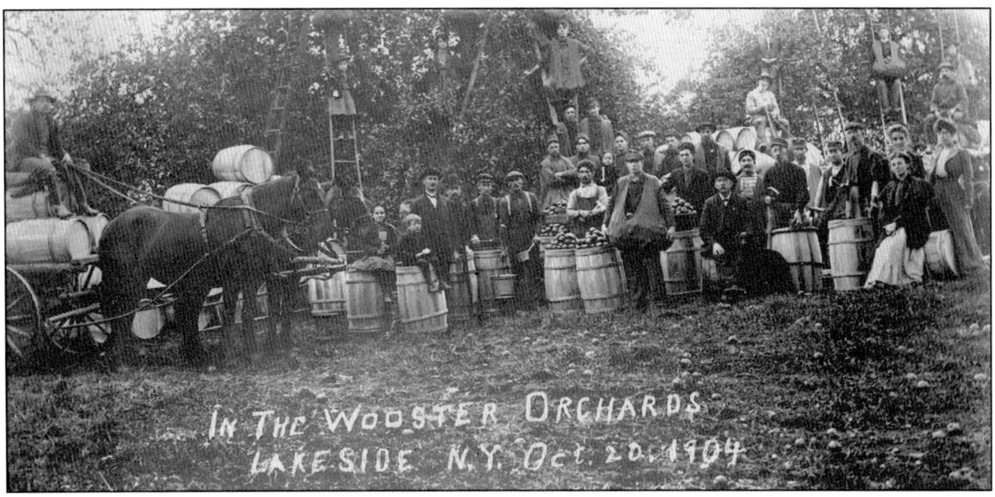

Gerald and Donald Wooster ran the farm their grandfather Fred started under the names of Wooster Brothers and Wooster Orchards. In the 1960s, the Wooster Orchards was the largest sweet cherry orchards in the East. The Wooster land extended from Lakeside to Union Hill. Today's businesses of Crown Electric and Andy's Auto Parts were once part of that farm.

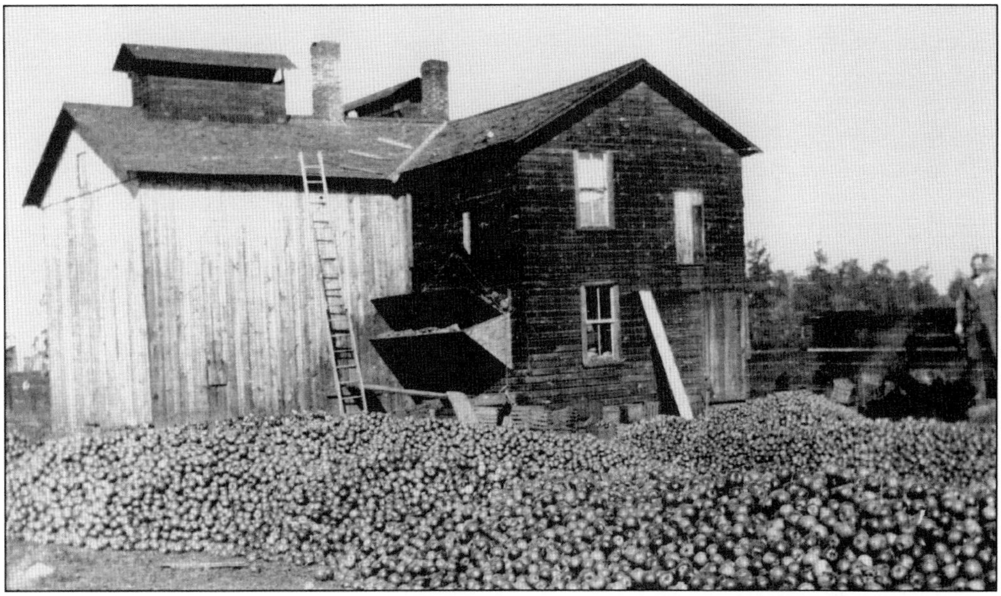

Before refrigeration, one way to preserve apples was to dry them in an apple dry house. Apples were sorted by size, peeled and pared, bleached by sulphur, and then sliced. The slices were piled about six inches thick on the kiln and leveled with a large wooden rake. The apple slices were turned several times a day using a shovel. It would take 20 to 24 hours to dry the apples. Wages were 50¢ for a woman, 75¢ for a strong boy, and $1 for a man. The heat for the kilns came from coal-fired hot-air furnaces. The dried apple slices were bagged or packed in wooden boxes for shipment by rail, or on the Erie Canal or Lake Ontario. The main markets were cities to the East and South. They were also shipped to markets in Europe. By the late 1920s, many of the individual apple dry houses were no longer operating. Instead drying was done by a few large commercial plants. In the 1930s, apples were canned, and by the 1940s freezing was more common.

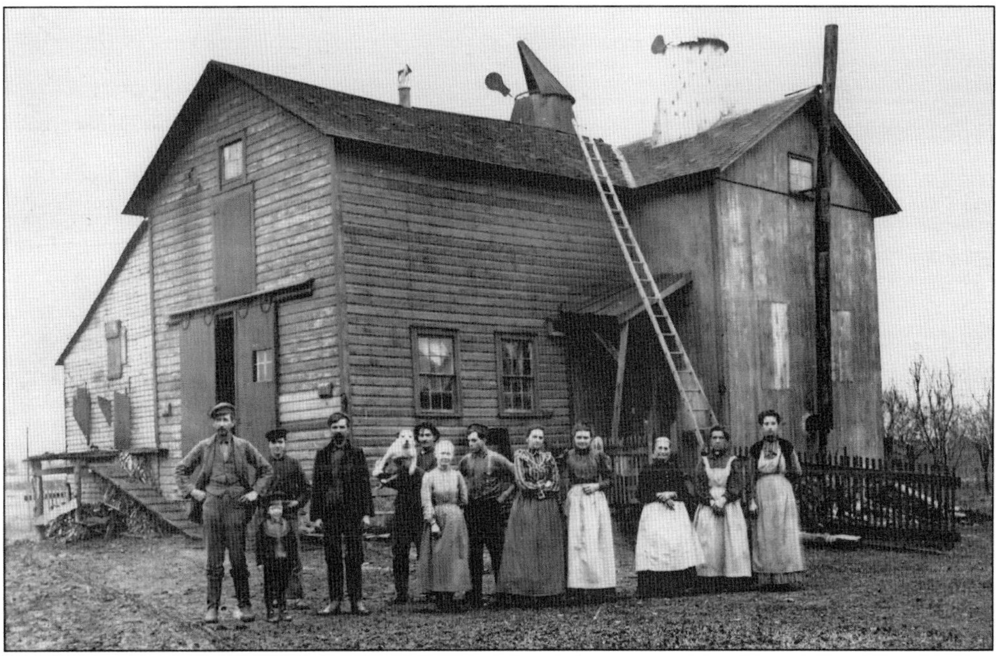

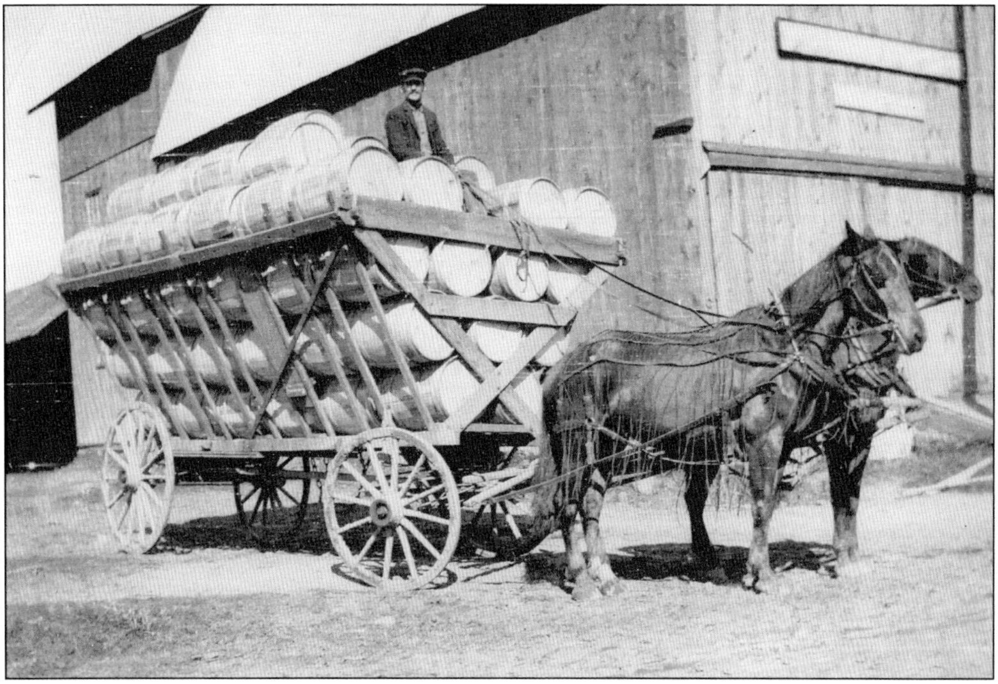

Jim Cowell is driving a wagon loaded with barrels filled with apples. Dried apples could be stored for long periods of time and made into apple pies. These pies were not as good as the fresh ones made with newly picked apples but better than having no dessert.

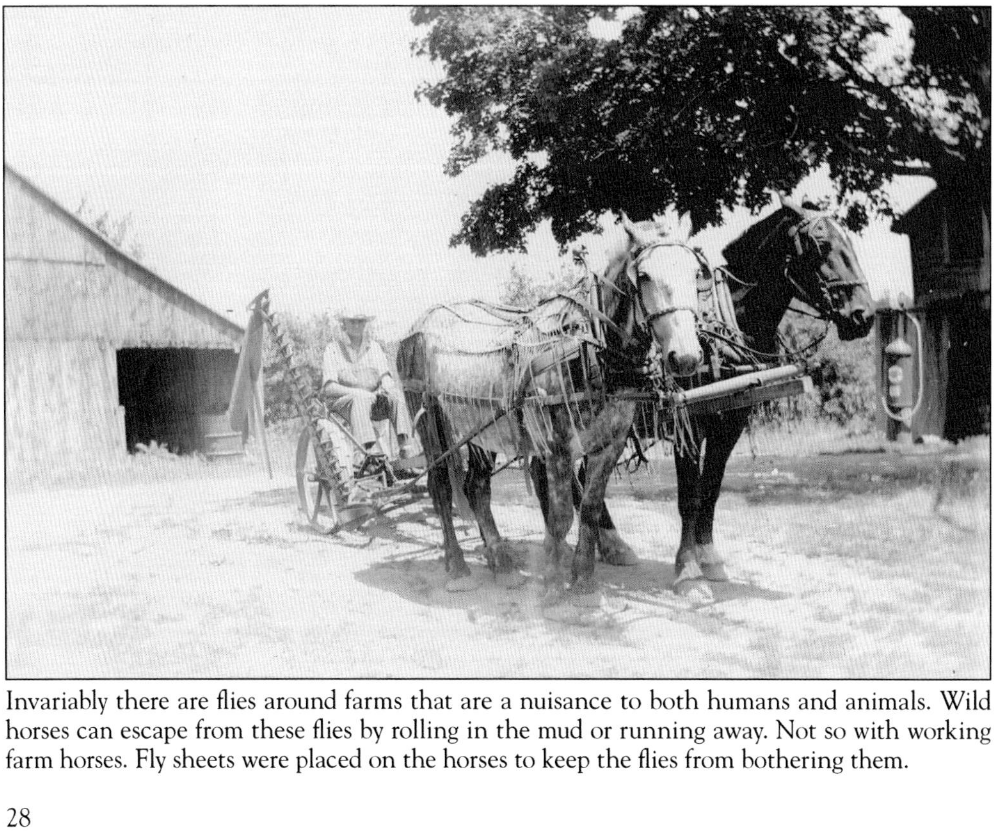

Invariably there are flies around farms that are a nuisance to both humans and animals. Wild horses can escape from these flies by rolling in the mud or running away. Not so with working farm horses. Fly sheets were placed on the horses to keep the flies from bothering them.

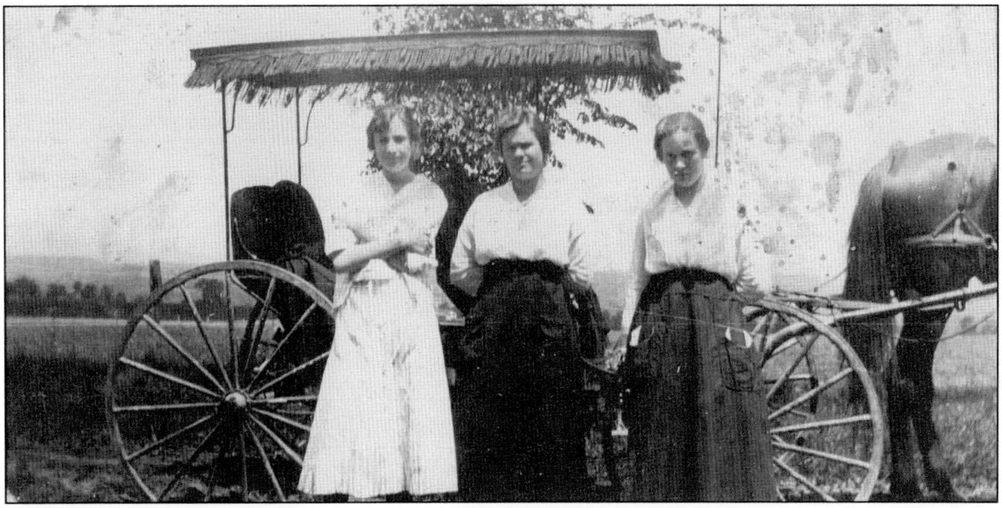

Zola Clark, Pete, and Lucy Geer are standing in front of a surrey with fringe on top. "Pete," born in 1902, is Edith Mae Clark Adams, Marian Wulfert's mother. This photograph was probably taken in the 1920s. The Adams family had a farm on Lake Road.

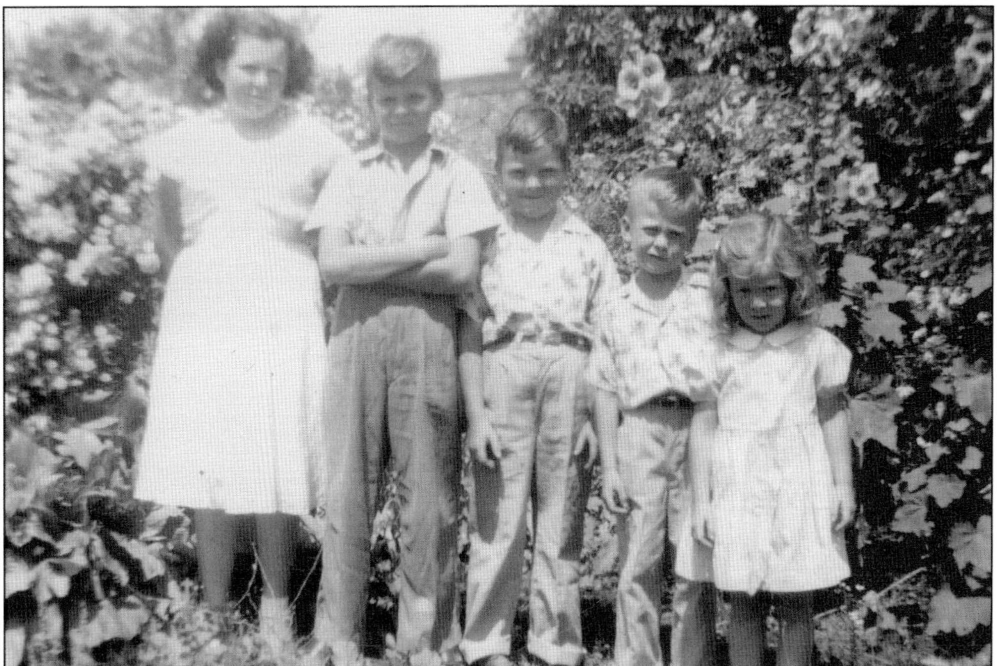

Shown here are Edith and Merritt Adams' children. From left to right are Emma, Durwood, Richard, Edward, and Marian (age three).

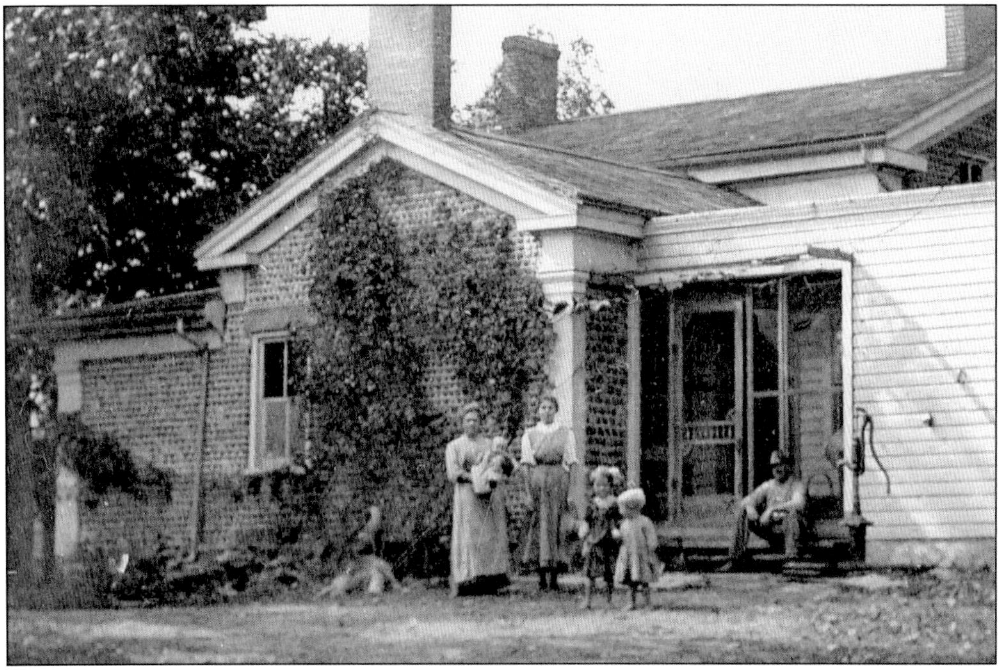

At the Lyman Brewer farmhouse on Lake Road, Kate is holding her baby, Robert. Next to her is Lillian, the oldest daughter. Leila is holding Orlando's hand. Notice he is in a dress. Their father, Lyman, was recovering from polio at the time.

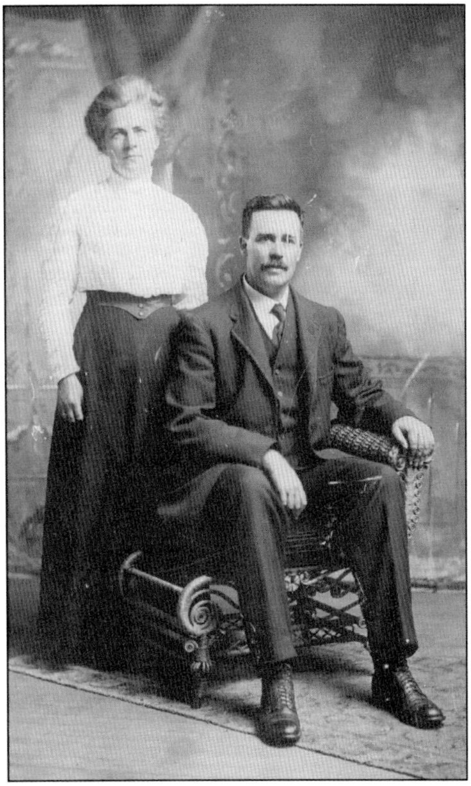

Kate and Lyman Hoste Brewer posed for this photograph in October 1913. They were married at Lakeside Methodist Church in 1896 and had their first farm on Boston and Lakeside Roads. They later purchased the 75-acre Eaton farm on Lake Road, which became known as the Brewer Cobblestone Homestead. There they grew berries, grapes, cherries, pears, and apples. They also raised cows, sheep, horses, and chickens. Lyman enlarged the farm with the help of his sister's son Ernest Adams.

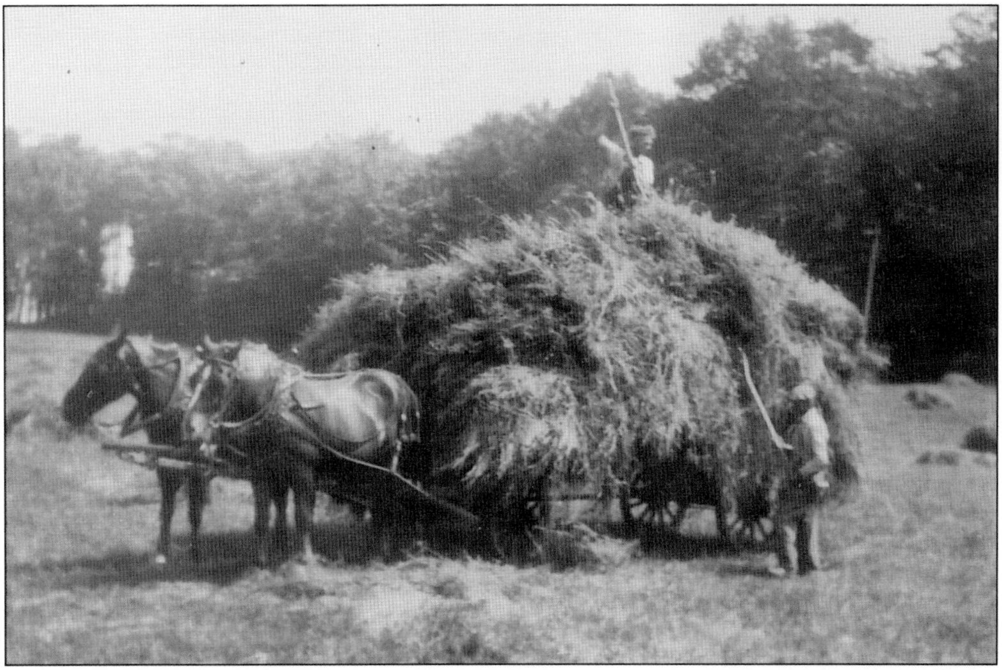

In 1928, the Brewers sold the farm to Helene Motley, who renamed the farm Wychmere Farm. She raised registered Guernsey cattle. Here, in 1935, hay is being loaded onto the horse-drawn hay wagon. Orlando "Landy" Brewer is on top of the hay. He continued to work for Motley after his parents sold the farm. Richard Bauch, on the ground, was Motley's farm manager.

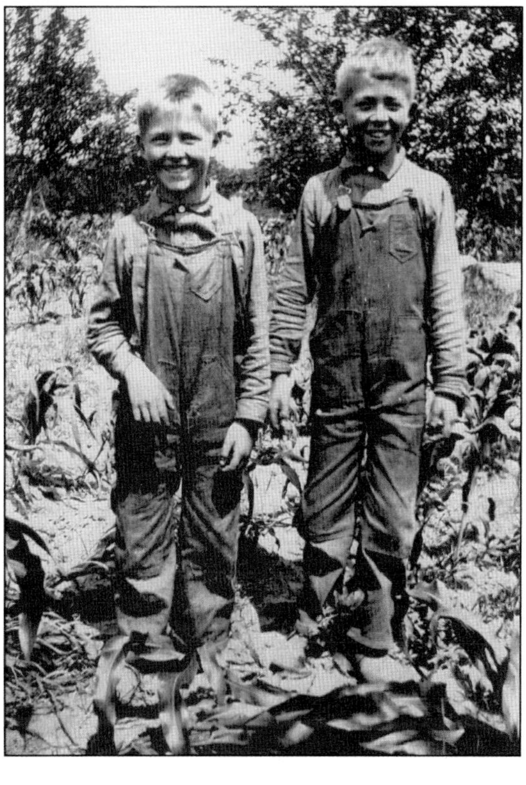

Robert (left) and Orlando Brewer are standing in a cornfield in this photograph, which was taken about 1920. They had been picking cherries on the farm. Often children were responsible for many of the chores around the farm.

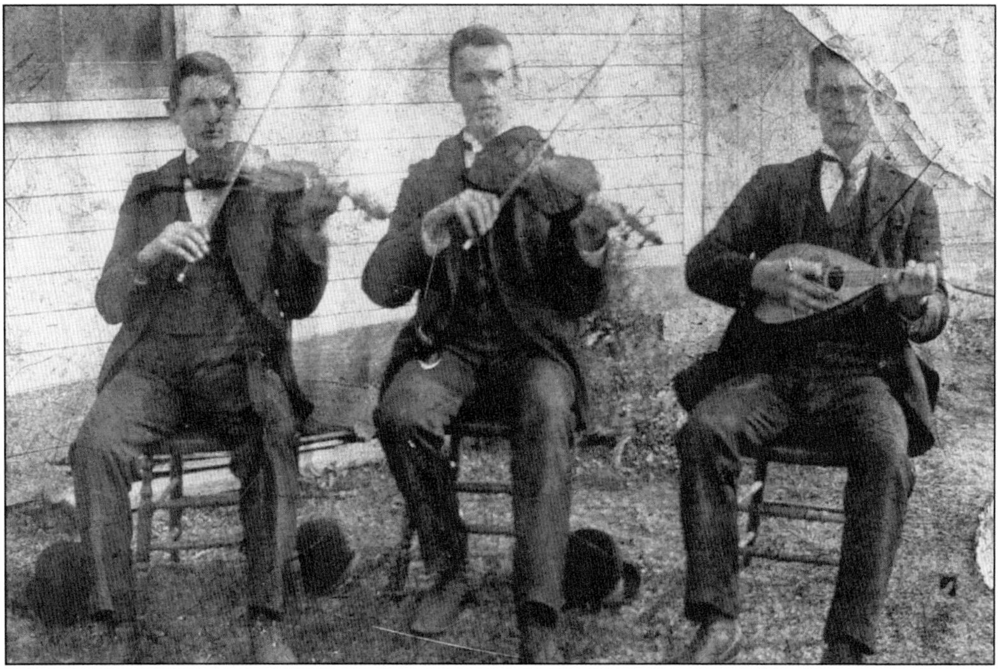

Fred Hodges (left), Lyman Brewer (center), and Jim Foley are pictured here, probably before 1900. Lyman's daughter Leila Brewer Irwin remembers that they played by ear, with no formal training. They played for square dances and parties at friends' and neighbors' homes. Carpets were rolled back, and good food and fun were had by all.

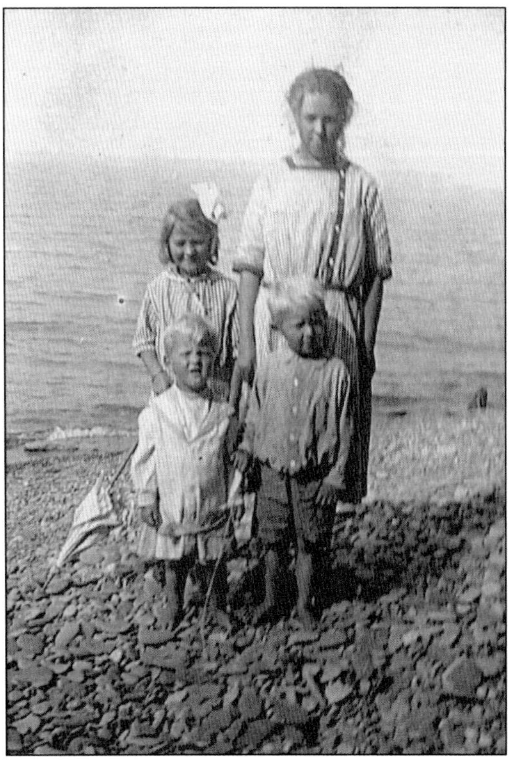

Children did have time to play. These children pose on the Lake Ontario shore. Standing from left to right are (first row) Robert Brewer and Orlando Brewer; (second row) Leila Brewer and Dorothy Brewer.

Three

Early Schools and Churches

Once families were settled into their new homes, they began to consider schooling and churches. One-room schoolhouses began to be built with limited amenities. Many of them did not have indoor toilets or electricity until the 1920s. Teachers for the schools were often housed with families as a way for the family to pay school taxes. Some of these one-room schoolhouses were remodeled over the years into private residences. Others were destroyed either by neglect or deliberately, as in the case of the Albright Schoolhouse. Only a single one-room schoolhouse remains in Ontario today. In many cases, church congregations met in various locations, sometimes private homes, until a church building could be erected.

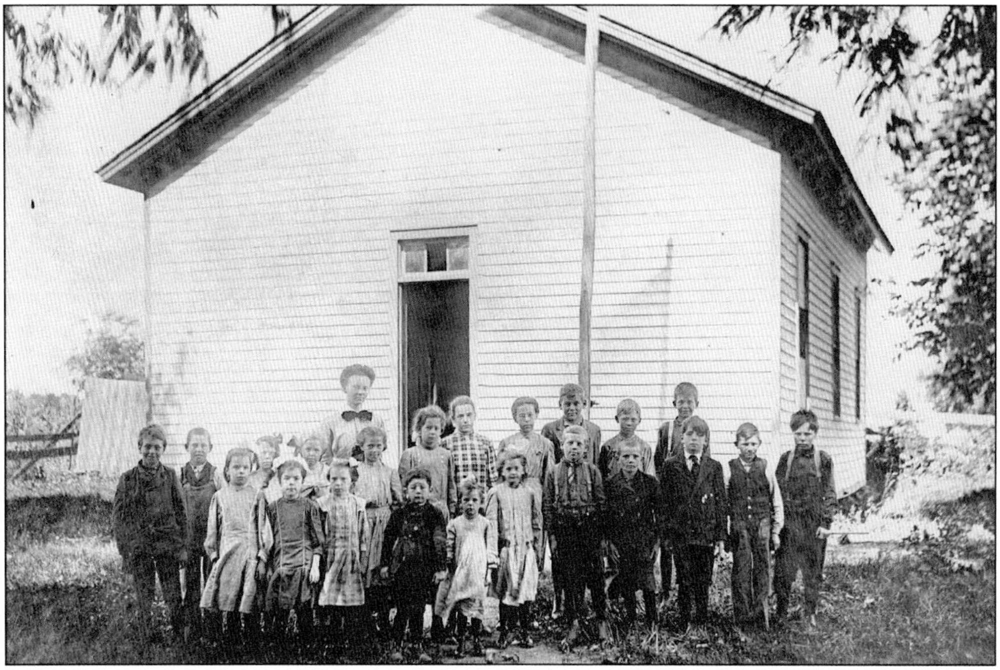

The Albright schoolhouse was the first built in Ontario as early as 1816. It was built of logs in the neighborhood where the first families (Hopkins, Thatcher, Leavins, Crowley, Davis, and Gates) lived. An early teacher, Lucy Barnhart was paid $5 per week for a 10-week term. In 1907, teacher Anna Gage Putnam (center back row) posed with her students. Used until 1949, this schoolhouse was replaced by the Ontario Water Department.

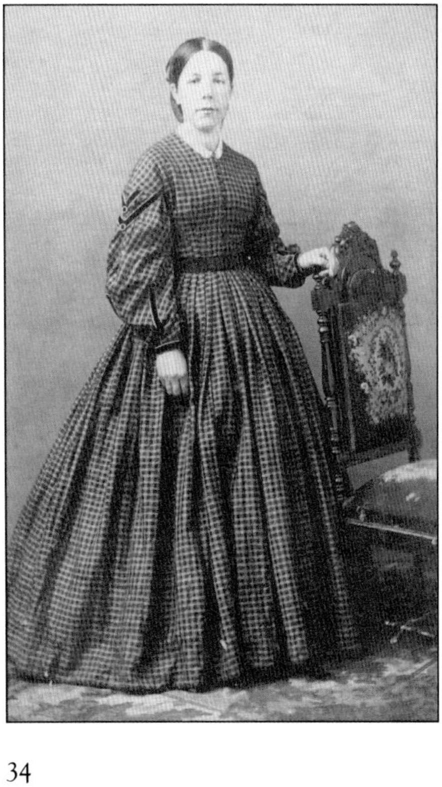

Shown here is Lucy Leavins. She and her husband, Joseph Gates, deeded land on December 31, 1835, to the Albright District No. 3 to rebuild the schoolhouse. The building was replaced twice with improvements each time.

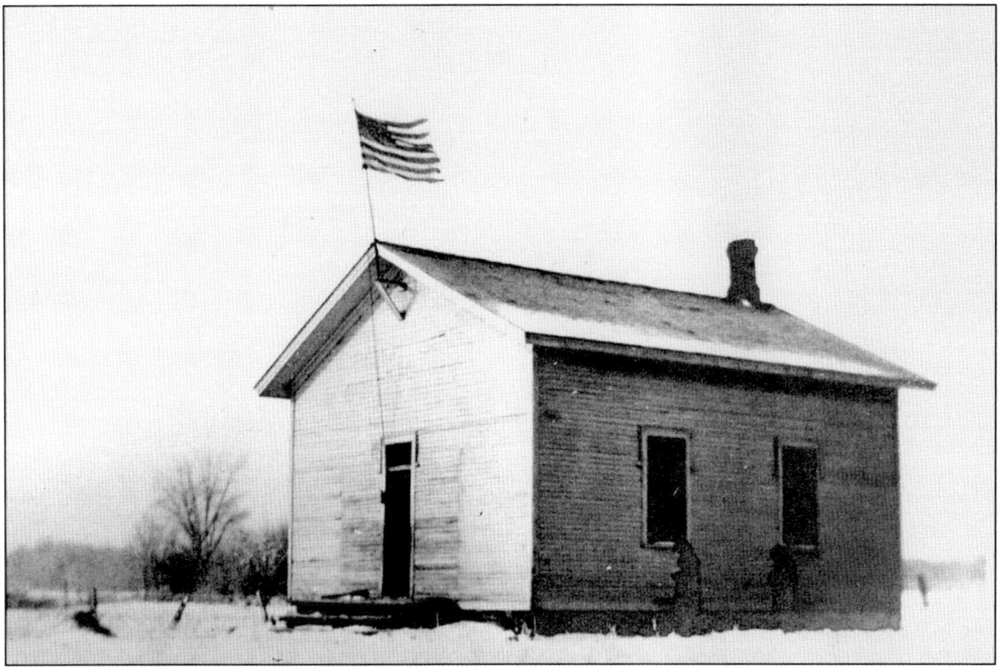

The Lake Road Schoolhouse, District No. 2, was situated on the south side of Lake Road one and a half miles east of the Monroe County Line. School records show that in 1826 the school year was three months in the winter and five months in the summer. The 1827 school board minutes say that taxes would include "good sound wood and if any man neglects to get his wood by the 10th of January, he shall pay 6 shillings per cord." In the school board minutes from the early 1860s, it was noted that the teacher's salary was $3 per week. By 1939, there were only two students and it was decided to close the school. The building was sold to Arthur Blanchard, of Webster, in 1946. The photograph below shows the crumbled remains of the Lake Road Schoolhouse.

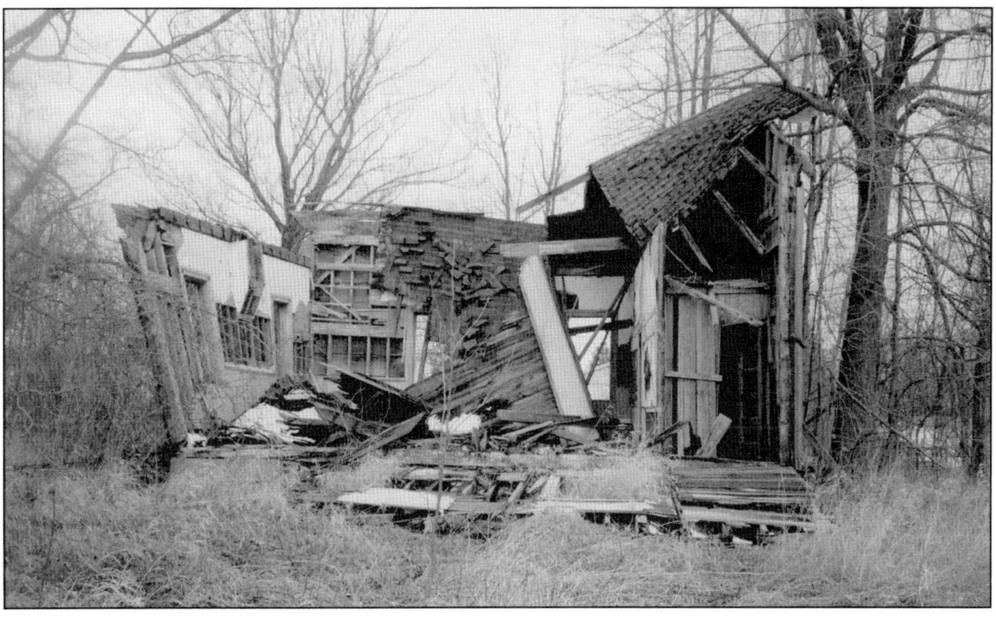

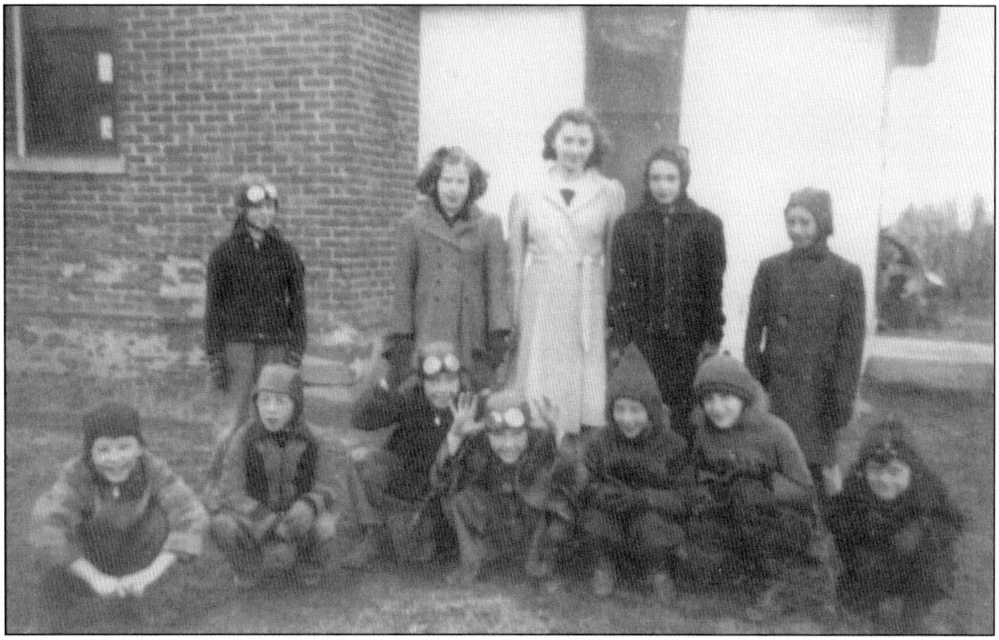

Schoolchildren pose with their teacher in front of the Brick Church Schoolhouse in 1942. They are, from left to right, (first row) two unidentified children, Norman and Nelson Leenhouts (twins), Phil Barnhardt, Beverly Barnhardt, and Pauline Hilligeer; (second row) Ralph Derleth, Phyllis Pratt, Elizabeth Fox (teacher, also known as Jane Gates) Thelma Harris (Russell), and Norman Hilligeer.

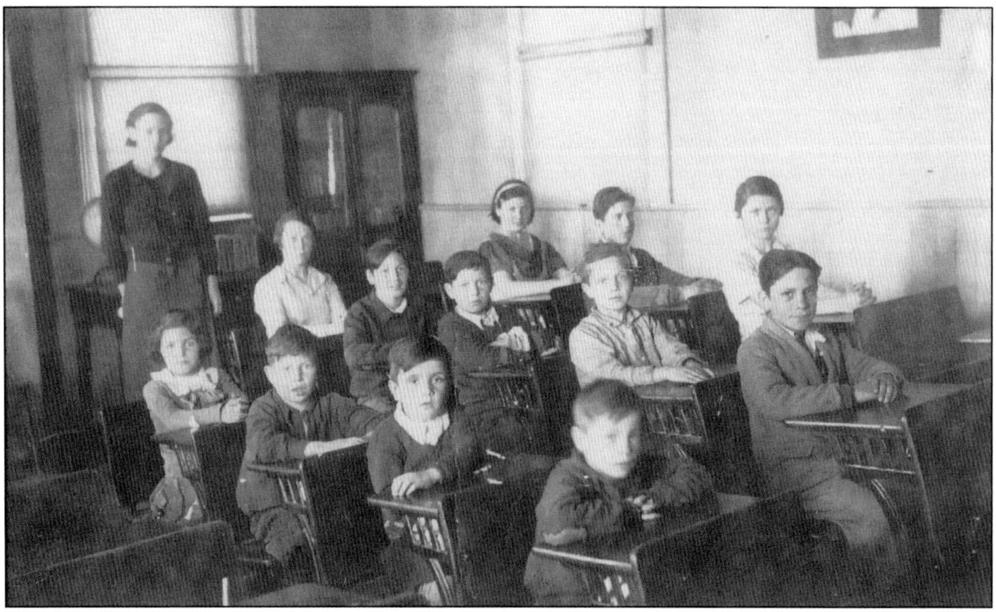

District No. 4 is the Brick Church Schoolhouse, which has been carefully preserved by the Town of Ontario Historical and Landmark Preservation Society at Heritage Square. Shown here in 1933 with teacher Lois Palmer Cass are, from left to right, (first row) Jenny Catalano, Floyd Palmer, Eddie Catalano, and ? Palmer; (second row) Arlene Thomas, Anthony Catalano, George Catalano, ? Palmer, and Joseph Fioco; (third row) Marie Catalano, Frank Fioco, and Ruth Thomas.

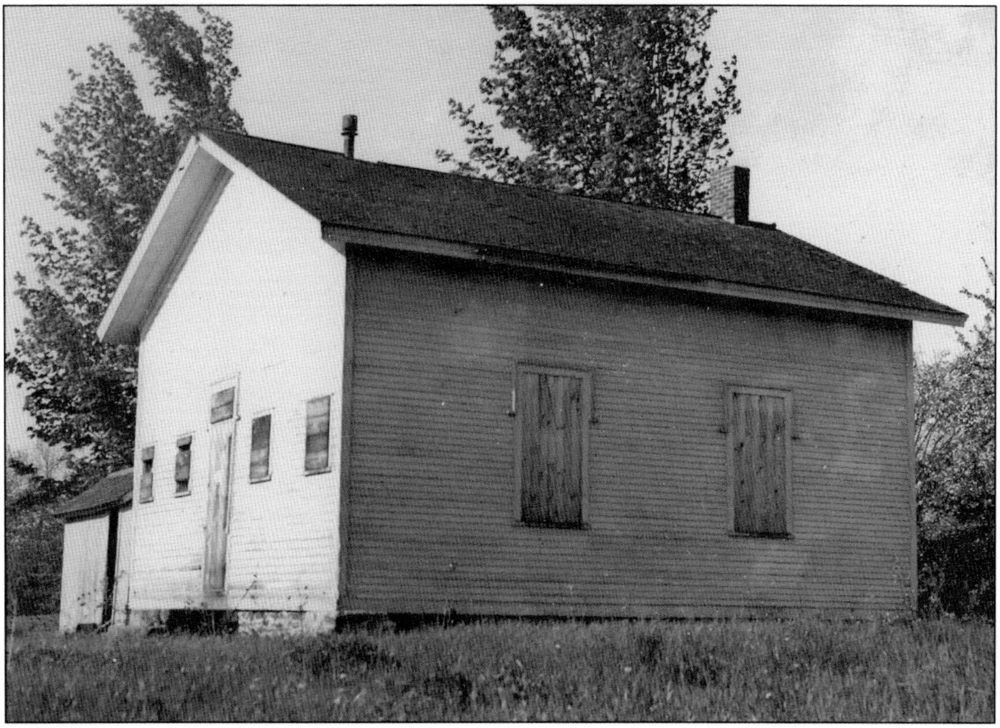

The Paddy Lane Schoolhouse, built in an area of many Irish families, was thought to have been built in the late 1890s. Wood and then coal were used to fuel the stove. Water came from a well and was brought into the school in a bucket. Often the children would drink from the bucket using a shared dipper. The school year had two terms. The summer term was often taught by a woman. The winter term was taught by a man because the older children would attend only during the winter months when they were not needed on the farm. In this farming area, there were cattle roaming freely. One even charged the students, but the teacher was able to hold it until the children were safe. The Paddy Lane Schoolhouse, shown below, is now a private residence located at 1846 Paddy Lane.

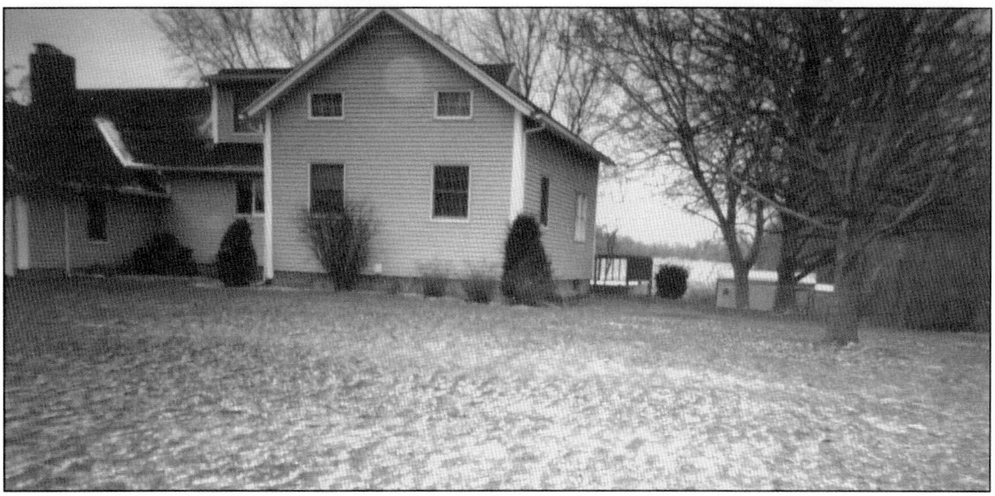

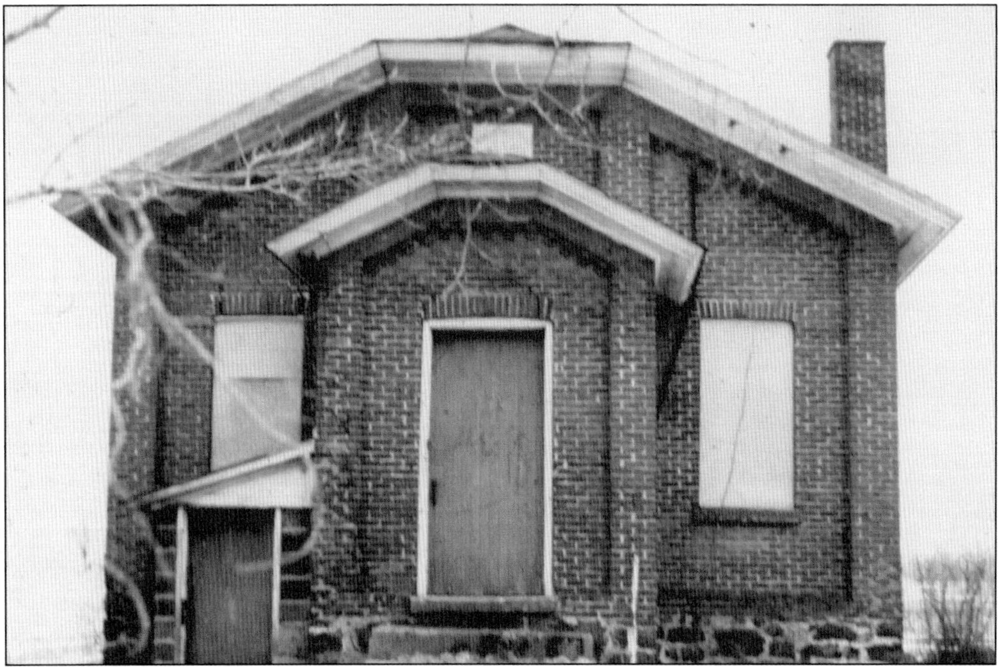

In 1878, this brick building replaced the wooden Town Line Schoolhouse. It was one of the later schools to be built. Surrounded on three sides by a stone fence built by Norman Meaker, the old wood building had stood for 77 years. Six hitching posts were placed in the front for those who rode to school on horseback. This district encompassed Putnam Road, Trimble Road, Kenyon Road, and the Town Line Road (Fisher Road).

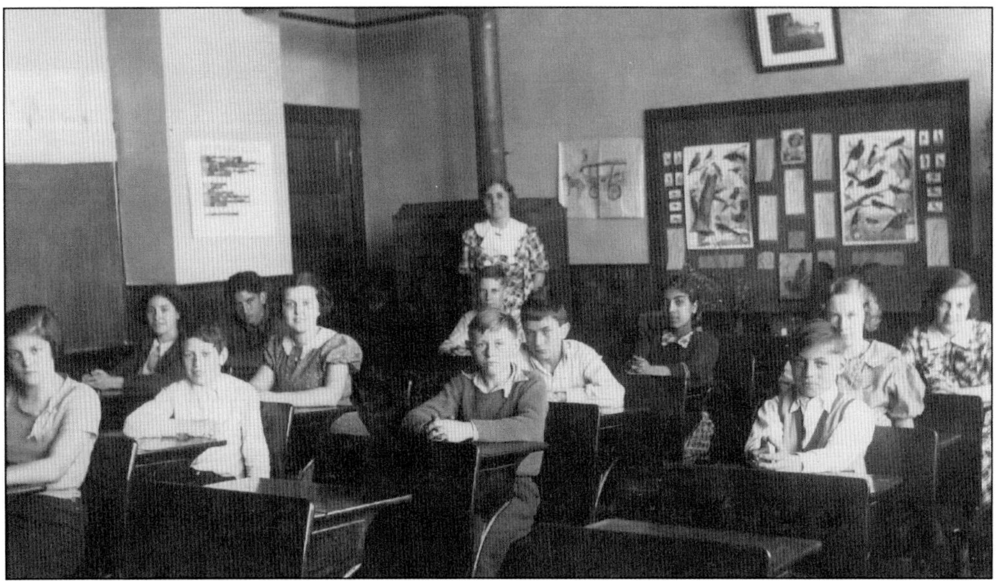

The Furnaceville Schoolhouse was built in the early 1830s. Shown here, almost 100 years later, is Augusta Trimble with her students Lila Meeker, Tony Catalano, Pearl Fisher, Grace Catalano, Ellsworth Thompson, Paul DeRight, Carmella Mitchell Koch, Jack Eaton, Allen Albright, and Elaine VerDow. In 1971, James Dwyer and his wife bought this school at an auction and converted it into a home.

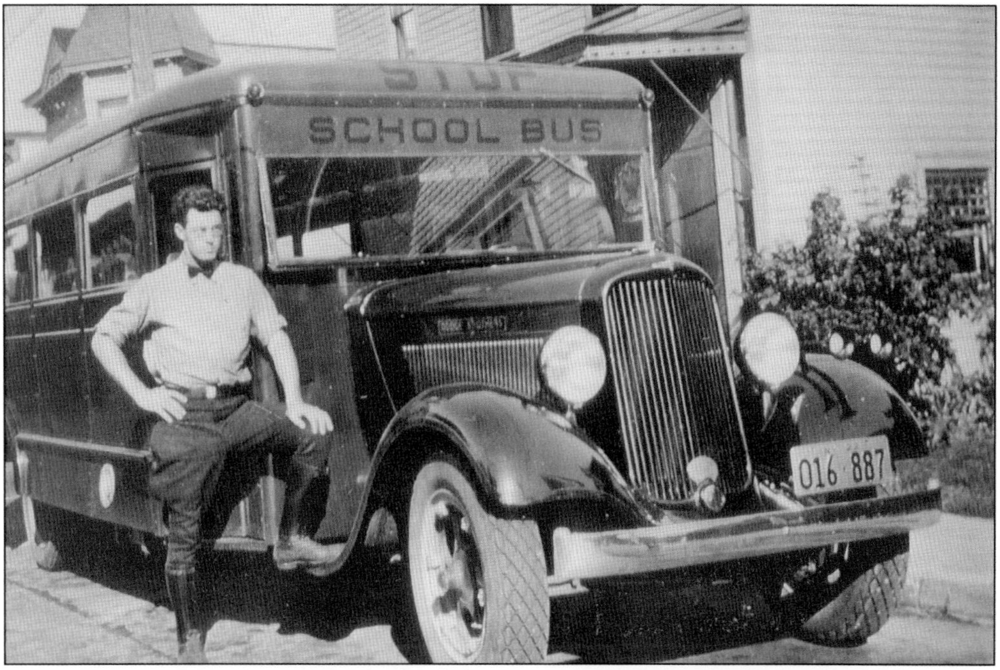

In 1933, an education law required school districts to provide transportation for rural schools. The first school bus combined a Dodge truck chassis with a school bus body (bought in Pennsylvania). The first bus driver was Scott Cass (in the photograph), who had recently graduated from Ontario High School.

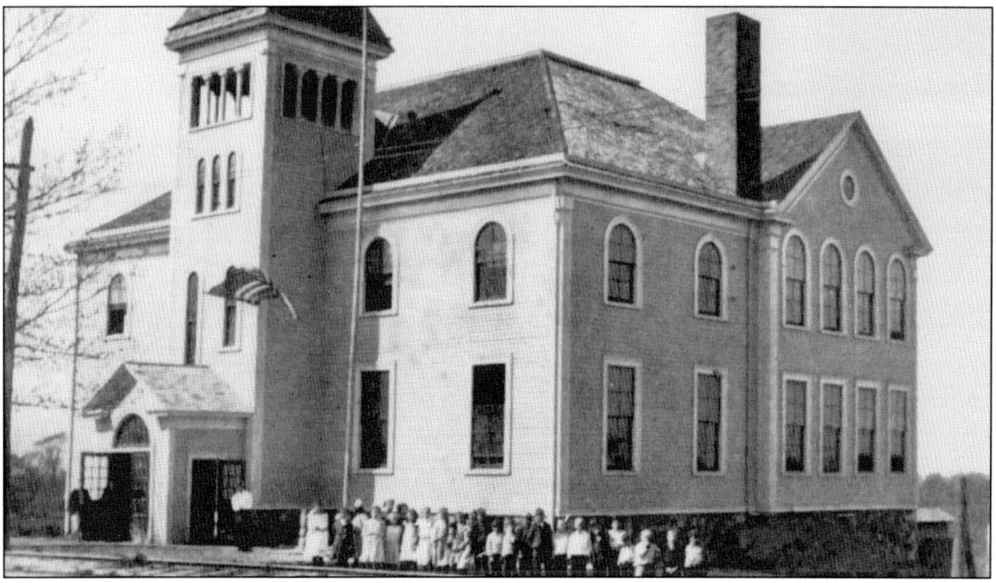

The Union Free School was built across from the current Ontario Elementary School on Ridge Road in 1895. Students from Ontario and Ontario Center, combining Districts 5 and 6, attended. It was the first opportunity to go beyond elementary school in Ontario and get a high school diploma without needing to attend a boarding school. Before this, it was common for Ontario high school students to attend the Walworth Academy, which was the nearest secondary school.

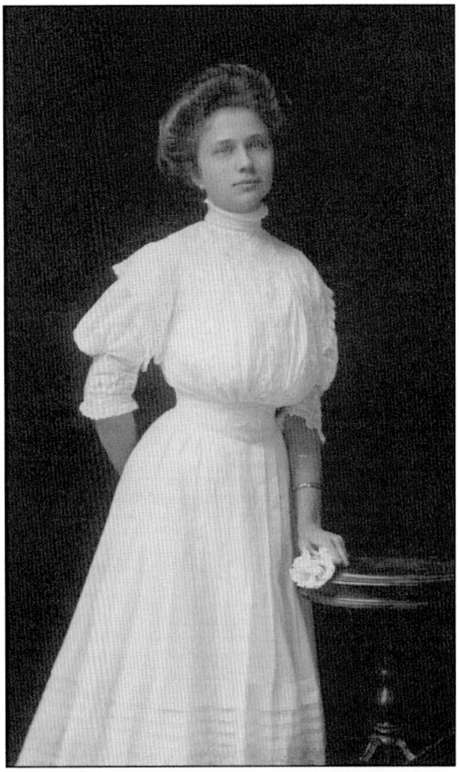

Maude VanIngen poses for her high school graduation photograph in 1908. Maude's father, John, owned the VanIngen General Store on Main Street. After Maude married Arthur Risley, John sold his business to Risley and Clifford Payne in 1919. When Clifford moved to Wolcott, Risley continued alone until 1942, when the firm A. W. Risley and Sons was formed. After Risley died, Maude moved to Florida.

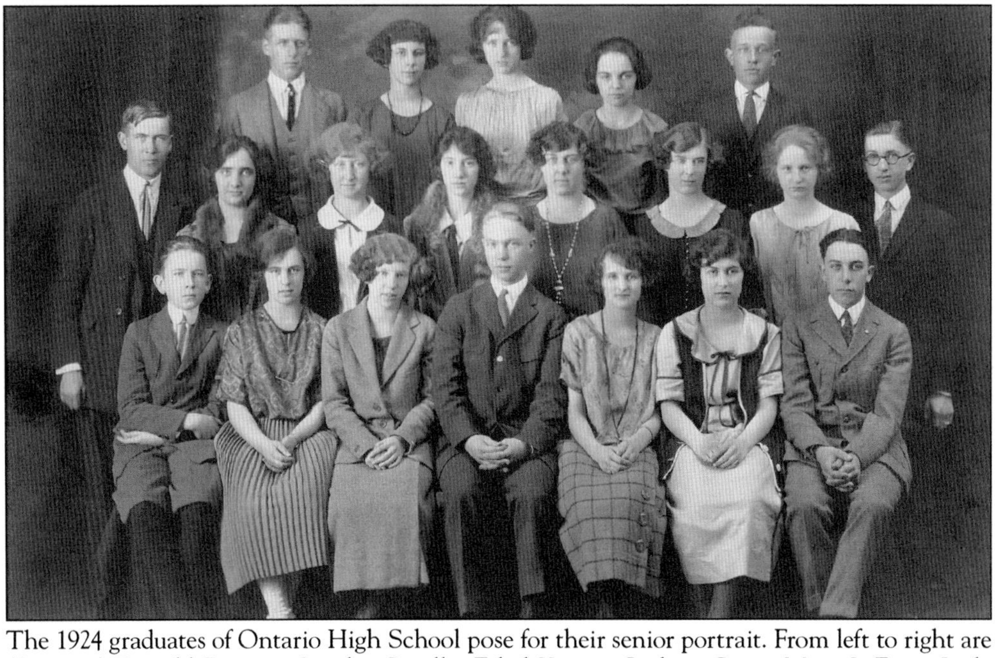

The 1924 graduates of Ontario High School pose for their senior portrait. From left to right are (first row) Donald Fewster, Coralie Coville, Ethel Young, Carlton Cone, Mary LeFrois, Leila Hise, and Smith Pratt; (second row) Harold Fewster, Louise Cann, Glenna Porrey, Lelah Rouch, Arrethea Verdine, Louise Verdine, Doris Huxley, and Melville Sheahen; (third row) Raymond Middleton, Genevieve Foley, Orian Stevens, Elsie Brown, and Mason Stevens.

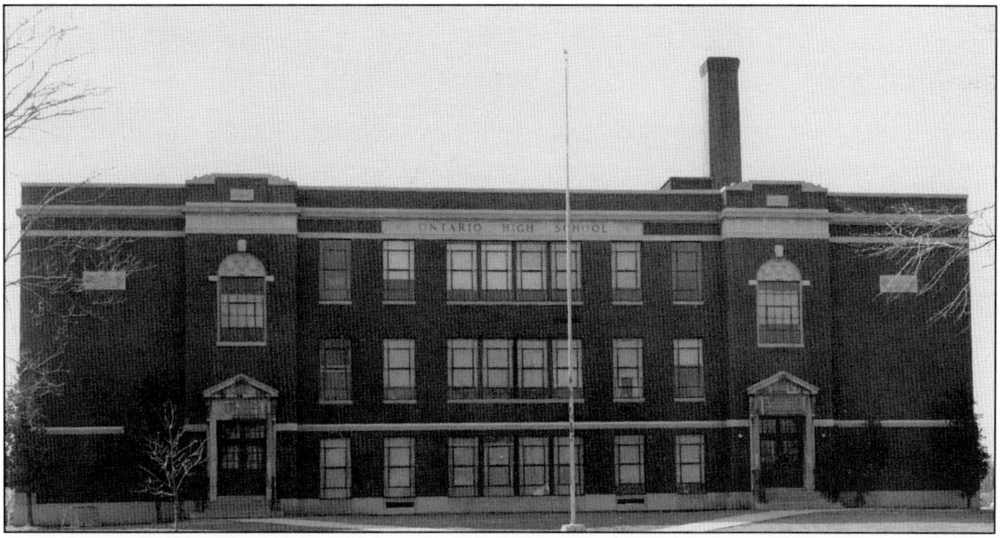

The current Ontario Elementary School was built in 1926 as the Ontario High School. Engraved above the main west doorway are the words, "Wisdom adorns riches and softens poverty" by Socrates; and above the east main doorway, "Enter to learn–Go forth to serve".

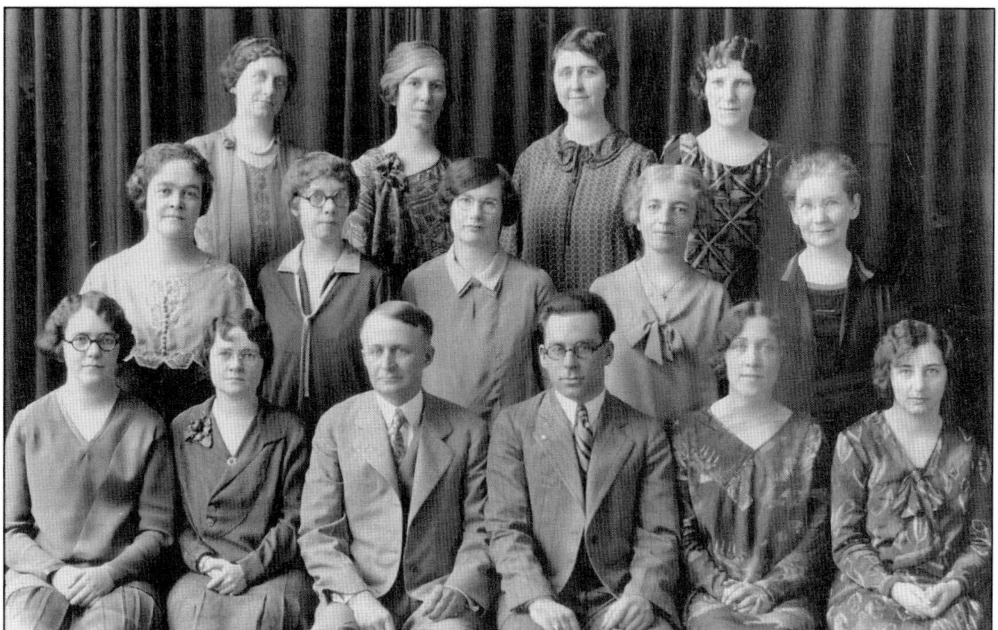

The 1928 faculty of the high school are, from left to right, (first row) Marjorie E. Wilson (French and algebra), Edna M. Butterfield (English and librarian), Edgar A. Lewis (principal), L. S. Summers (history, science, and physical training), Grace M. Brinkerhoff (domestic science), and Winifred F. Petteys (music and drawing); (second row) Maude Englesen (eighth grade), Ada Belle Suter (sixth grade), Merle Hodges (seventh grade), Sena M. Clark (fourth grade), and Helen M. Eaton (second grade); (third row) Florence M. Weidrick (fifth grade), Jennie Brown (third grade), Marion DeLong (Latin, civics, and history), and Leona Fleming (first grade).

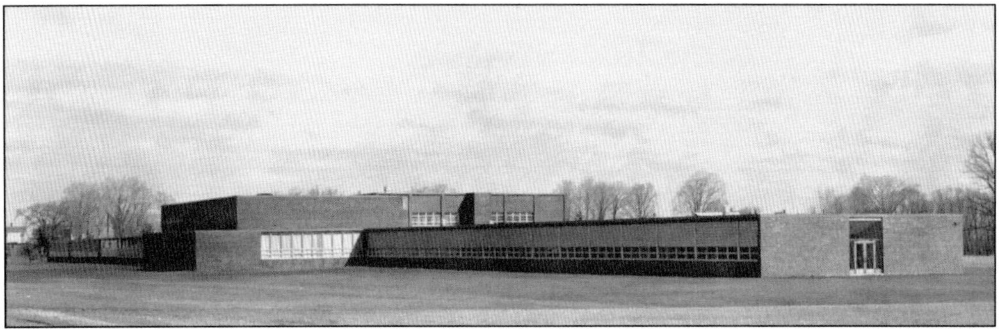

The current high school on Ontario Center Road was built in 1951 and named for James A. Beneway. Beneway retired from the board of education in 1967, after serving for 18 years. The last 13 years he served as the district's school board president.

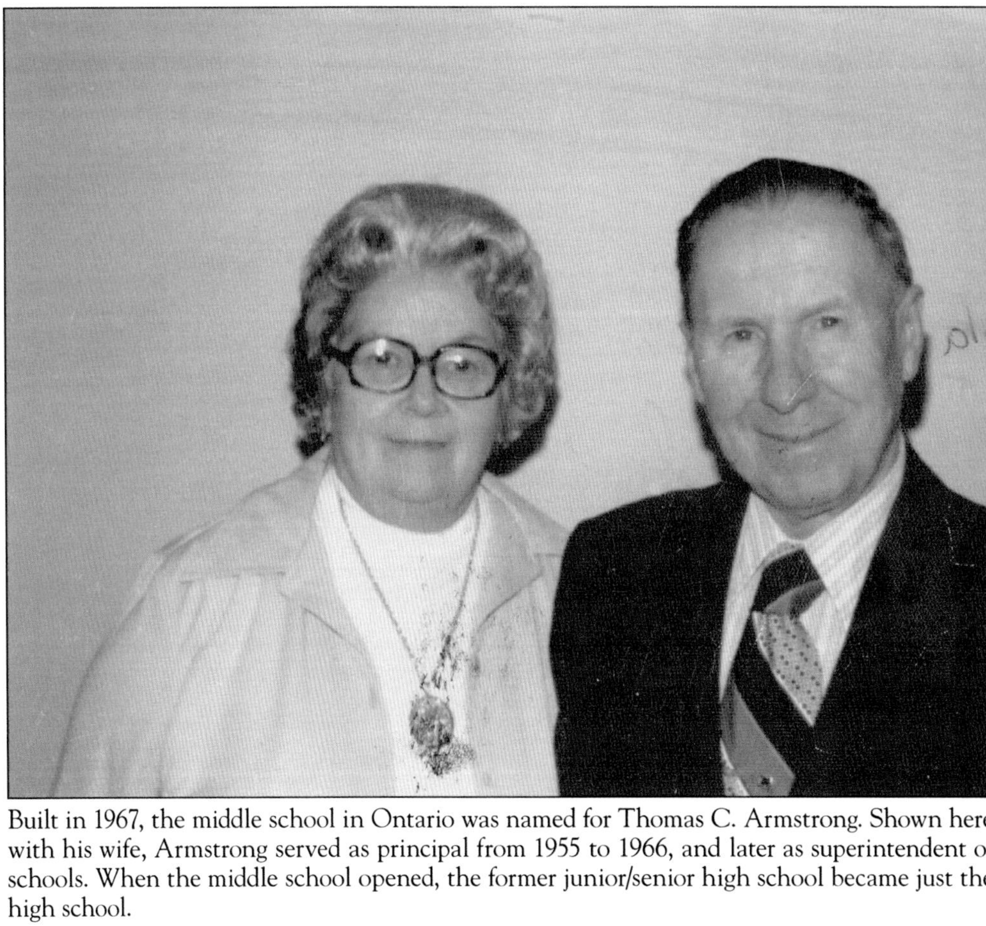

Built in 1967, the middle school in Ontario was named for Thomas C. Armstrong. Shown here with his wife, Armstrong served as principal from 1955 to 1966, and later as superintendent of schools. When the middle school opened, the former junior/senior high school became just the high school.

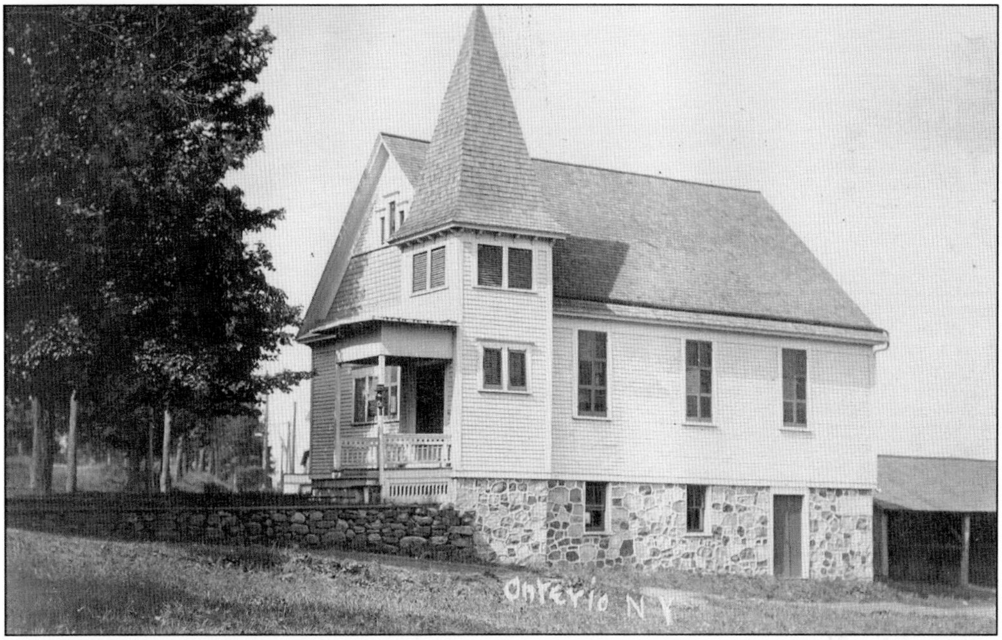

Is a church the building or the people who come together to worship? The Dutch Reformed Church was first organized in the summer of 1884 by a group of people from Holland who wanted to have a church service in their native language. By 1885, there were 33 members of the congregation. The group tried to raise enough money to build a church building but found that funds were not available. Church membership declined and then ended. In 1896, a group of Hollanders again established the church. It was not until 1898, after all those years of increasing and decreasing membership and several relocations of church services, that the church building was constructed. Since 1957 the church has been remodeled and the kitchen modernized. The interior was paneled, painted, and carpeted. Unfortunately, in 1976, this church burned to the ground (shown below).

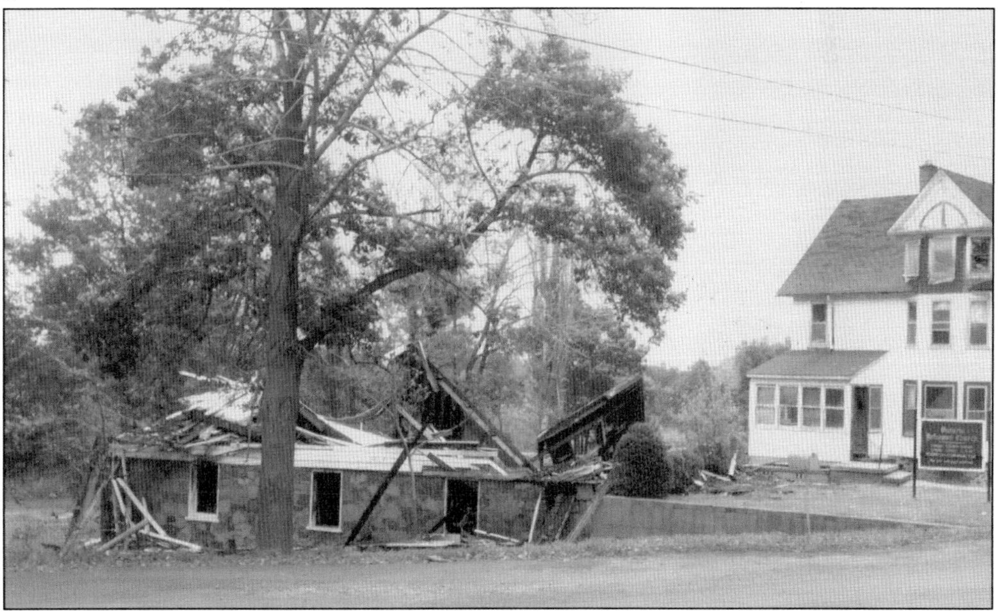

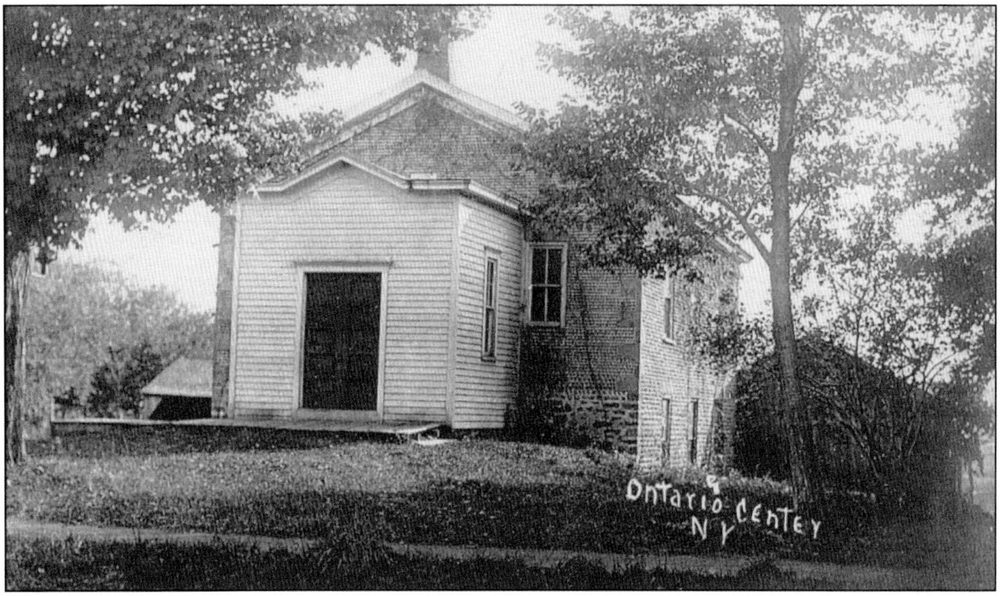

In 1833, under the leadership of Reverend Bliss, a meeting was held to organize the Presbyterian church. By 1842, the project of erecting a church building was begun with cobblestones and sand for mixing the mortar taken from the lake. This original cobblestone structure was replaced. The present church building was erected and dedicated on July 15, 1915.

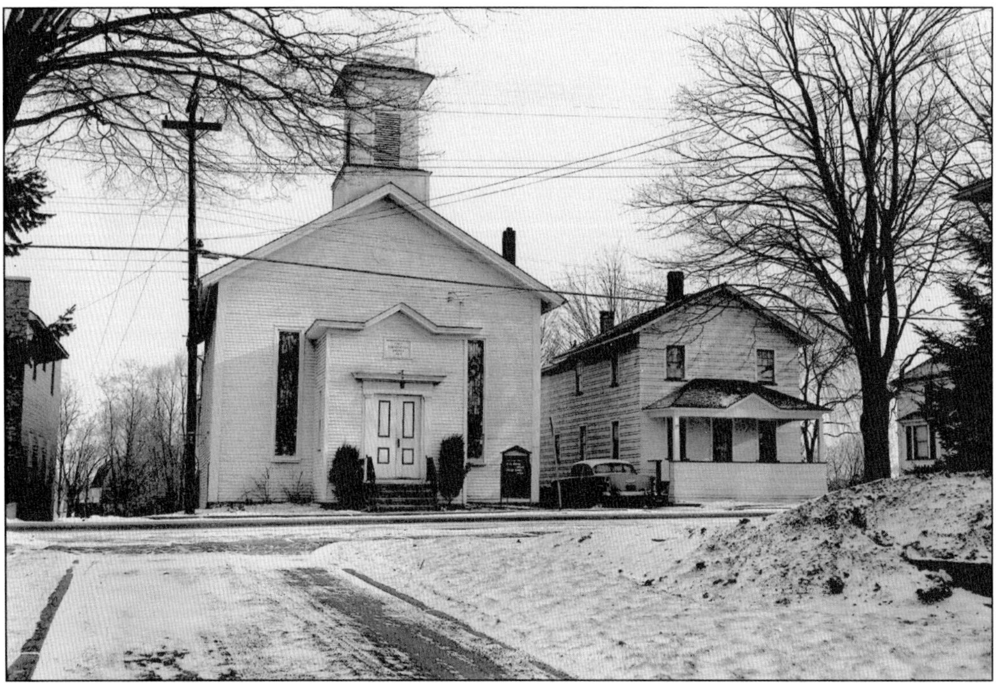

The church currently known as the Immanuel United Church of Christ was originally organized as a Wesleyan Methodist church in 1857. Services were held in various locations around the town until the current church building was constructed in 1865. It was dedicated in 1869, and an addition was built in 1950. Located at 1973 Ridge Road, as seen here in 1957, the church celebrated its 150th anniversary in 2007.

Four

HOMES AROUND TOWN

Early pioneers to Ontario had the task of building a suitable home for their families. Clearing the land involved chopping trees, which were often turned into log homes. As time went on and the pioneers became more settled, frame homes were built. Some homes were elaborately made of brick. Some utilized the cobblestones that were readily available along the shoreline of Lake Ontario and in the fields that were cleared for crops. Over 90 percent of cobblestone houses are located within a 60-mile radius of Rochester. Twelve of them are in Ontario. Building cobblestone houses was a folk art that flourished in Upstate New York from 1825 until the Civil War. It is thought (but not known for certain) that cobblestone construction was brought to this area by laborers who came to work on the Erie Canal. The genealogy of some of the early homes of Ontario is as complex as the history of the early families.

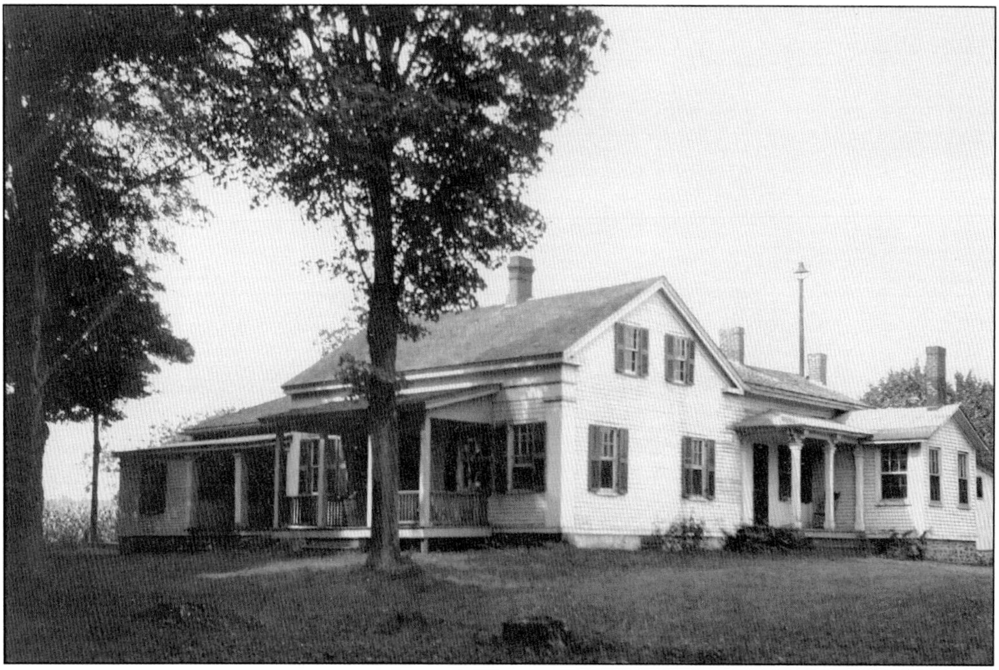

The Palmer home, located on Lakeside Road, was built by Daniel Jennings in about 1815. The home and farm of 200 acres was bought by Oliver Hazard Palmer in 1864. It was also the home of Van Rensselaer Palmer. His son Wilbur was born here.

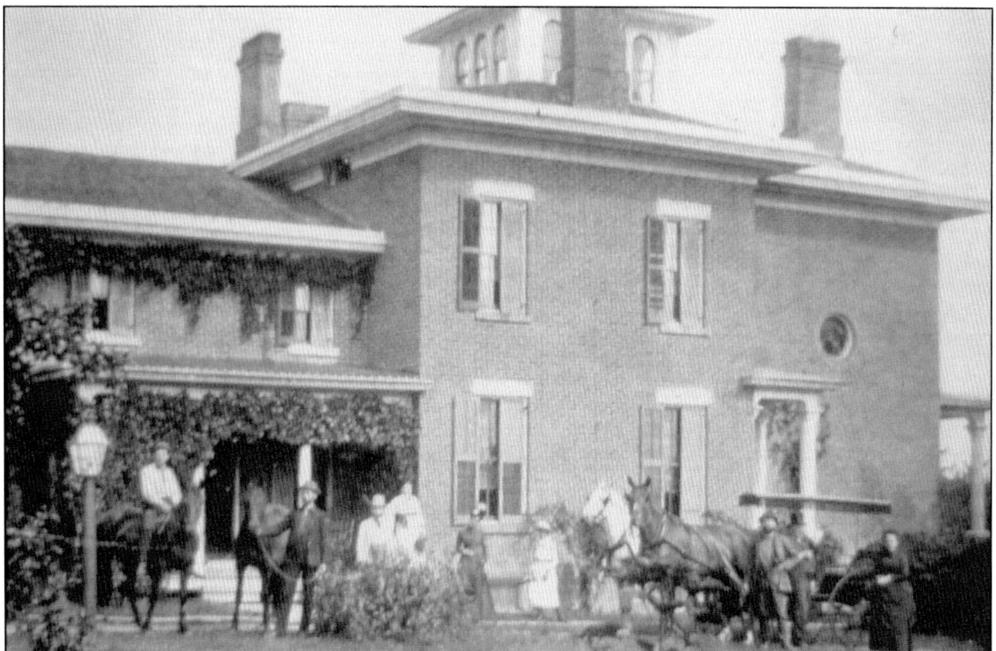

Lorenzo Boynton built this two-story brick Victorian-style home in 1862 with bricks made at Burnett's in Webster. His wife, Mary Hopkins, was the daughter of the first settler, Freeman Hopkins. Frederick Douglass was said to have visited this house to make an Underground Railroad contact.

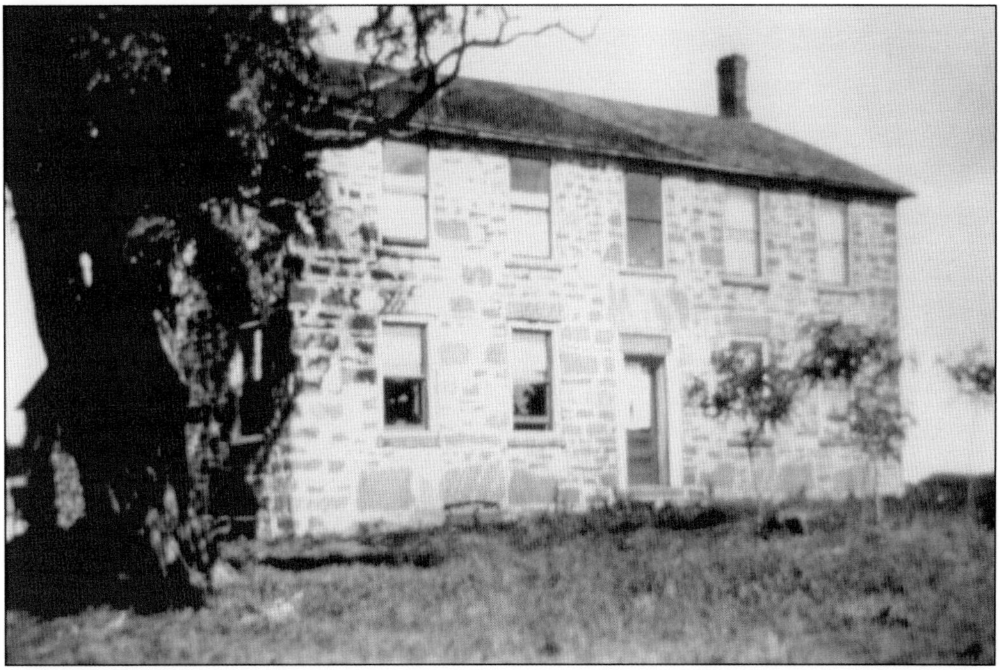

Peter Thatcher was one of the first settlers of Ontario. Arriving in 1806, he built a log cabin and a log blacksmith shop. He later had this home, made of fieldstone, built in the Georgian style in about 1827. Located at 7434 Knickerbocker Road, this home was also owned by the Crowleys and the Lugerts.

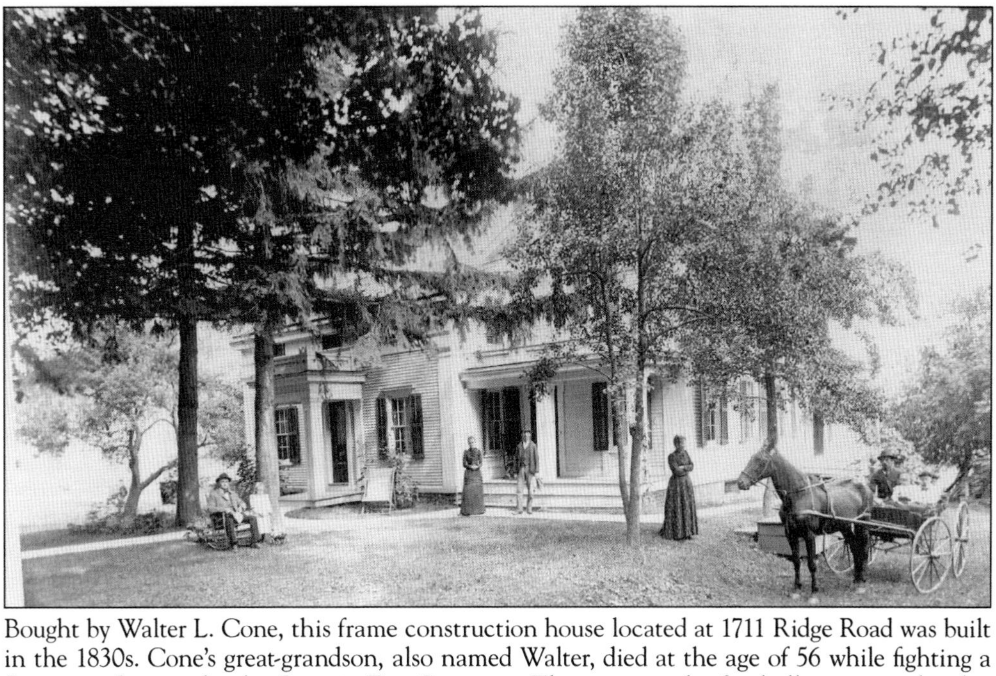

Bought by Walter L. Cone, this frame construction house located at 1711 Ridge Road was built in the 1830s. Cone's great-grandson, also named Walter, died at the age of 56 while fighting a fire as a volunteer for the Ontario Fire Company. The street to the fire hall was named in his honor. Pictured here are, from left to right, Walter L. Cone, Ada Belle Suter, Mrs. Glen C. Cone, Glen C. Cone, Nellie Cone, Floyd Gates, and Floyd's wife and his children.

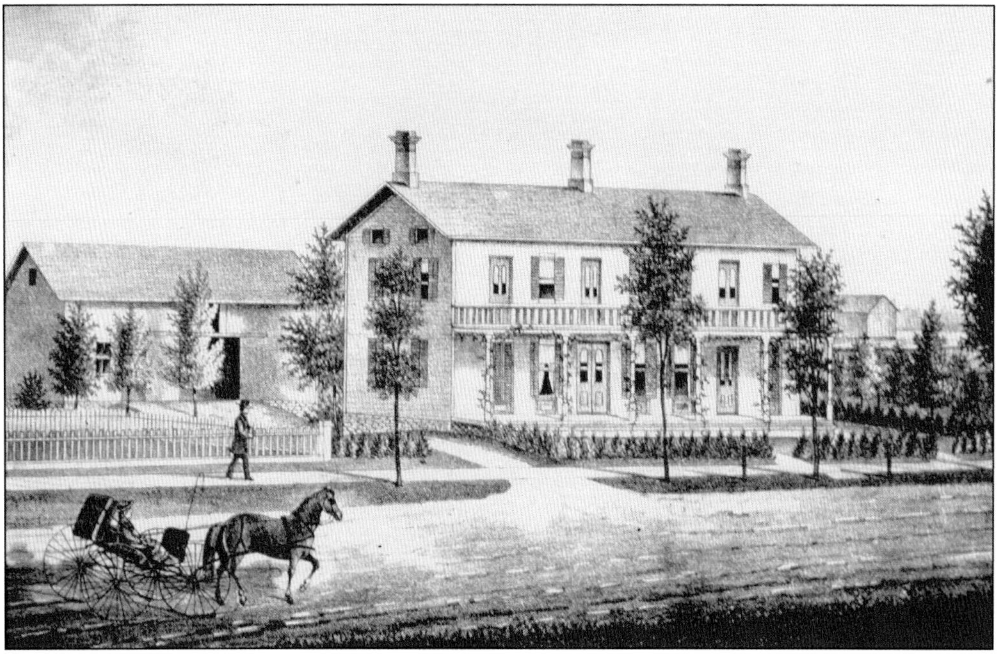

The old Hezekiah Hill farm was also a hotel that was known as the Allen House. Beginning in 1910, it was run by Charles Allen. The hotel had guests from as far away as New England, New York City, Brooklyn, and New Orleans. The rates were $2 per day. The food was prepared by Charles's wife, Ada, and was well known in the area. A full-course chicken dinner cost 50¢; a big breakfast cost 25¢. Schoolteachers would often board here. Other guests included traveling salesmen (drummers), who would stay here while they were working in the area. In the summer of 1910, the New York Telephone Company opened an office in the rooms in back of the main dining room. The hotel closed in 1918. It was purchased in 1941 by Gus VandeWater, who converted it into an apartment building with five apartments as shown below.

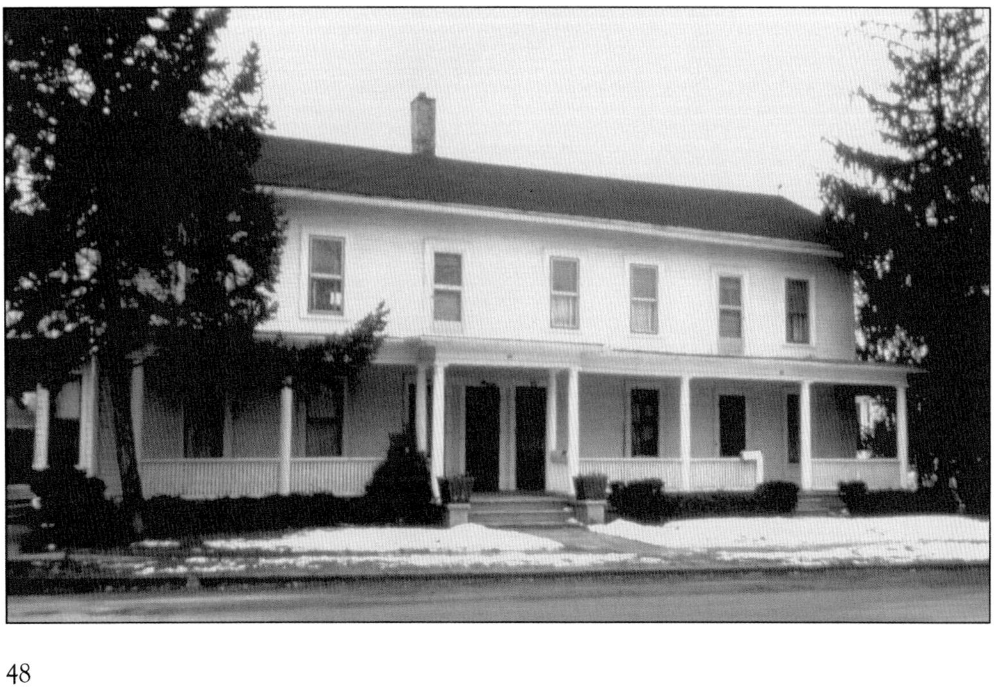

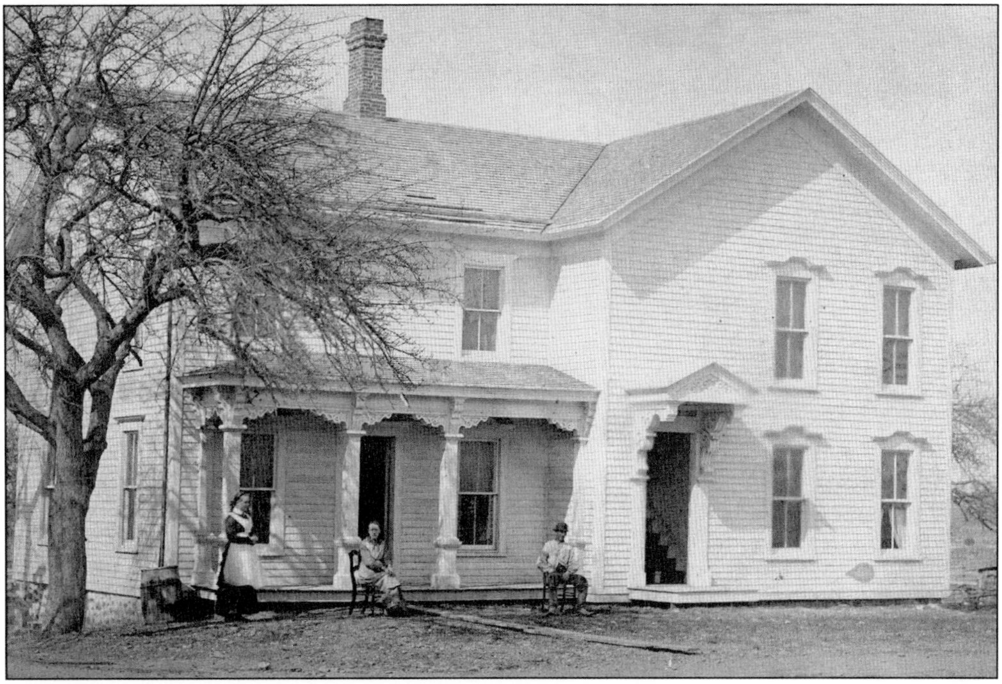

The Austin Clark homestead, built in 1877, was located on Main Street. Shown here are Alice Goodnow and the Clarks.

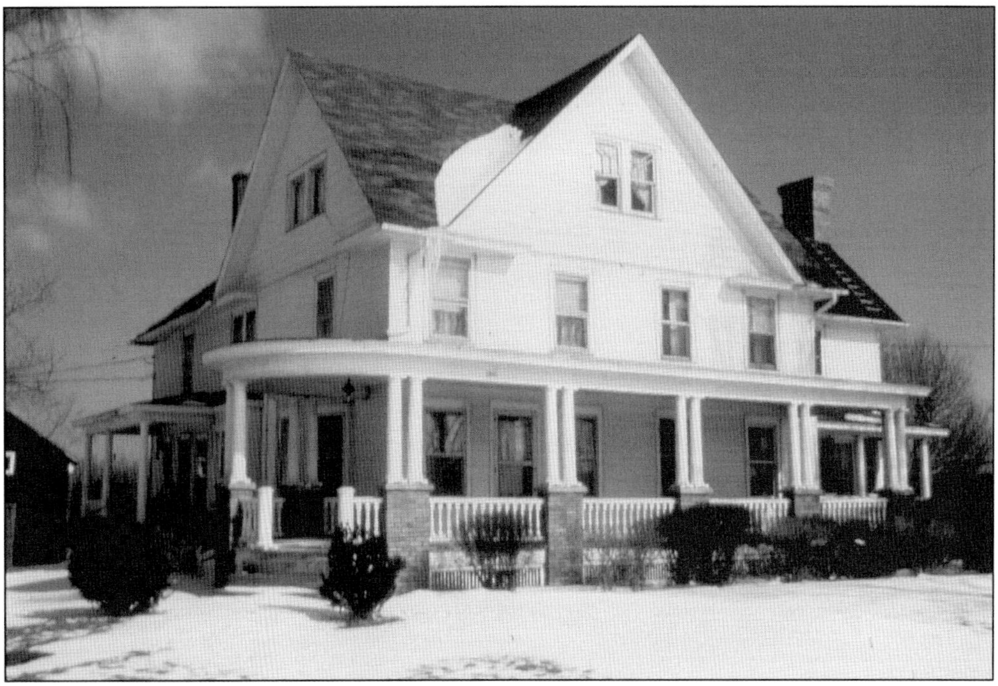

The Gates farmhouse was made into a double home by Floyd Gates when his son Ross married Alice Sheldon in 1912. In 1987, Ross Gates celebrated his 100th birthday at the Sheldon Cottage, Gates Grove on Lake Road. The Gates' 230-acre farm was bought by Rochester Gas and Electric in order to build the nuclear power plant.

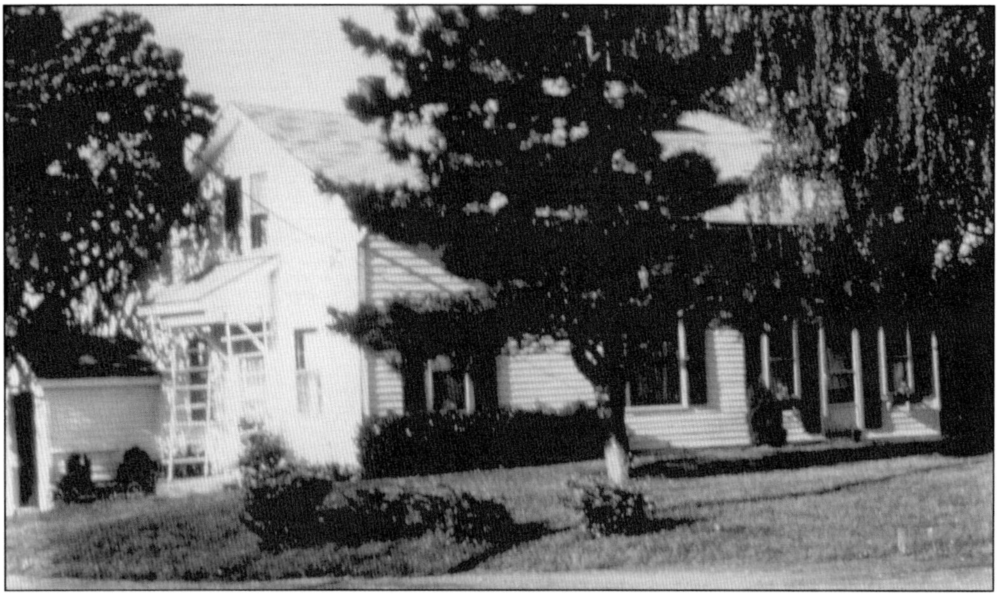

The Slocum-Boughton home was the first home built on the ridge between Webster and Ontario in 1827, in an area then known as Wray's Corners. On December 29, 1863, Benjamin Slocum and his wife, Catherine, came to Ontario and bought the 70-acre farm on the corner of Slocum and Ridge Roads for $4,200. He was the highway commissioner then, as his great-great-grandson William is today.

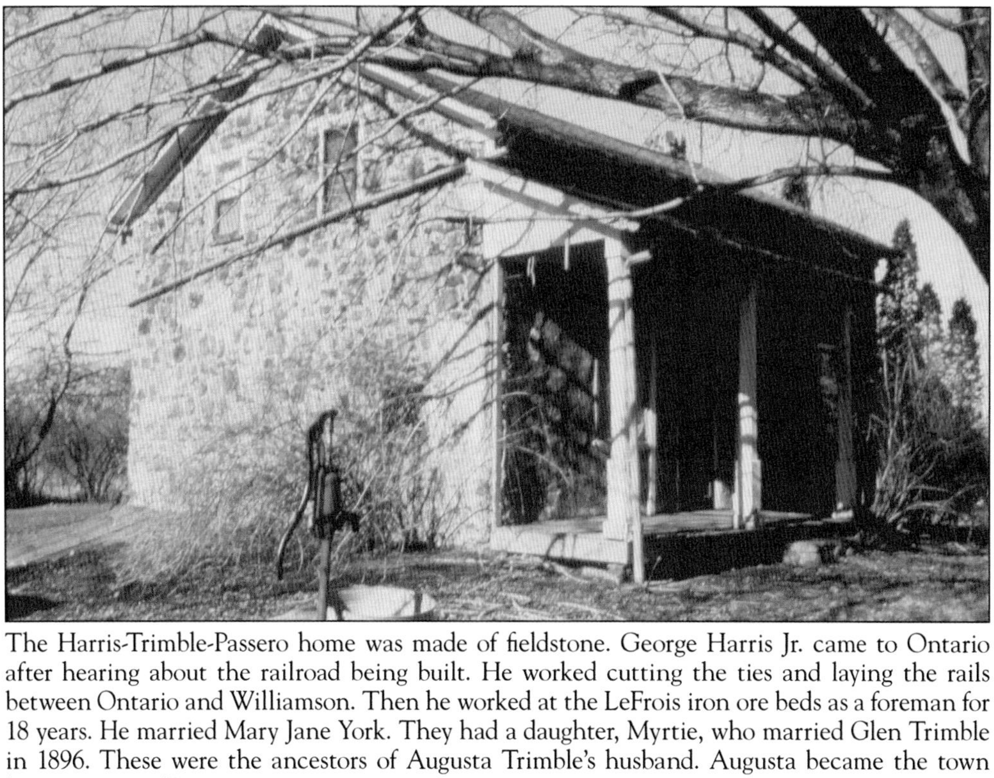

The Harris-Trimble-Passero home was made of fieldstone. George Harris Jr. came to Ontario after hearing about the railroad being built. He worked cutting the ties and laying the rails between Ontario and Williamson. Then he worked at the LeFrois iron ore beds as a foreman for 18 years. He married Mary Jane York. They had a daughter, Myrtie, who married Glen Trimble in 1896. These were the ancestors of Augusta Trimble's husband. Augusta became the town historian in 1957.

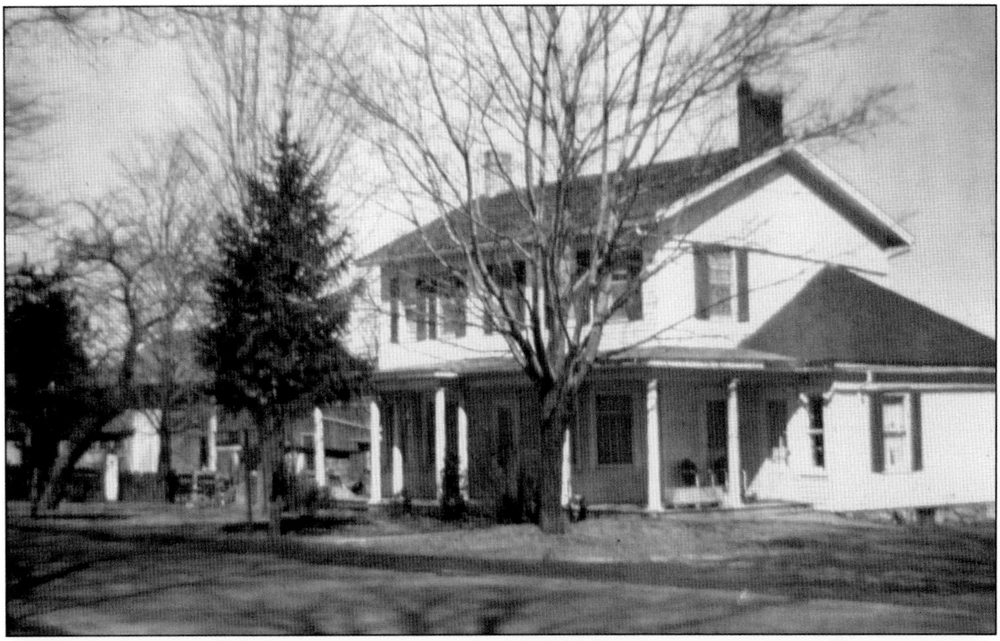

This is the Hurum Harrison farmhouse located at 2435 Ridge Road. It was the home of Zella Clark Albright's mother, Phebe Harrison Clark. This farm has remained in the family for 175 years.

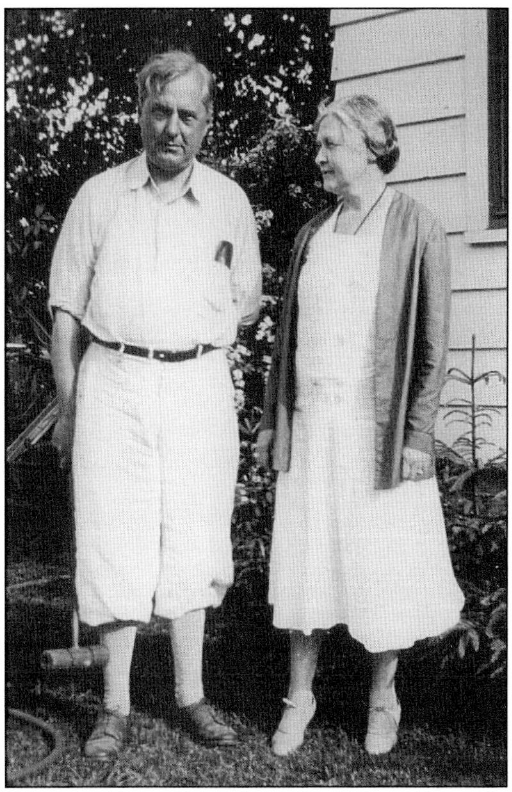

Johnson Stanley and Zella Clark Albright are pictured here on June 19, 1932, celebrating their 25th anniversary at their cottage on the lake at 1969 Lake Road.

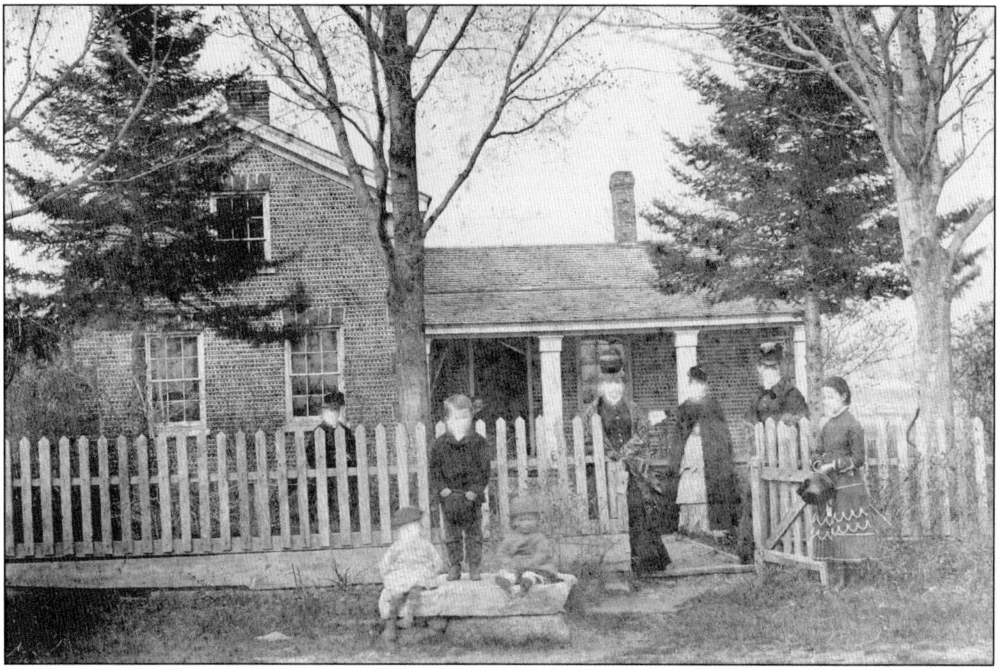

The Clark-Freeman-Buck cobblestone house, located at 5820 Walworth Road, was built in 1838. Shown above in 1879, it was later expanded with an addition when extra space was needed (shown below). The cobblestones selected are lake-washed stones with some light pink and grey ones mixed in. Sometimes the lake-washed stones are so carefully selected for size, shape, and color that the homes, when complete, look like they were machine made. Sorting of the stones was often done in "bees" where the neighbors would get together to help. This house has two entrances sharing a common porch. The first owners, John and Elizabeth Clark, who came from Yorkshire, England, in 1829, originally lived in Williamson. They later moved to Ontario and lived here in this house.

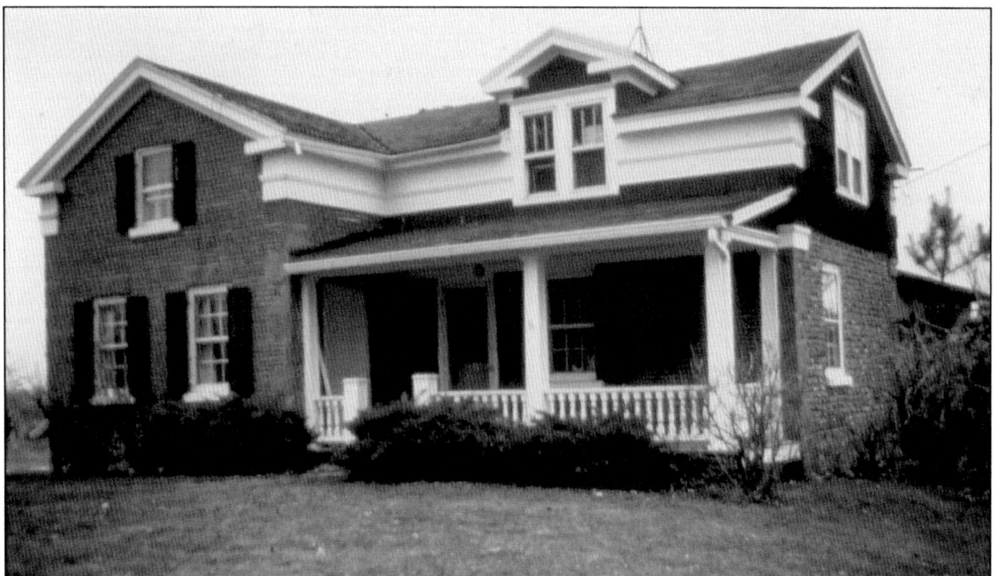

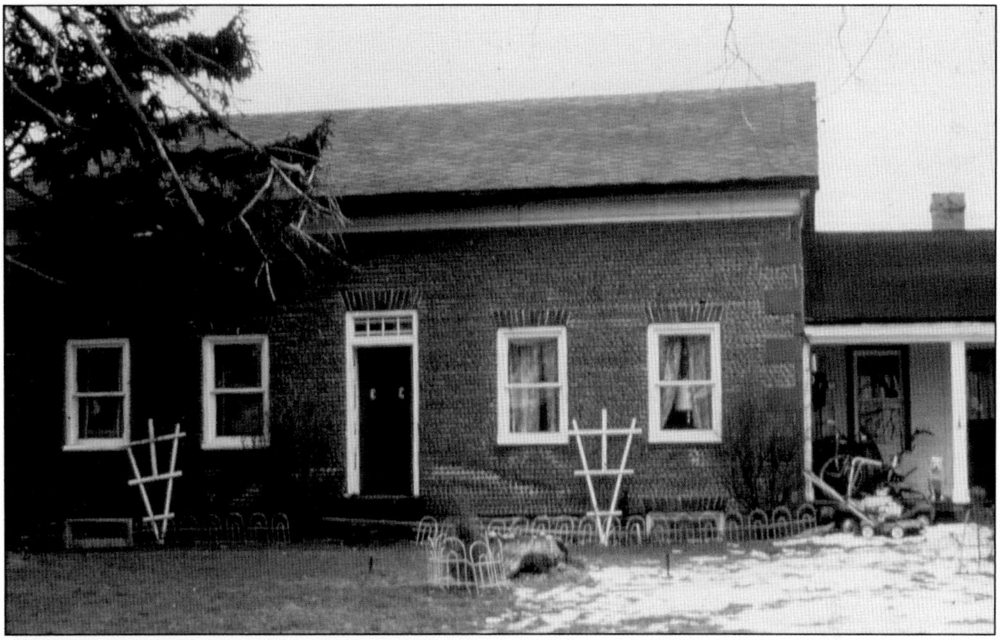

The Riker-Enderlin-Hatch cobblestone house located at 7235 Knickerbocker Road was built by a mason named Potter in 1842. A north wing was added in 1868. John Riker and his wife, Mary Thorne, came to Ontario by horse and wagon. John would wade out into Lake Ontario to carefully select the cobblestones for this house. John is the great-grandfather of Natalie Slocum, Diane Doyle, and Marcia DeHollander.

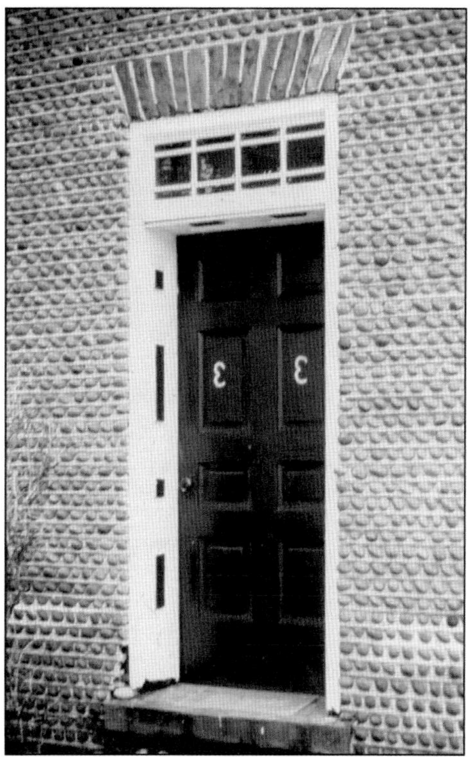

A close-up of the door of the Riker home gives one a good look at the cobblestone pattern. Notice the rows of evenly spaced stones. The mortar has no distinctive pattern. The eight-paneled, recessed door has a rectangular transom over it.

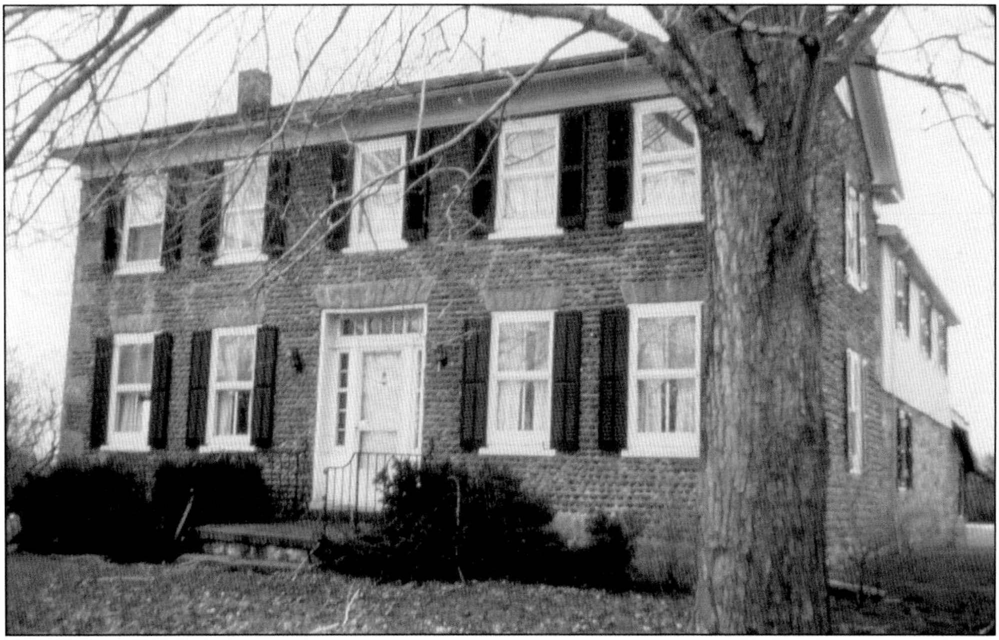

This is the Cook-Camp-Scully cobblestone house located at 5656 Walworth Road. The history of this house goes back to the Phelps and Gorham land purchase. The original 101.2-acre farm was surveyed in 1836 by George Mathewson. Then Joseph Fellows, who was a land agent, got the title from Phelps and Gorham. Fellows sold it to Orin and Matilda Moss, who sold it to George and Jane Russell in 1864. Andrew Cook bought it from the Russells in 1883; Dr. Camp bought the home in 1912, and the Scullys in 1956.

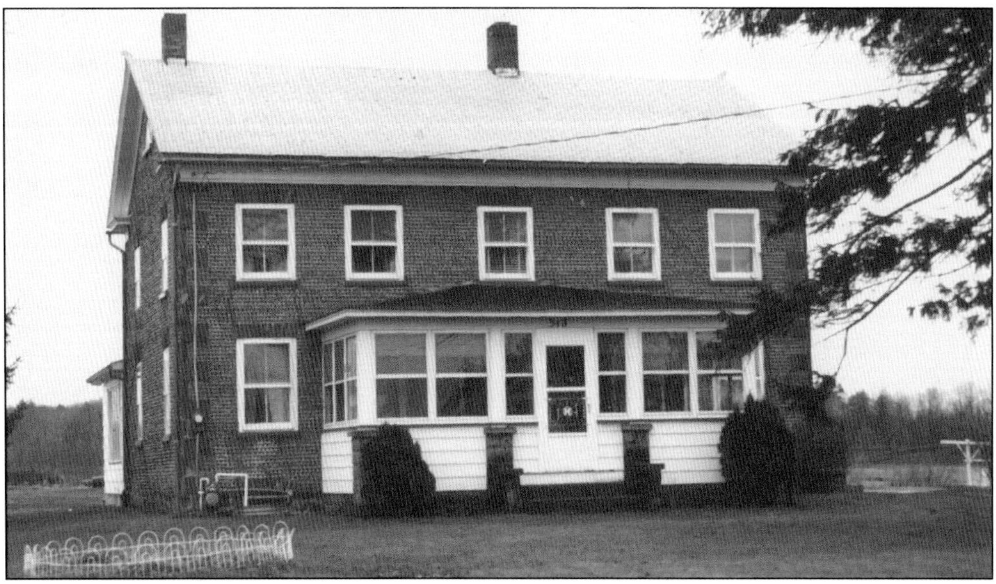

This cobblestone house at 6952 Ontario Center Road was built by a mason named Clark for Marvin Gurnee in 1845. It was sold in 1899 to Dr. J. S. Brandt. Other owners of this house were the Albright brothers (Jacob and James), Debolt, Taft, and Hillegeer. Many of these cobblestone houses had walls that were a foot thick. The front of the house has lake stones, the sides have stones of larger size, and the back has field stones.

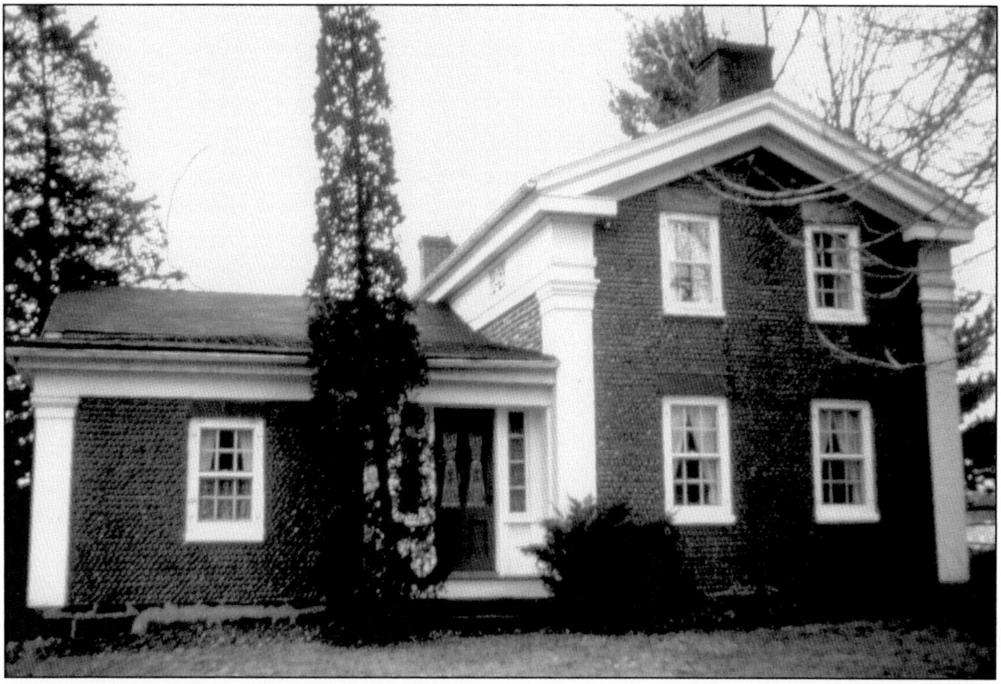

The Bigsby-Pratt-Eaton-Brewer-Motley-Wilson cobblestone was built in the Greek Revival style. It is the only cobblestone house in Ontario with wooden pilasters instead of stone quoins at the corners. It is located at 1695 Lake Road.

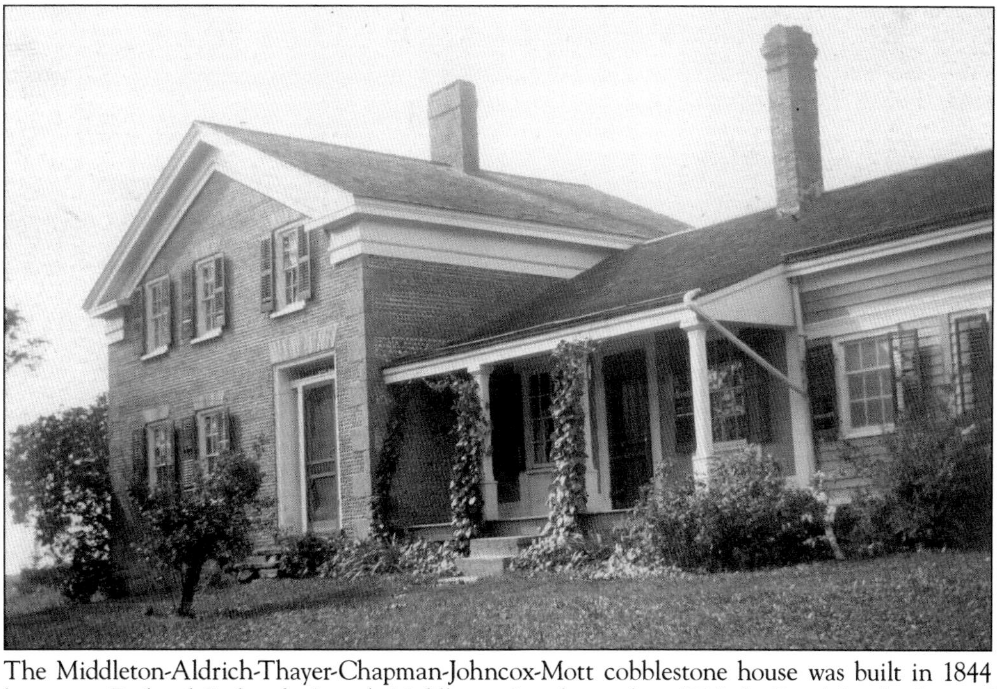

The Middleton-Aldrich-Thayer-Chapman-Johncox-Mott cobblestone house was built in 1844 by mason Richard Stokes for Joseph Middleton. It is located at 487 Lake Road. In the front of the house the cobblestones are lake-washed red sandstone. There are six courses per quoin. The quoins are the large stone blocks at the corners of the house.

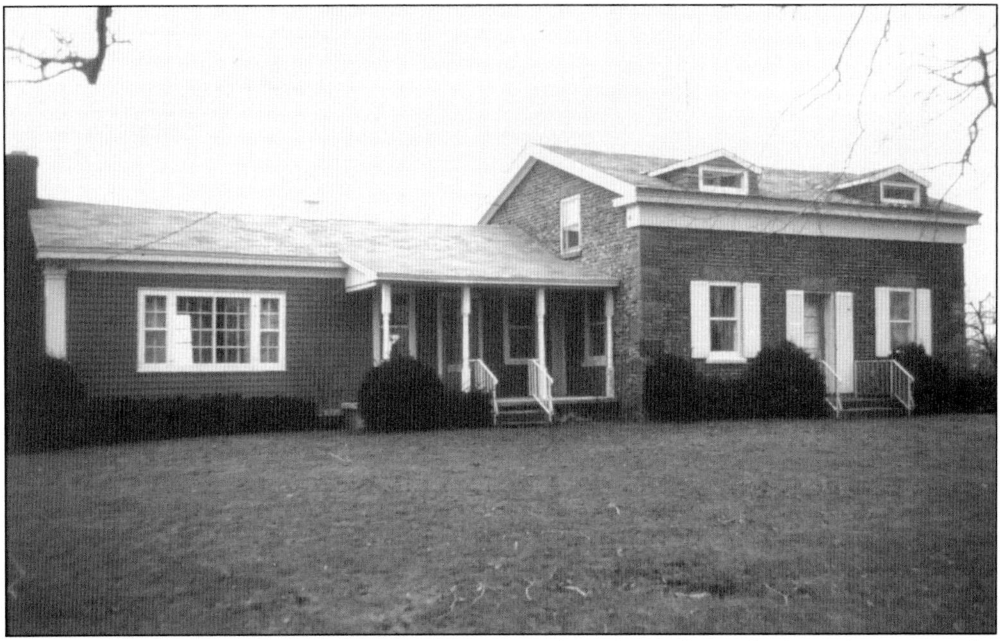

The Casey-Bebernitz cobblestone home, at 5708 Walworth Road, was built in the 1830s. The walls are built from various colored round and oval lake cobblestones with grey limestone quoins supporting the corners of the house. The masons who created these beautiful houses were very distinctive about their designs and styles.

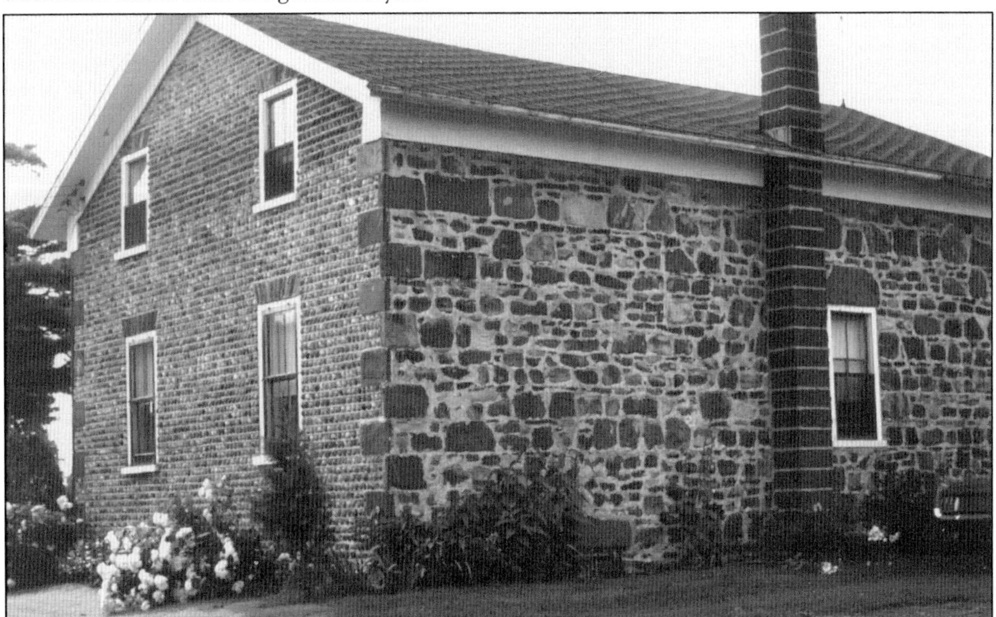

The Gage-Verberg cobblestone home, at 7101 Knickerbocker Road, was built with red sandstone quoins and cobblestones in the herringbone pattern. Sometimes a cobblestone pattern of stones would be neater in the front of the house and more random on the other three sides, which is really obvious in this view of the house. The first Gages to arrive in Ontario were Jesse and his wife Marcy.

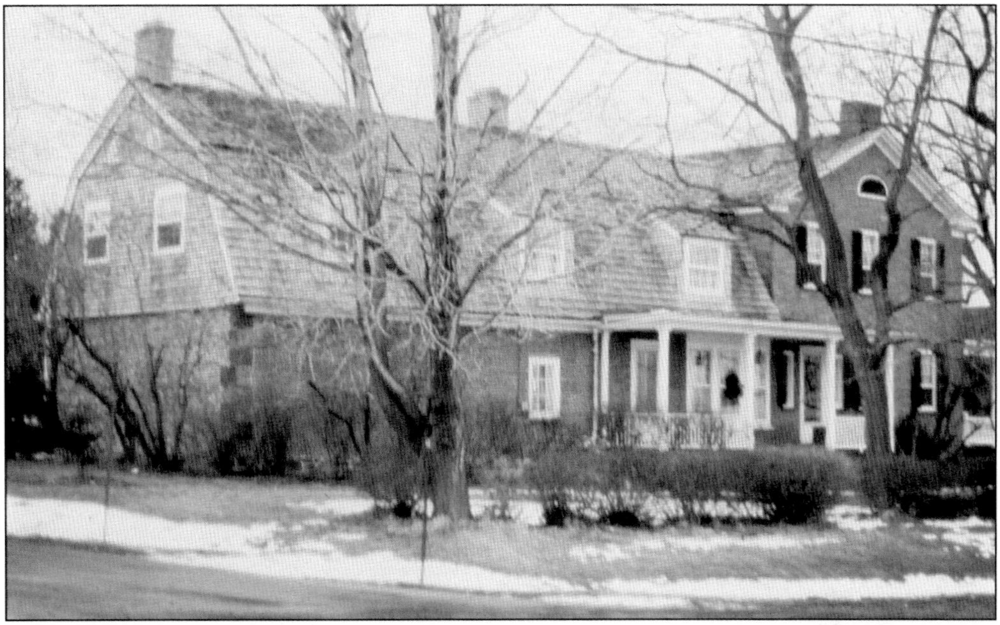

The Teats-Sherburne-Wickes-Loomis-Allen-Holm cobblestone house is at the corner of Lake Road and Ontario Center Road at 1556 Lake Road. The cornerstone dates it as 1835. For many years it was known as the Sherburne Homestead. Mrs. Sherburne Teats later sold it to the Wickes family. Norman Loomis and his wife, Laura (Jinny), bought it from the Wickes. They sold it to the Allens, who recently sold it to Dave Holm. The cobblestones used are carefully selected lake-washed red sandstone for the front. It combines a one-and-a-half-story cobblestone wing, which was added to a two-story brick gable roofed main section. The photograph below is a close-up of the cobblestones of this home. It shows that color was not an important factor in choosing the stones for the sides.

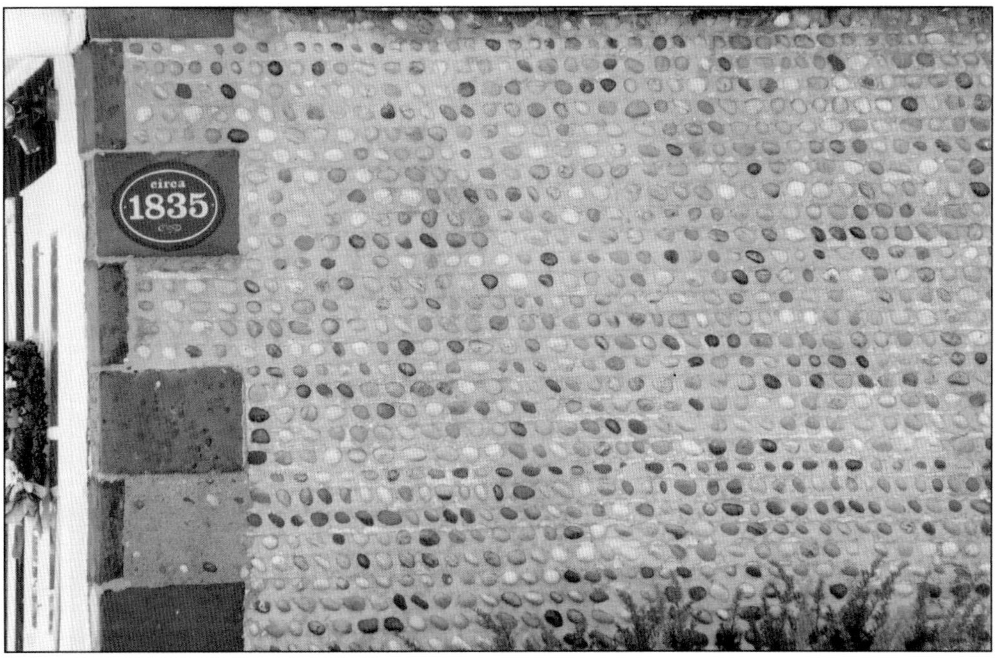

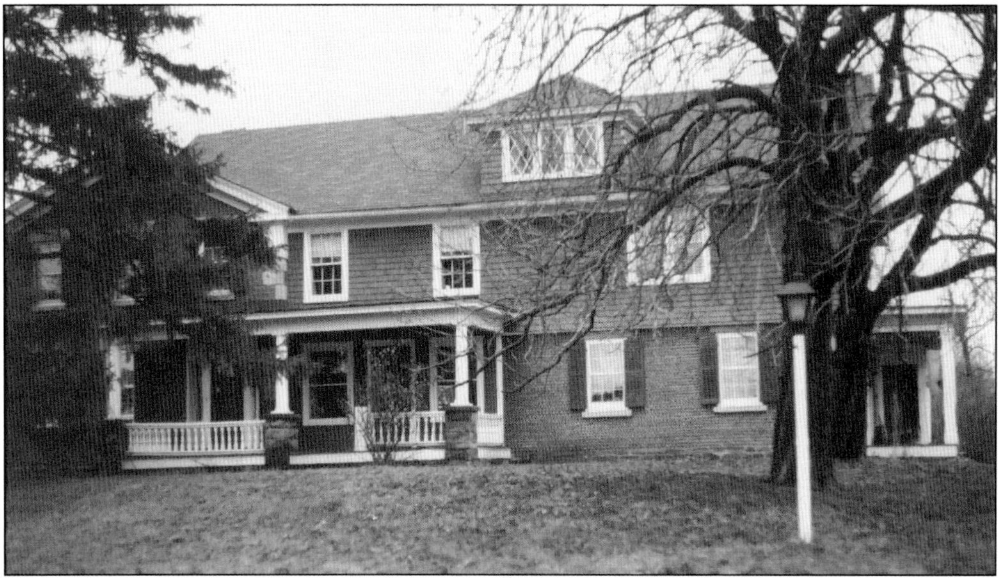

Zebedee Hodges had this cobblestone house built by a mason named Clark in 1840. It is located at 7272 Ontario Center Road. It is made of lake-washed, oblong-shaped red sandstone in the herringbone pattern. It has two main entrances and 14 rooms. Much of this house has been shingled over.

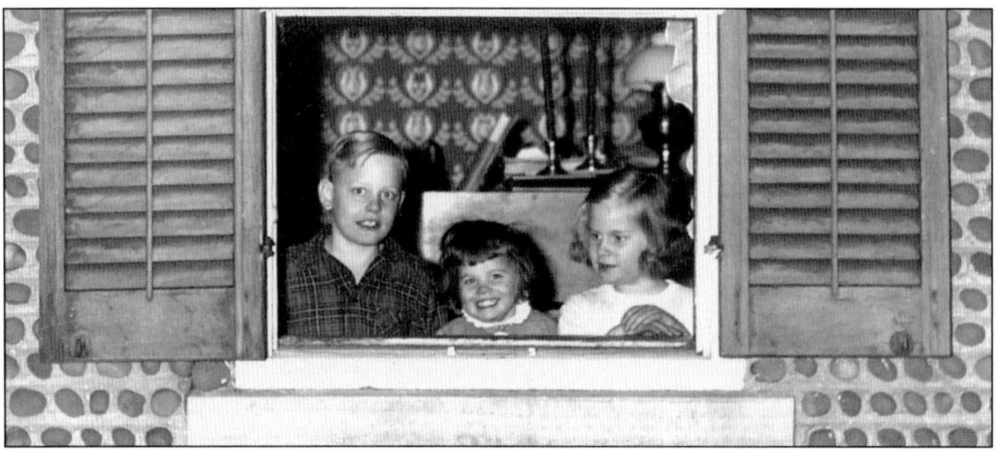

This close-up of the front of the Hodges-Peterson-Taillie home shows the detail of the cobblestone pattern. In the window are, from left to right, Glen, Sue, and Mary Gwen Peterson. Children were often enlisted to gather stones and sort them by size by passing the stones through an iron ring called a "beetle" ring.

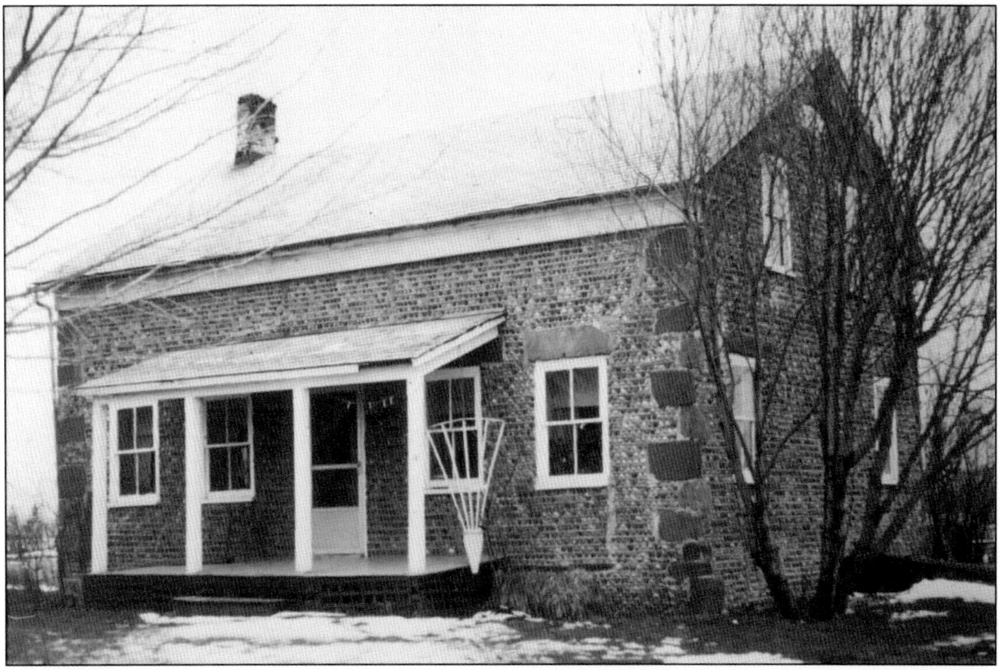

The Jobse-VanEnwyck cobblestone house is located at 7105 Fisher Road, formerly known as East Town Line Road. Charles and Alice Van Enwyck bought this house from Henry, Charles's father. The stones used to build it were carried by oxcart from Sodus Point. It took two weeks to transport a single load. Perhaps that is why color was not important here. The close-up (below) shows the layers of stones and mortar. Here the mortar pattern with raised ridges is more distinctive. A mason could lay three rows of cobblestones in a day, working 10 to 12 hours per day. It is said that the masons would work on several nearby houses at the same time since they could only do a little work at a time on one house before stopping to wait for the mortar to dry.

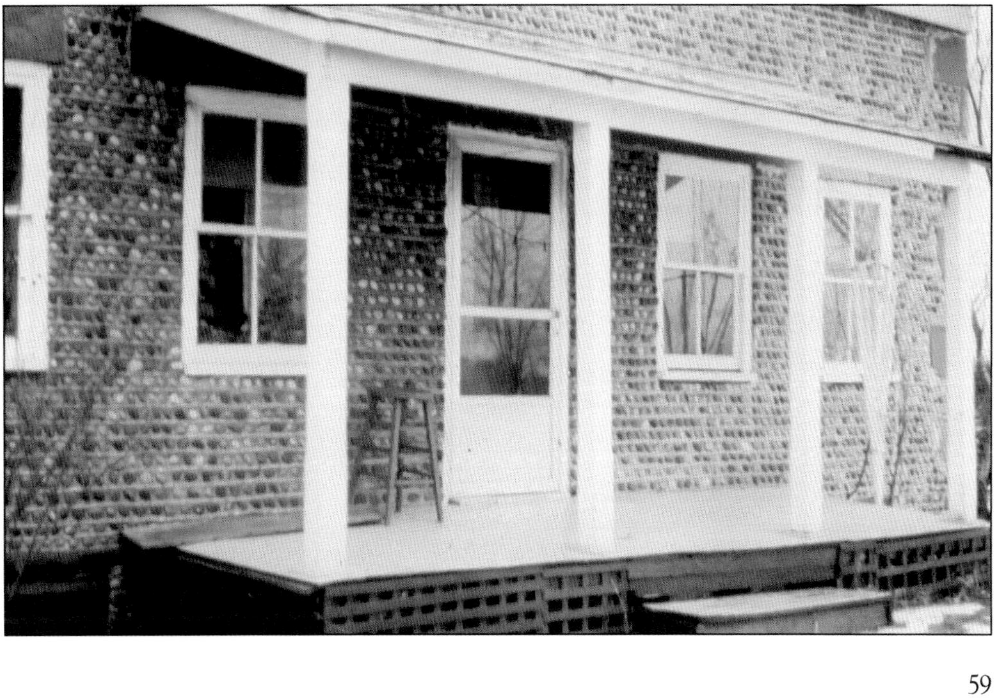

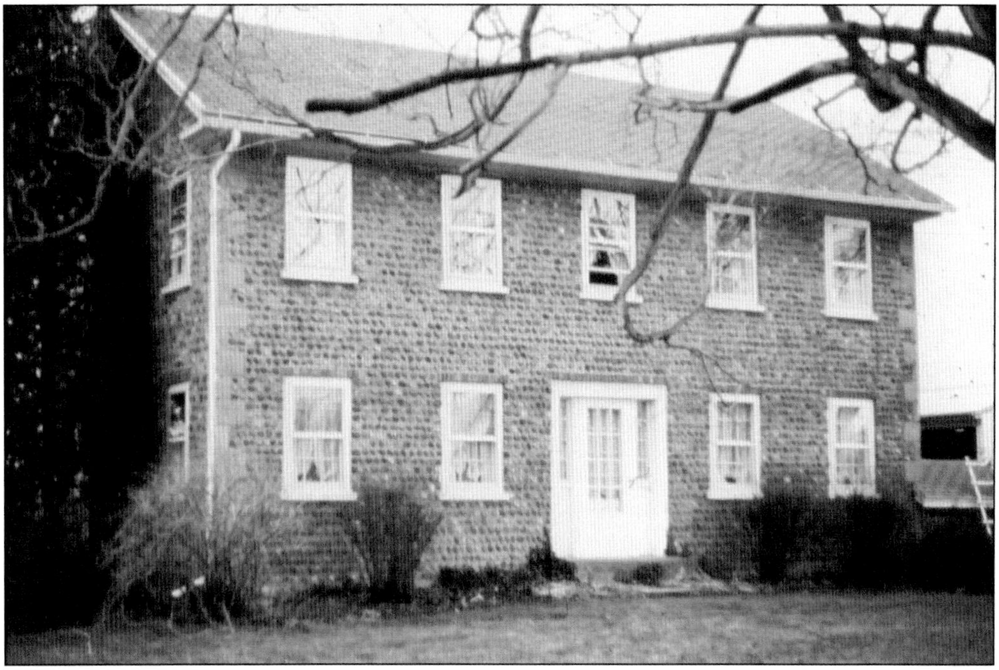

This is the Whitney-Raymour cobblestone home located at 5668 Lincoln Road. It is a two-story, five-bay house. The stones are an assortment of colors and shapes.

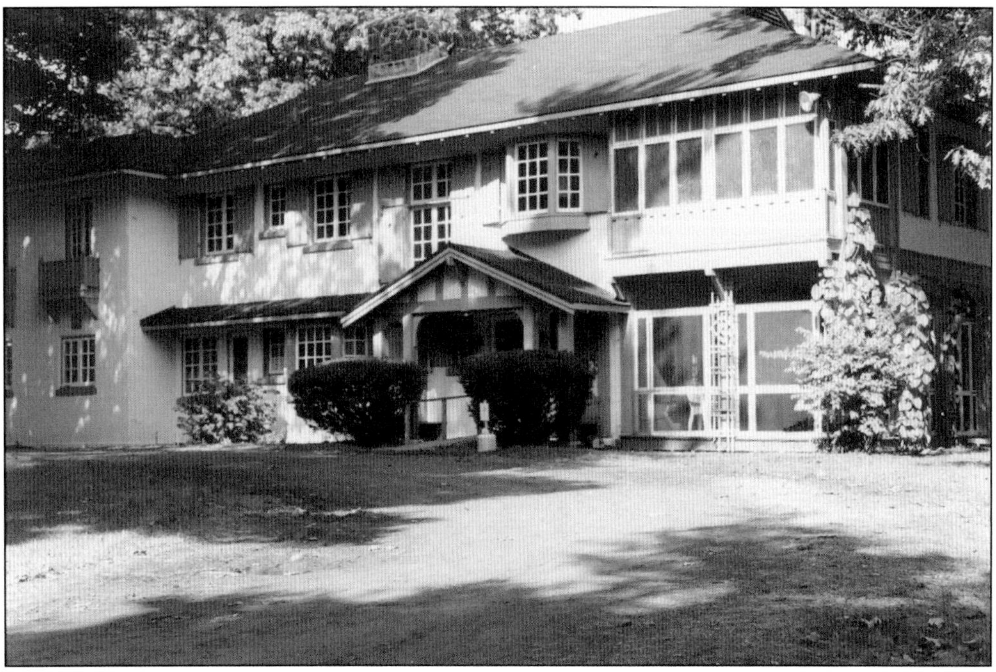

The Ellwanger-Fields Manor House is located on the grounds of the Ginna Nuclear Power plant. Built in the 1920s as a summer home, this two-story home features four bedrooms facing the lake and servants quarters on the opposite side. There is a hidden transom near the ceiling by the main staircase that is accessed from the attic. This is where the owners hid their summer home valuables during the winter months.

Five

Along Main Street

Ridge Road in Ontario Village is also known as Main Street. This chapter includes images captured long ago traveling along Main Street from east to west. It would certainly be a fascinating journey to take this same route today, along with this information, and compare what is along Main Street today with what remains of the buildings from long ago. While some of these homes and businesses are still intact, others have had additions made, and some are disguised with modern alterations. Others have been gone a long time.

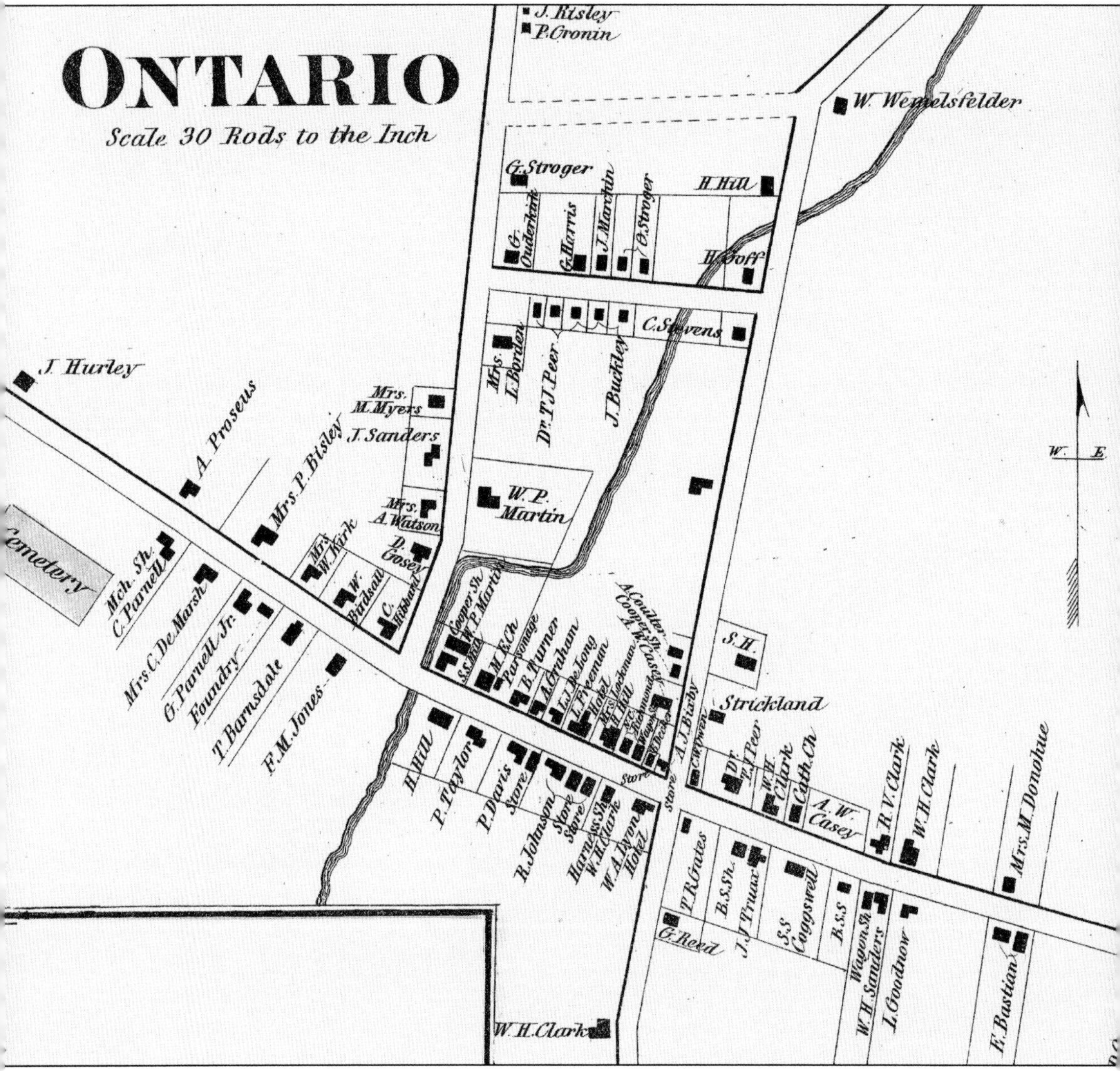

This map of Ontario is taken from D. G. Beer's and Company *Atlas of Wayne County New York, 1874*.

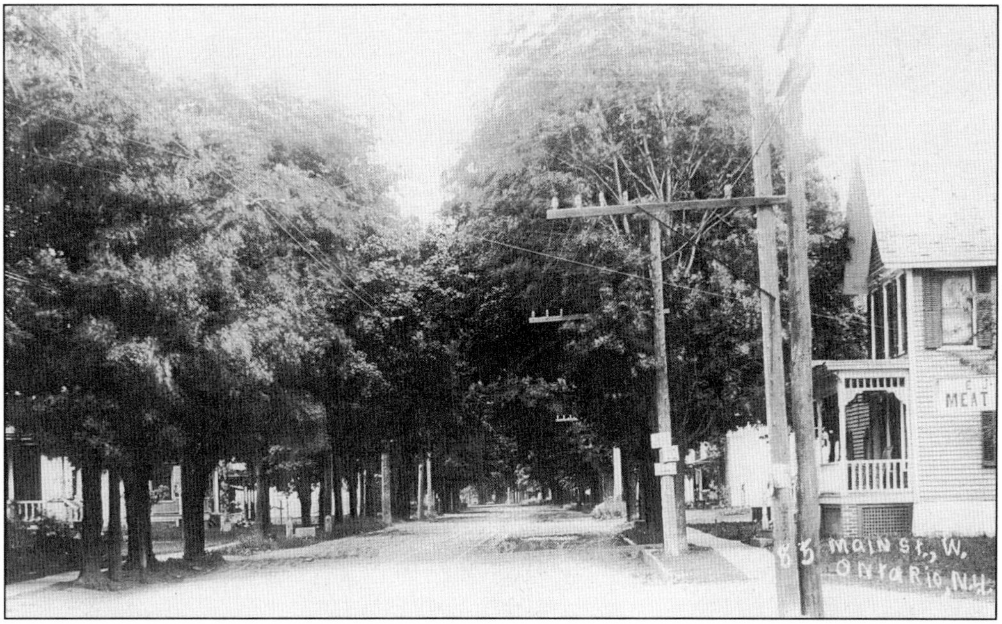

This is a tree-lined view of Main Street looking east at Furnace/Walworth Road during the summer.

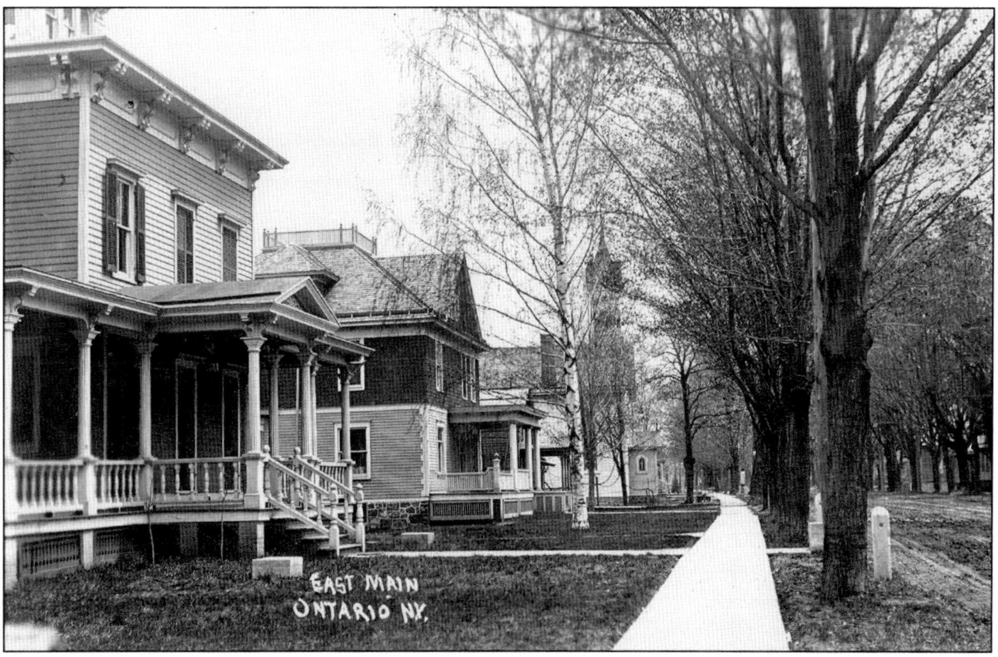

An easterly view of the north side of Main Street at Furnace/Walworth Road shows the Peer house, the James Maher home, and the Catholic church in 1910.

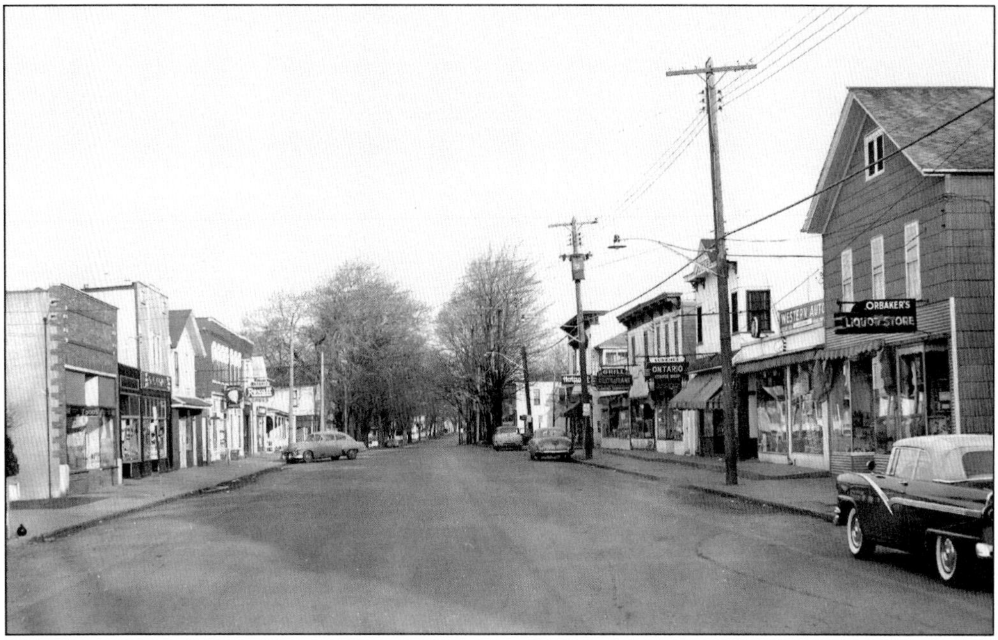

This view of both sides of Main Street, looking west from Furnace/Walworth Road, was taken in 1957.

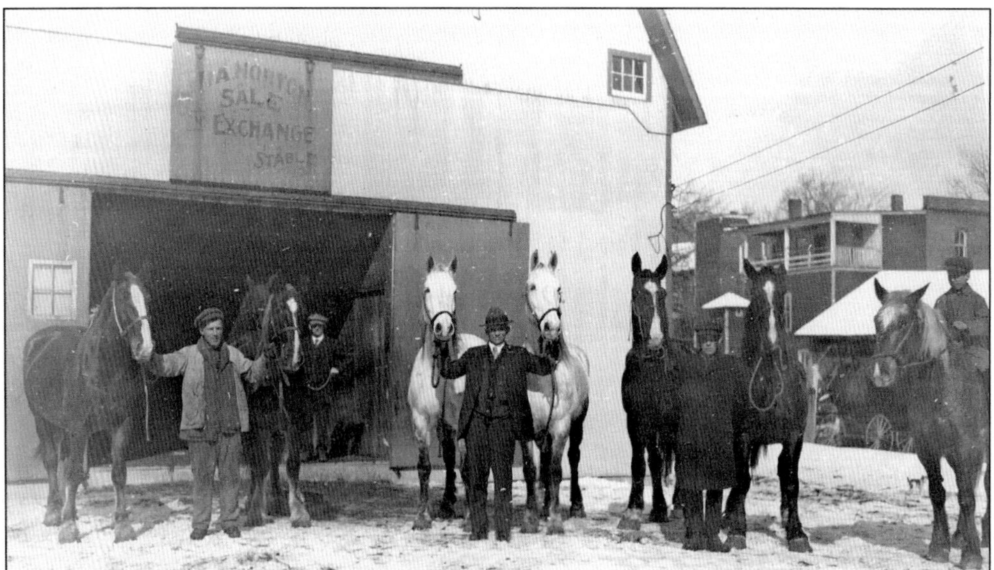

On the west side of Walworth Road, just south of Main Street, is where Ira Norton, a horse trader, had his barn. Horses came by railroad from the West and were driven loose to the barn where there were 25–30 stalls. They were then auctioned.

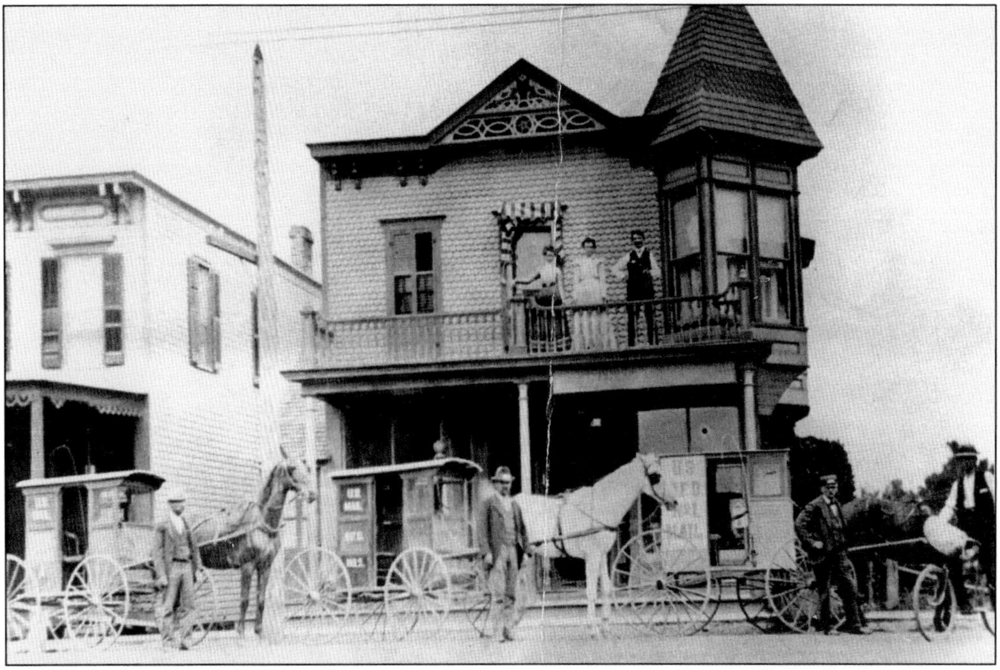

Mail delivery was much different in 1895. Shown here at the post office on the north side of Main Street, with mail wagons, are (from left to right) Charles Anthony, Rass House, Jim Prentice, and Emmet Teats (on the bicycle). Harvey Selleck and his wife are on the balcony.

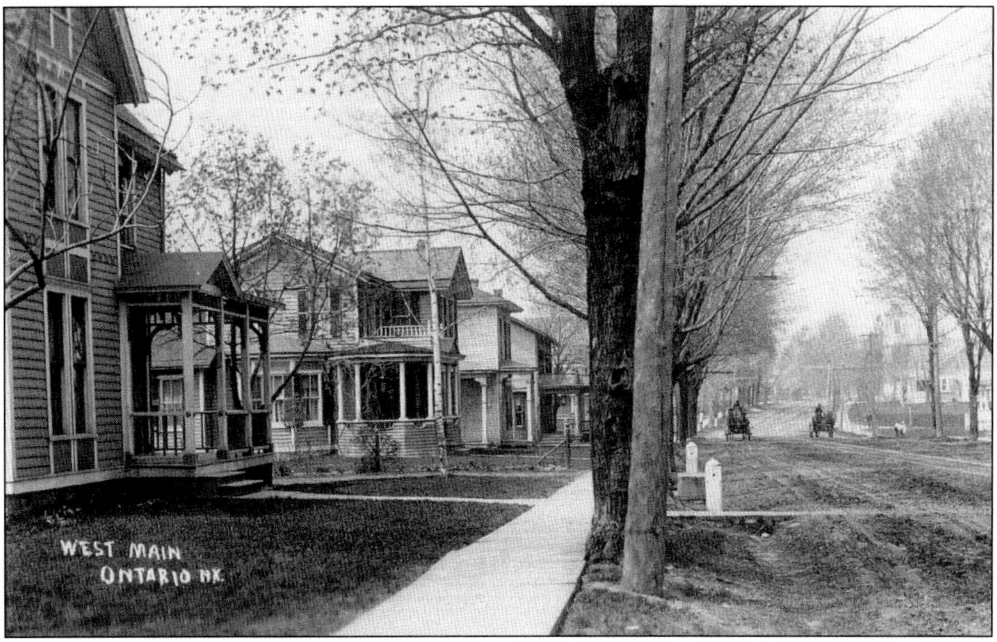

Shown here, looking west, are four Main Street houses. The first house on the left is 1988 Ridge Road. The second house is 1980 Ridge Road. The third house was Dr. Thompson's house at 1974 Ridge Road. It burned in the 1930s and was completely remodeled and rebuilt. The fourth house, 1968 Ridge Road, is the old Hezekiah Hill house. The Baptist church is on the right in the background.

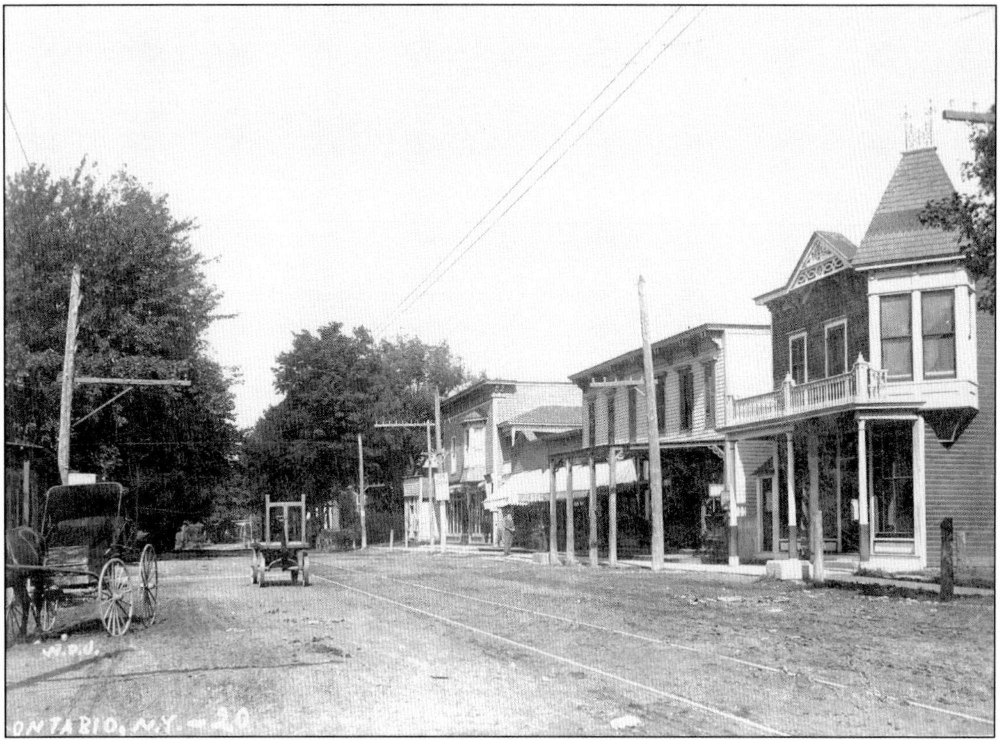

This is a view, looking west in 1908, of the north side of Main Street. The trolley tracks go down the center of the road with the electrical wires overhead.

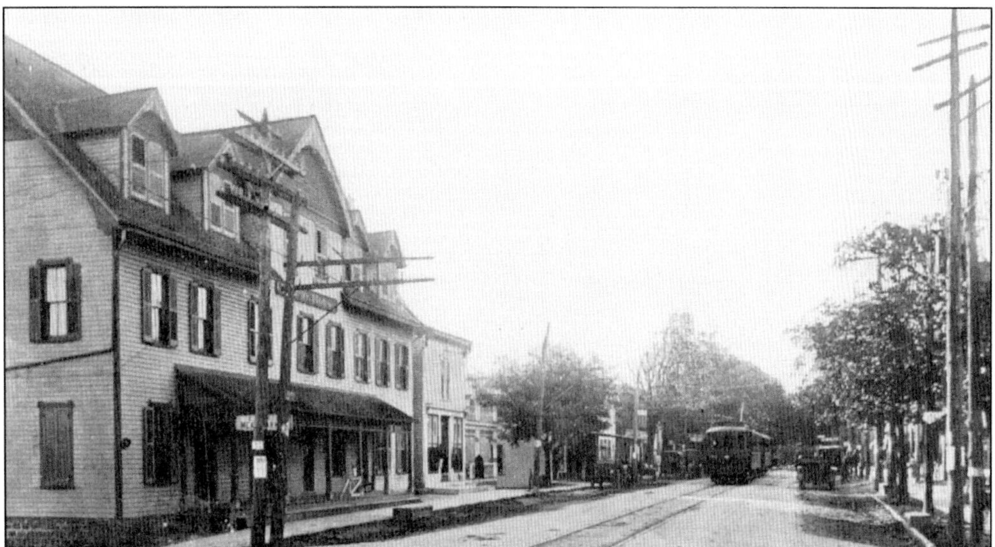

Looking west, at the south side of Main Street, the Ontario Hotel can be seen. A hotel on this site burned in June 1885 when a fire started in the loft of the barn behind it. The fire burned nine homes, four barns, three stores, two hotels, two sheds, two meat markets, two millinery shops, a marble shop, and a barbershop. This rebuilt hotel was torn down in 1944.

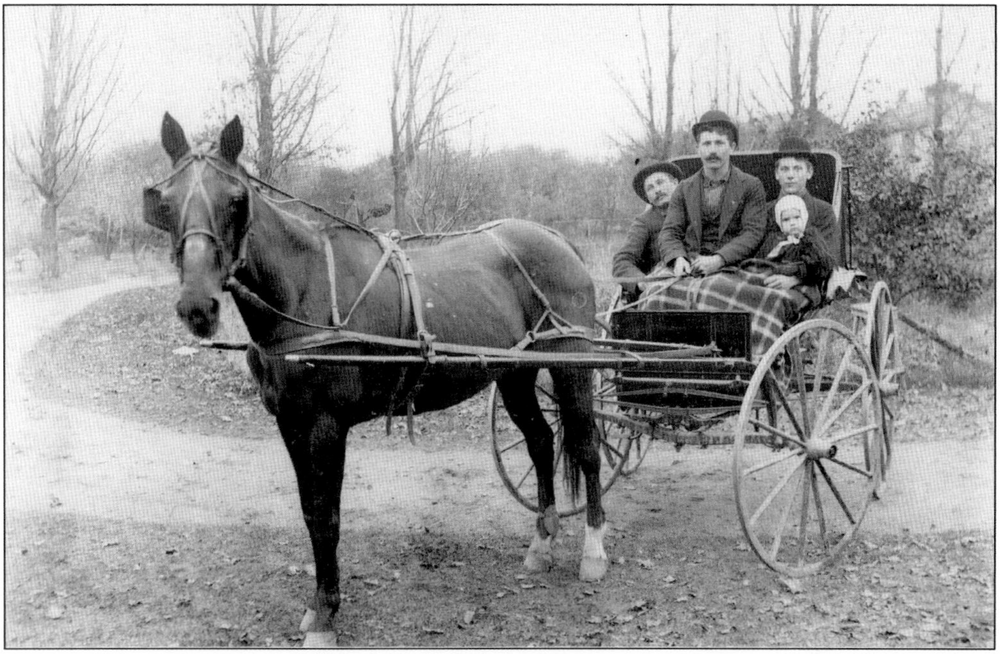

The horse and buggy was once the typical form of transportation (above). The trolley became an important addition to Ontario, traveling down Main Street between 1900 and 1929. The Rochester and Sodus Bay Trolley traveled from Rochester through the Main Streets of Webster, Union Hill, Ontario, Williamson, and into Sodus, turning north and ending at Sodus Point. From Ontario to Sodus the route passed through apple orchards. Below is the Kearns Homestead at 1058 Ridge Road. It was also the location of trolley stop No. 16. Many of the stops were labeled not by number but according to the person who lived in the home where it stopped.

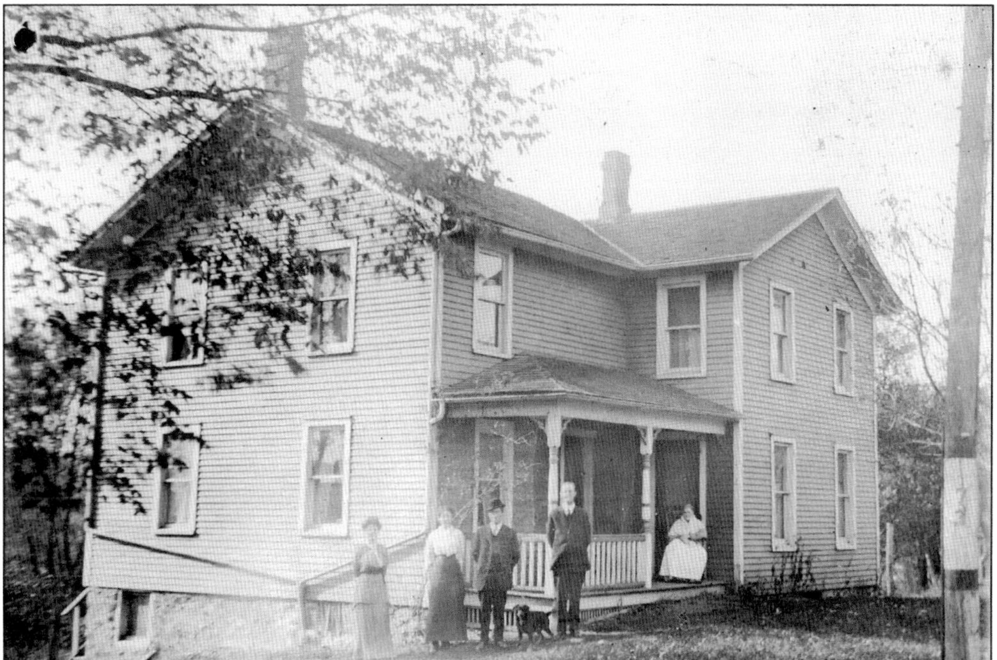

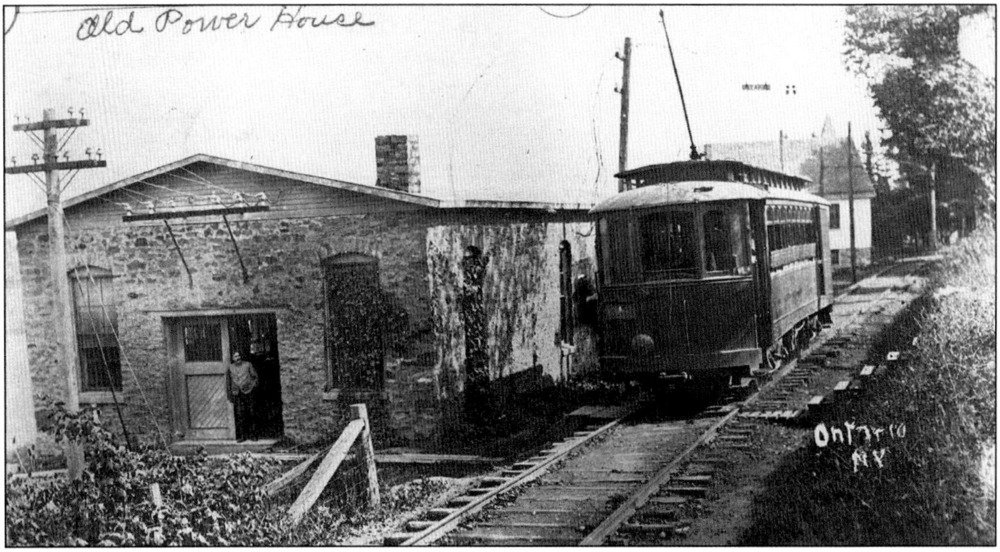

This early power booster station for the trolley was replaced in 1914 by the brick building. Located across from the Ontario Elementary School, it is currently a private home. The fare for the trolley was 2¢ per mile. The ride was noted for having a view of "forty miles of blossoms" in the springtime.

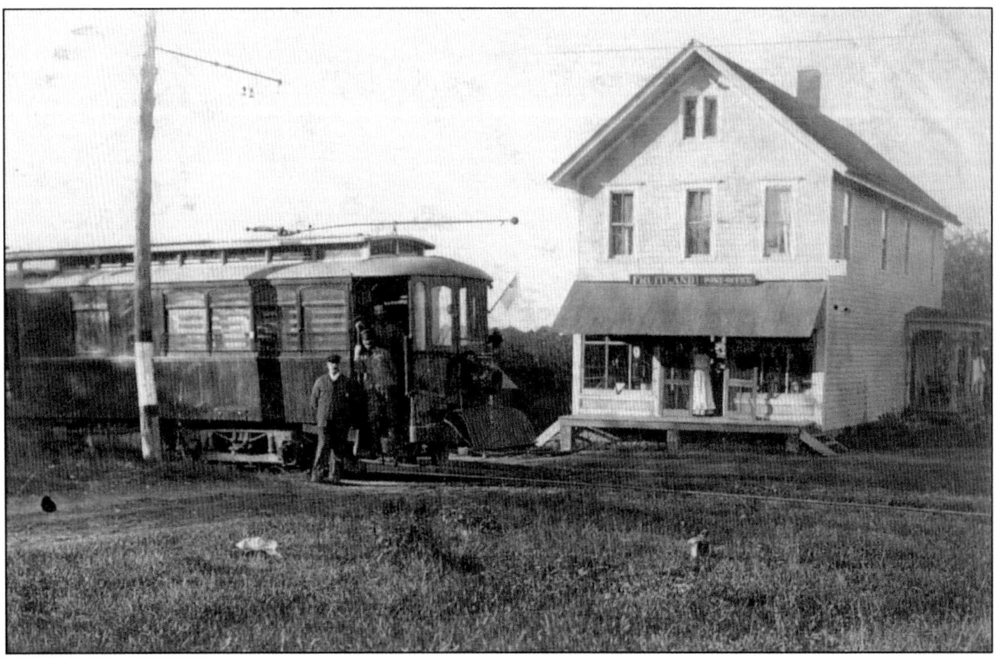

This shows the trolley at the store in Fruitland. The trolley carried both mail and freight, delivering to these Ridge Road businesses.

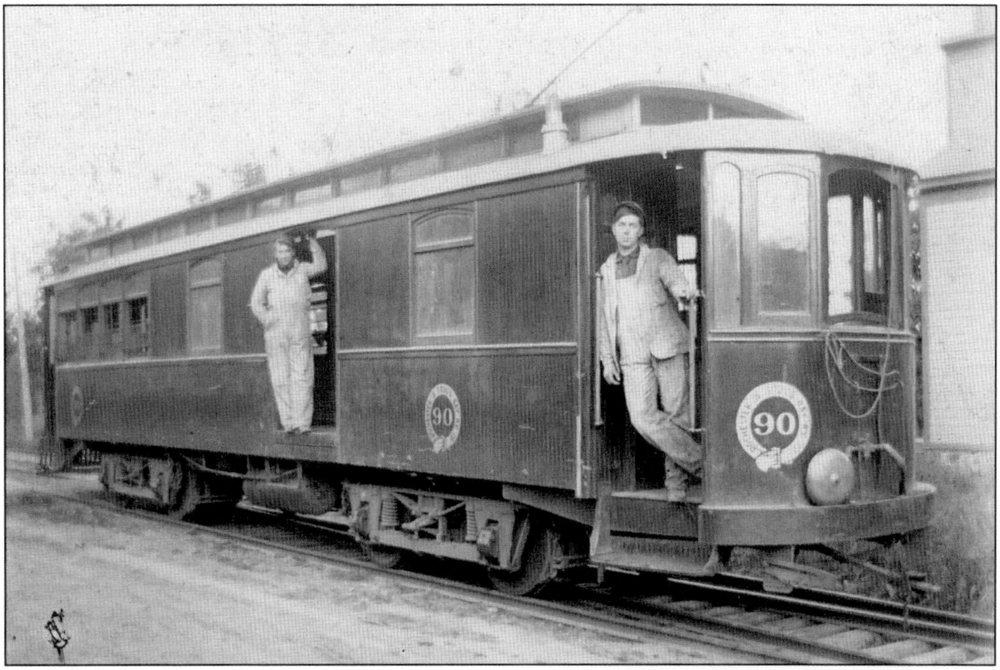

The first trolley to carry passengers to Sodus employed "Yank" Gloor as the motorman and "Shorty" Winslow as the conductor. Shown here from left to right are Gordon DeVille (conductor) and Bernie Stark (motorman) in 1903.

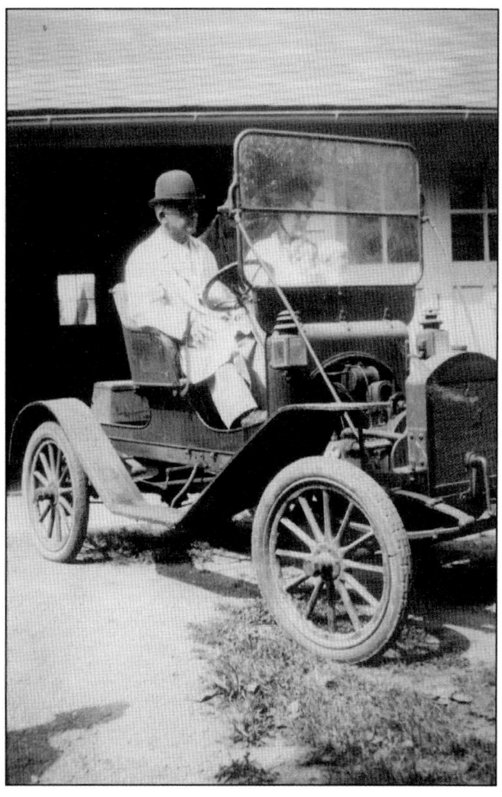

As time went on, more and more townspeople were able to have a car. By 1920, the automobile began cutting into the trolley business. The trolley was no longer an important mode of travel. James and Lena Maher and children are in Dave Craven's old 1931 Maxwell car.

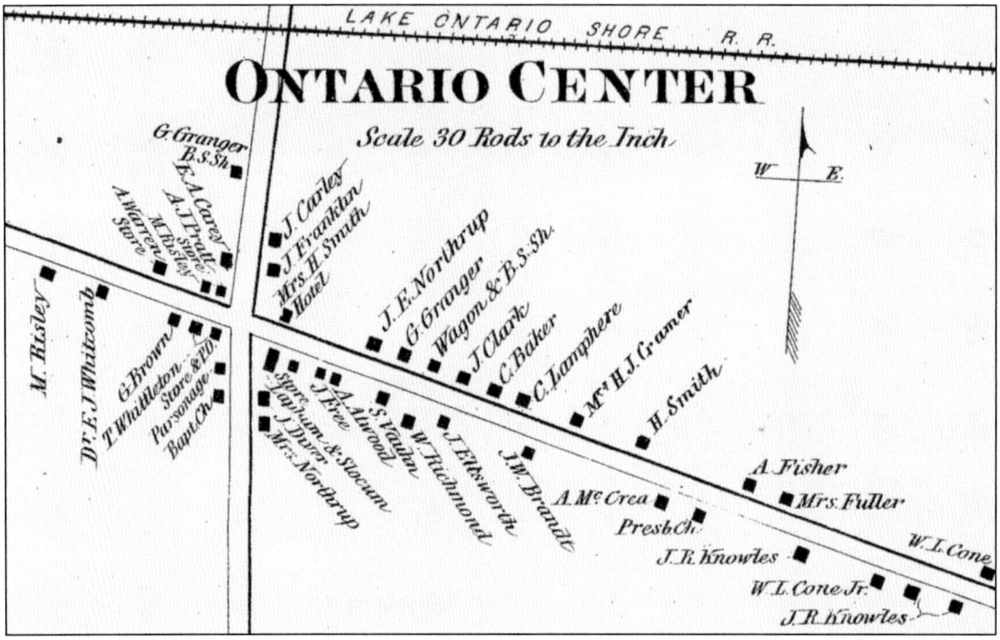

This map of Ontario Center is taken from D. G. Beer's and Company *Atlas of Wayne County New York, 1874.*

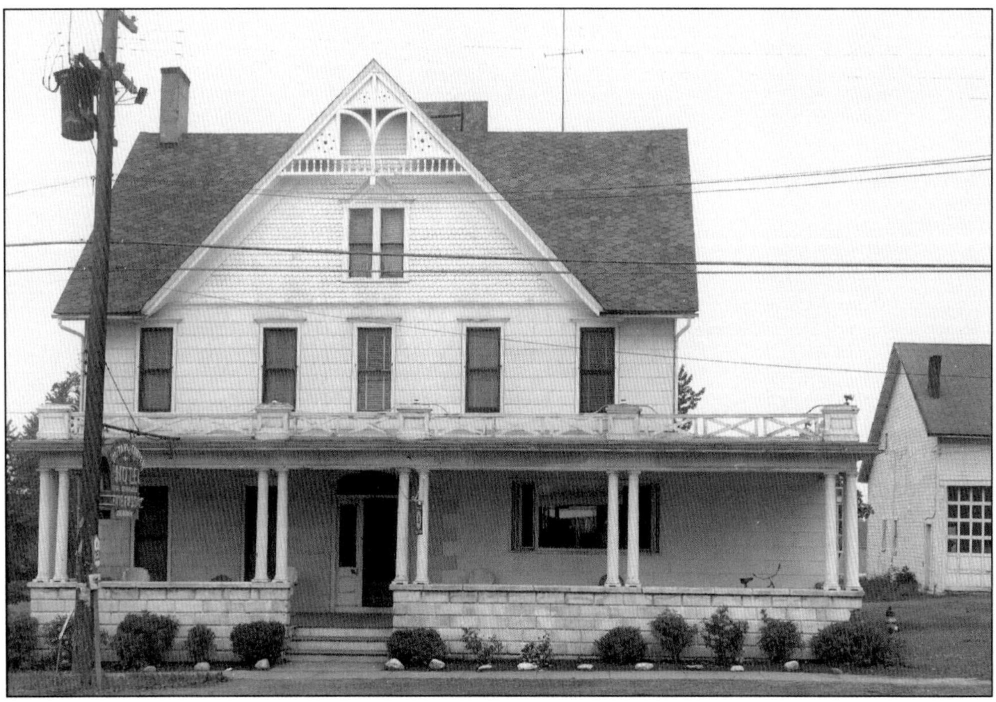

The Ontario Center Hotel is located on the northeast corner of Ontario Center Road and Ridge Road. On this same corner was located a tavern owned by Reynolds K. Northrup in 1830 and a hotel that burned to the ground in 1886. A replacement was built by E. A. Booth. When this photograph was taken in 1957, the hotel was used by the Rotary Club for its meetings on Tuesday nights.

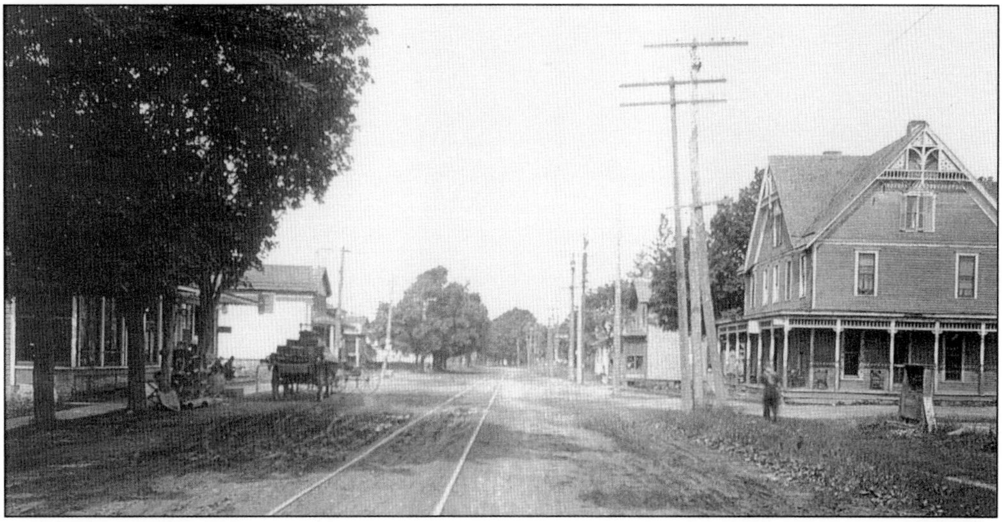

This photograph, taken in 1900, shows Ontario Center's Main Street looking west. Note the hotel on the right and the trolley tracks going down the center of the road.

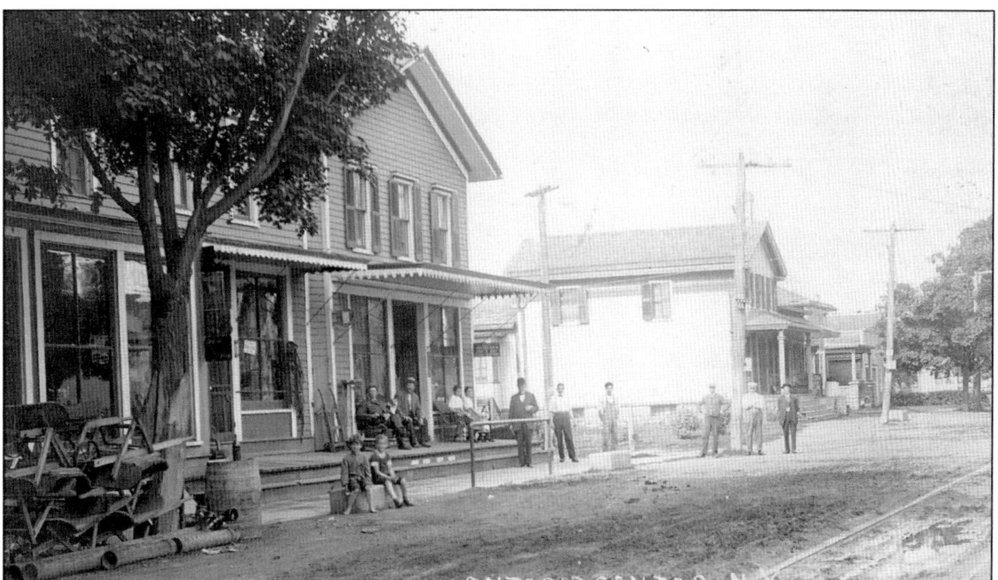

In the early 1900s, Main Street of Ontario Center had trolley tracks and yet the cement blocks used for getting in and out of horse-drawn wagons were still visible. This photograph shows a westerly view of the south side of the street.

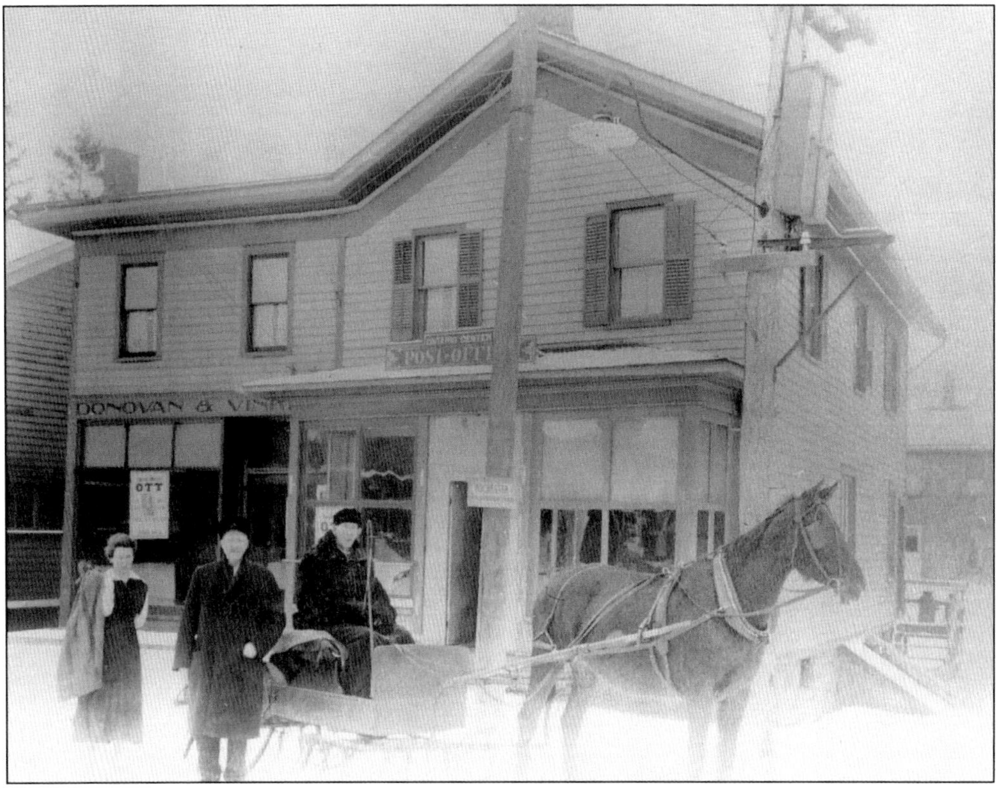

On the northwest corner of Ontario Center Road and Ridge Road is the Foley Building. In 1911, it housed the post office on the east side and Donovan and Vinkey hardware store on the west side of the building. Shown here are, from left to right, Mamie C. Foley (clerk), William J. Foley (postmaster), and John Stevens (mail carrier). During her years as clerk and then postmistress, Mamie would collect the string used to tie packages. When she retired in 1951, the ball of string weighed six pounds, six ounces. Jim Foley had his Hudson Sales and Service (shown below) is in the same location in Ontario Center in 1946.

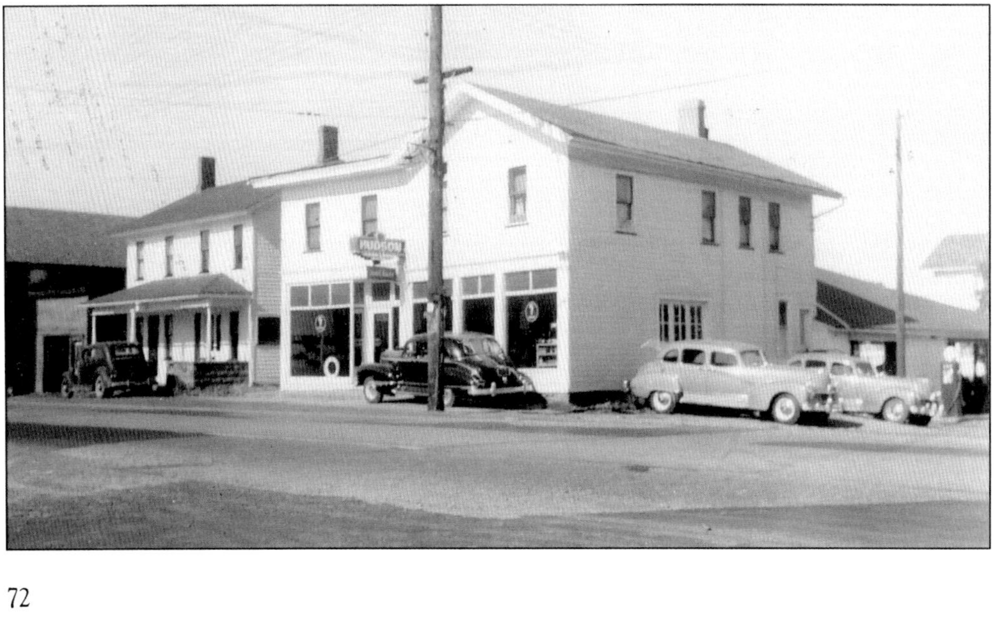

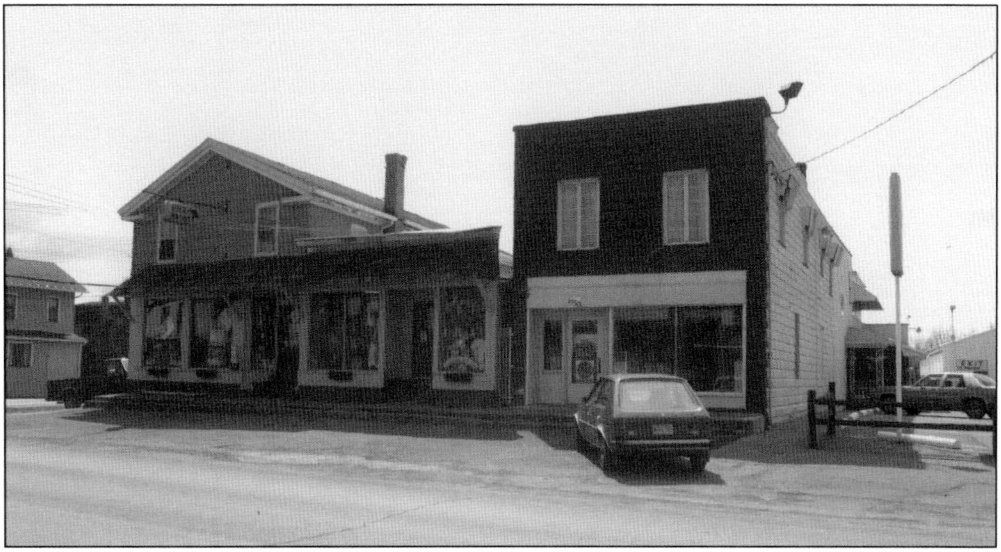

This 1988 photograph shows the Steven's Hardware Store located on the southwest corner of Ontario Center Road and Ridge Road. On January 2, 1992, a gas explosion and fire destroyed the hardware store and the attached video store.

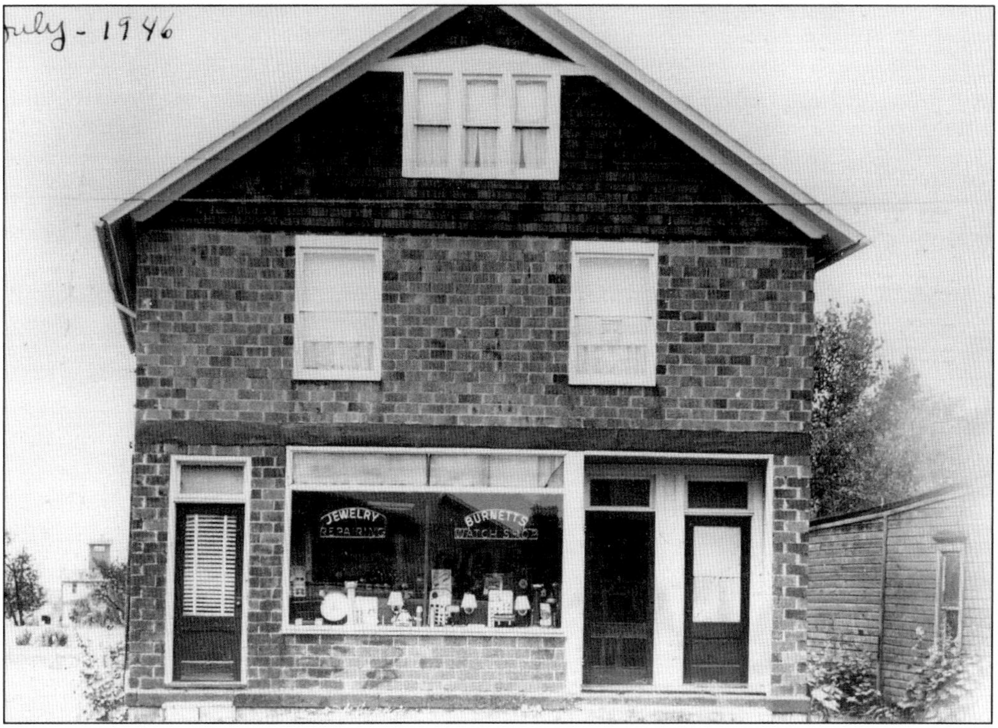

In Ontario Center in 1943, Bill Burnett had a watch, clock, and jewelry shop. Next door was a small barbershop and poolroom owned by Charles McCarty. In 1922, McCarty built the present Burnett building where he moved his barbershop and poolroom. In 1945, Burnett moved his watch repair and jewelry shop there. The earlier building was torn down, and an addition was made to the Burnett building. Bassage's grocery store was there in 1950. Radios, televisions, and appliances were sold in the west end of the building.

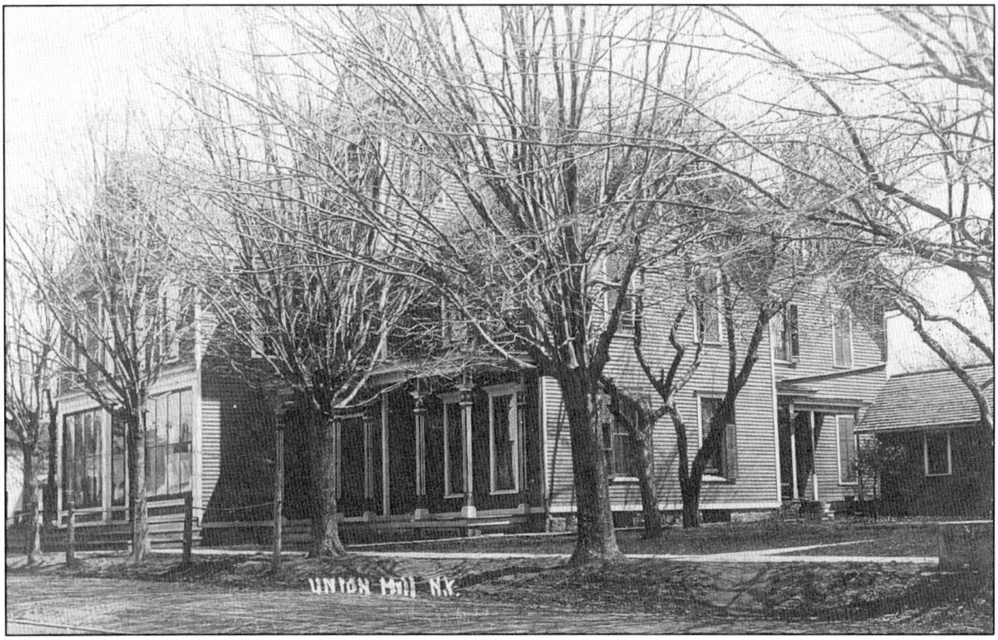

This building, now known as the Grill at Union Hill Country Store, was built by Frank M. Jones around 1865. Jones sold the building to William Stokes, who had a store here until his death in 1929. William and Thomas Elliott purchased it in 1932. A second building behind the store held horse-drawn carriages, which were sold there. That building was removed, and the space is the current restaurant's parking lot.

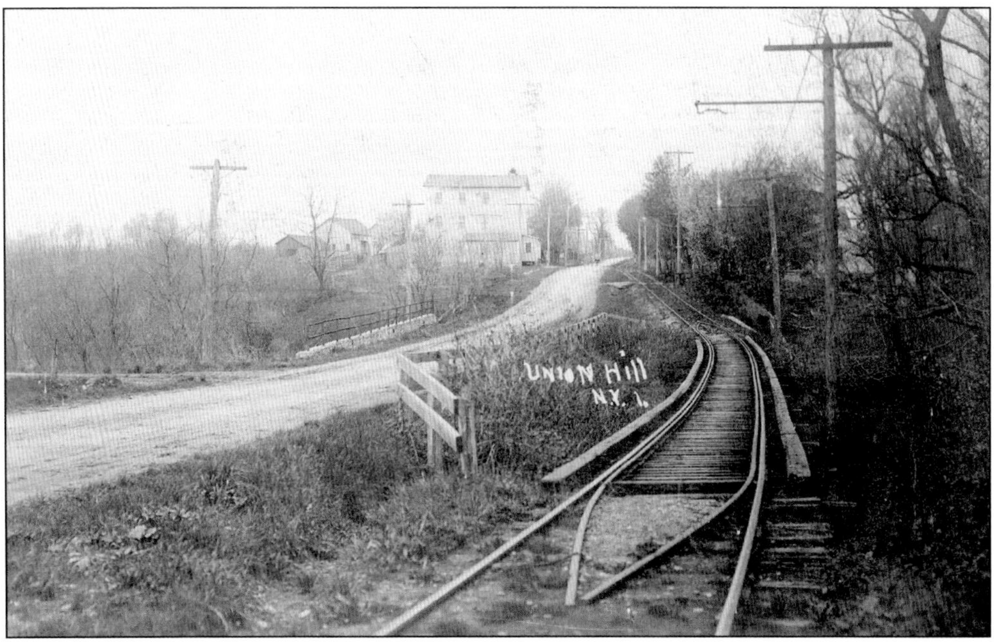

This photograph, taken in Union Hill, shows the railroad tracks for the Rochester and Sodus Bay Trolley. Supplies for country stores were shipped to the Union Hill railroad station and then taken to nearby stores by horse-drawn wagons. The Union Hill station closed in 1940.

Six

"Apples to Atoms"

In the early 1970s, the town officials adopted the slogan "Apples to Atoms." It is a fitting description of the business aspect of the town. The area is rich in fruit growing, especially apples, with the proximity of the lake helping to moderate the temperature and the growing season. As a result of the glacial deposits, farmers found the soil rich, so many crops were grown. The area is relatively flat, so the grazing of farm animals was easy. Alongside these agricultural aspects of the town also grew the town's businesses. First were those that helped enhance the farmer and developed out of his needs. Businesses like mills and blacksmithing became the first businesses to grow. Soon the region found new wealth by tapping an underground treasure—iron ore, and the iron ore industry came to be. In more recent years, Ontario became the home of atoms, with the building of the Ginna Nuclear Power Plant in the midst of an apple orchard. Ontario businesses and industries are truly an "apples to atoms" story.

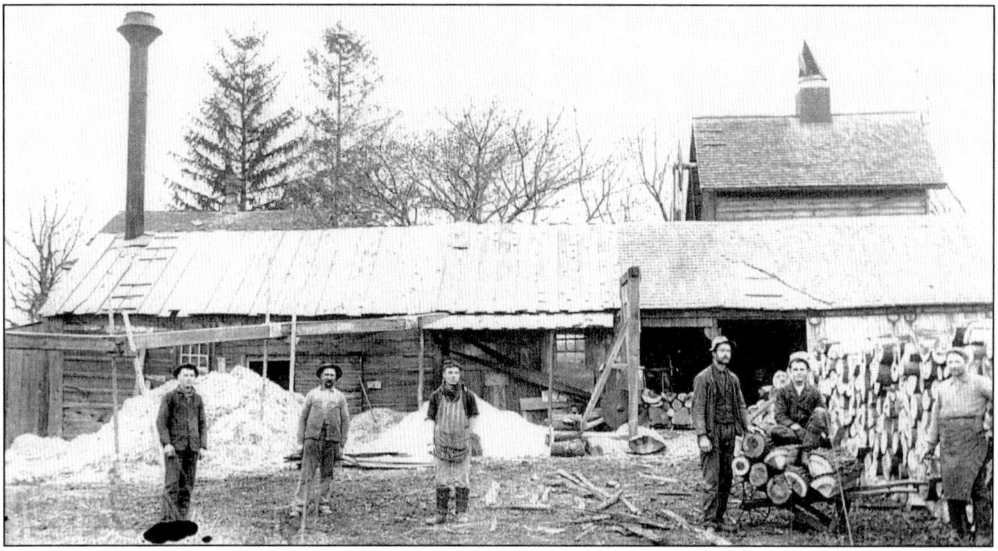

Early businesses developed out of the initial needs of the new arrivals to town. Sawmills were needed to cut the trees into usable lumber to build homes. This is a steam-driven sawmill.

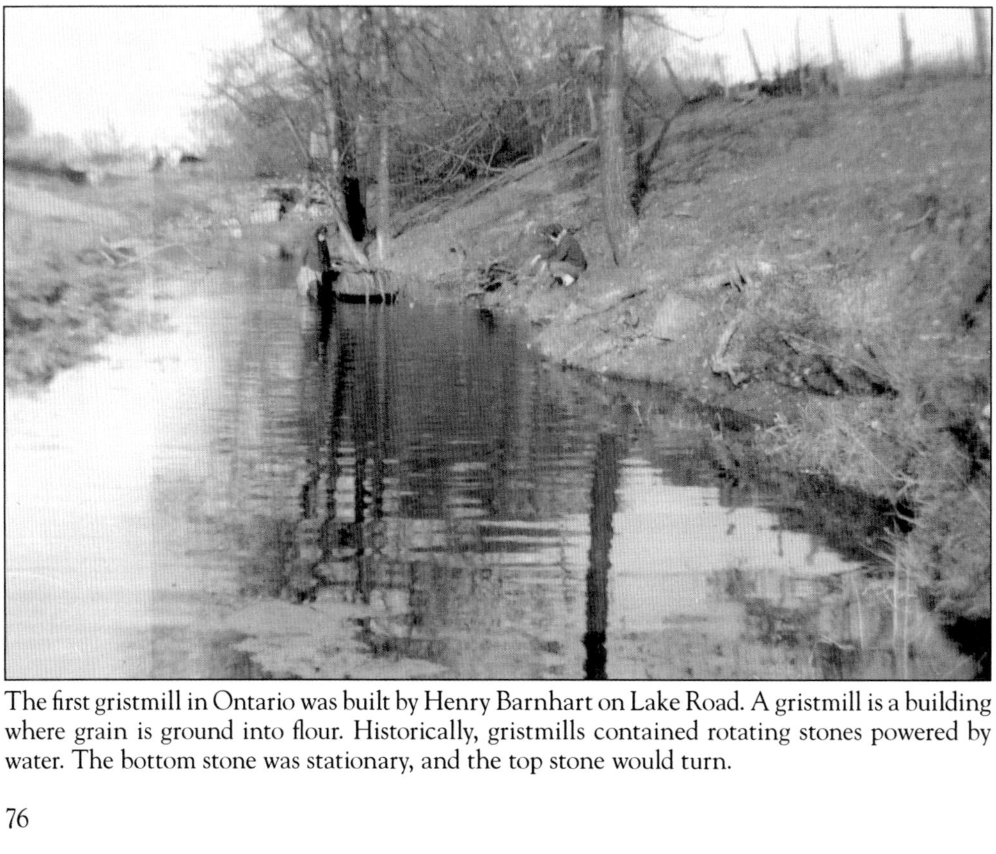

The first gristmill in Ontario was built by Henry Barnhart on Lake Road. A gristmill is a building where grain is ground into flour. Historically, gristmills contained rotating stones powered by water. The bottom stone was stationary, and the top stone would turn.

Ernest Adams, a soldier in World War I at the time, sits on one of the old Barnhart millstones.

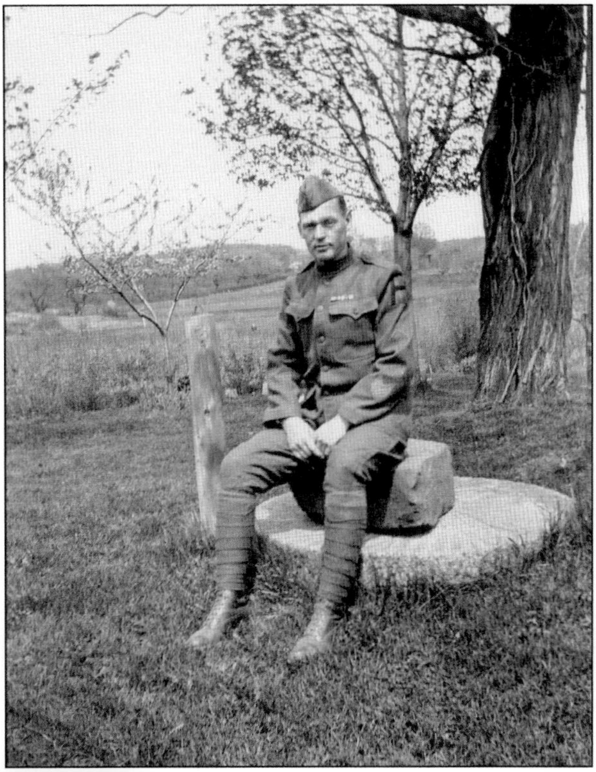

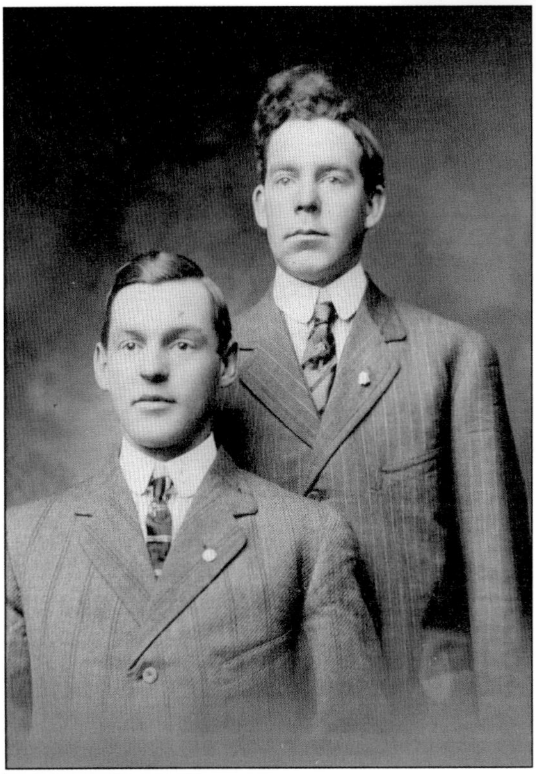

Ernest Adams (left) poses with his brother, Merritt Adams. They grew up on the Barnhart/Brewer farm, which subsequently became the Adams farm, located between what is currently 1338 through 1362 Lake Road.

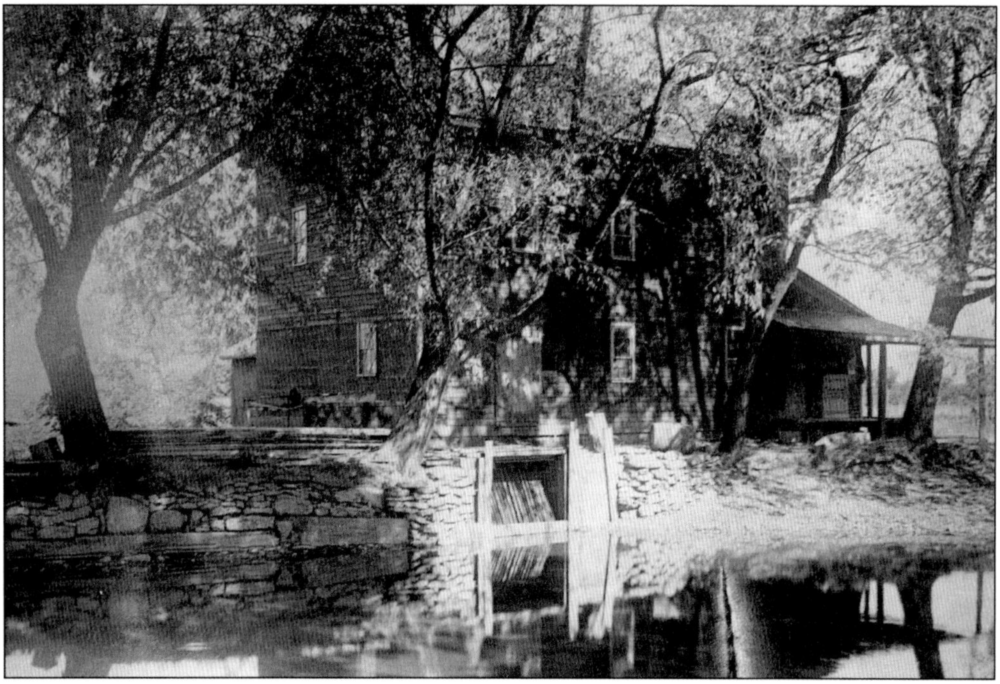

Ira Hill came to Ontario in 1835 and built a log house on 300 acres in what became known as Fruitland. He built a flour mill and a sawmill at the property's pond. He dammed the stream to increase the speed of the water to better turn the wheels that powered the mills. In 1862, he transferred ownership of his property to his son Francis Abner Hill.

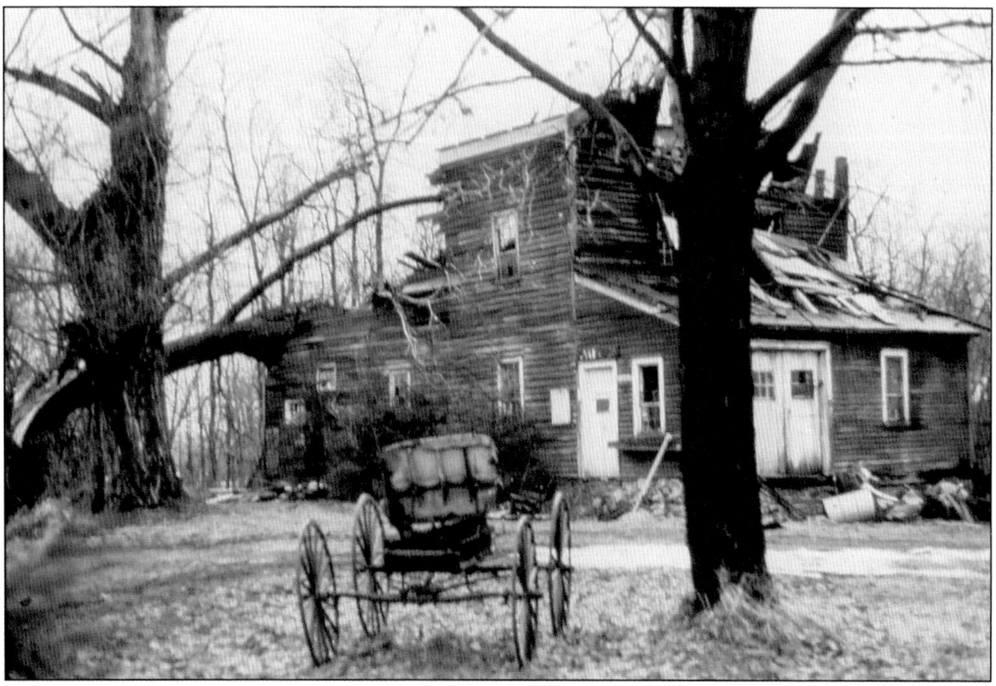

During a windstorm in December 1972, a huge tree fell on the old Fruitland mill, destroying this reminder of early businesses of the past.

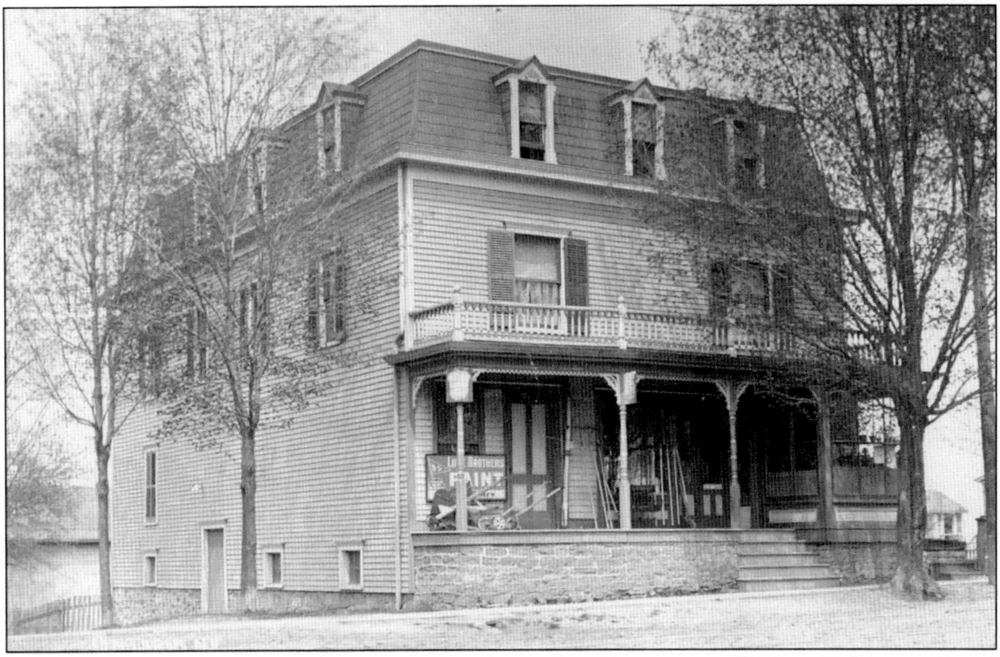

The Owen Tinsmith and Hardware Store was located on the corner of Walworth/Furnace Road and Main Street. C. Wooster Owen, also known as "Woos", came to Ontario at the age of 19 to learn the tin trade. In 1870, he built the three-story building. One side of the store had paints, brushes, and oils and the other side had pots, pans, and pails. The town bought the property in 1959, and it is now a parking lot.

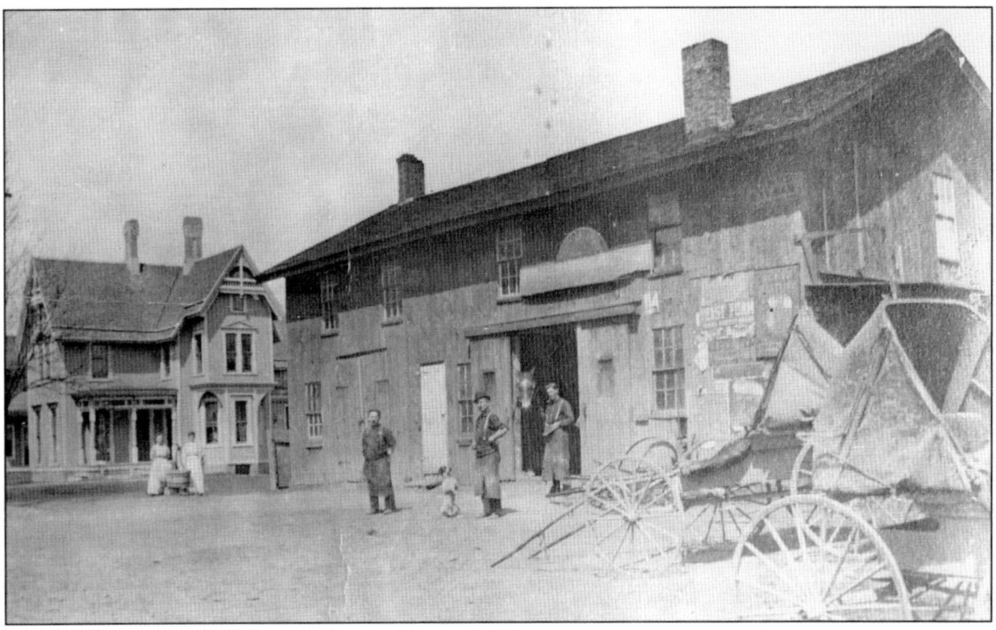

One of the earliest buildings in Upper Corners (Ontario Center) was Stuber's Blacksmith Shop. John Ellsworth operated the first shop here. In 1875, Seymour Stuber took over and ran the shop for 40 years. Then his son William operated the shop and went into partnership with his brother Grover. Eventually Grover ran the shop alone.

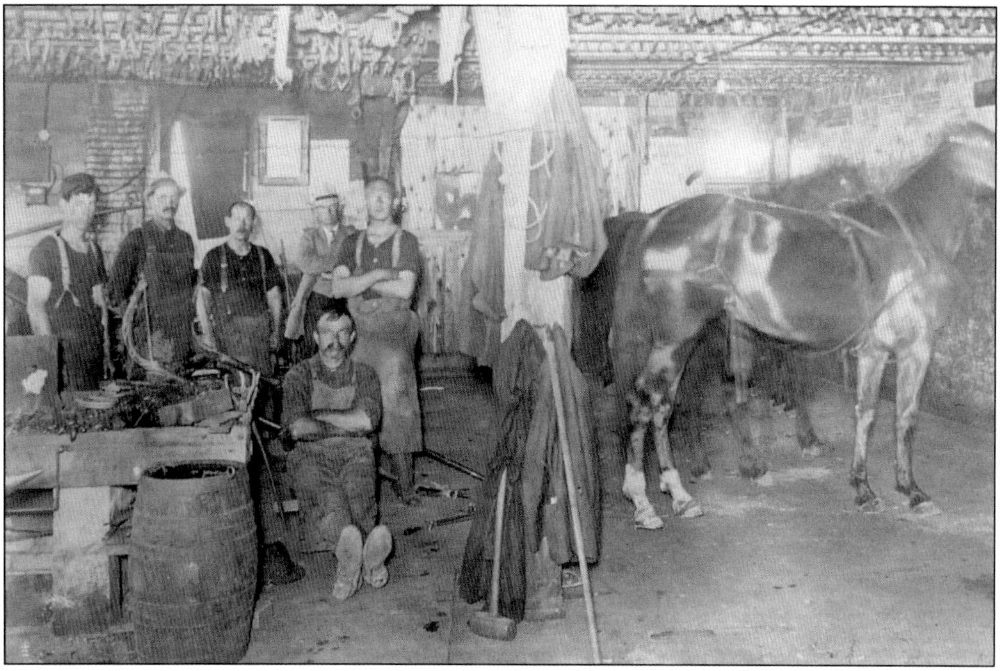

These workers are inside the Stuber Blacksmith Shop. Standing from left to right are William Stuber, unidentified, Seymour Stuber, unidentified, and William Cunningham. The man seated is unidentified.

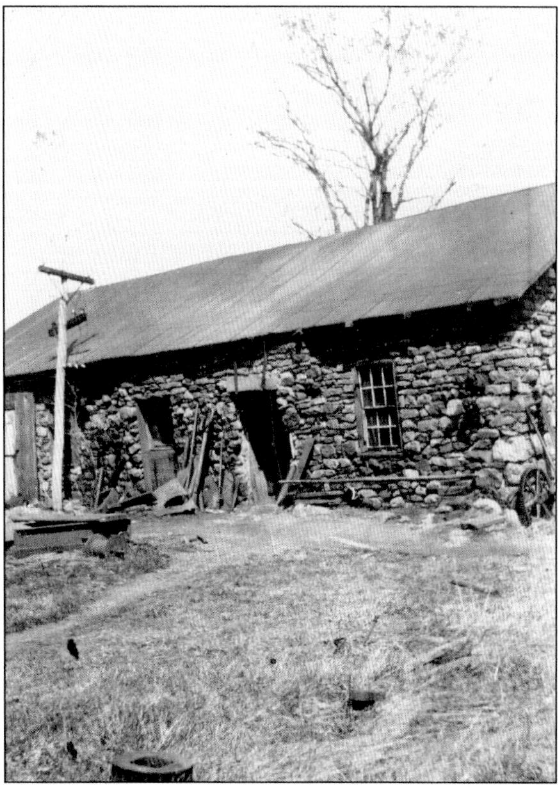

In the late 1800s, Sam Davis was the blacksmith at this shop on Ontario Center Road.

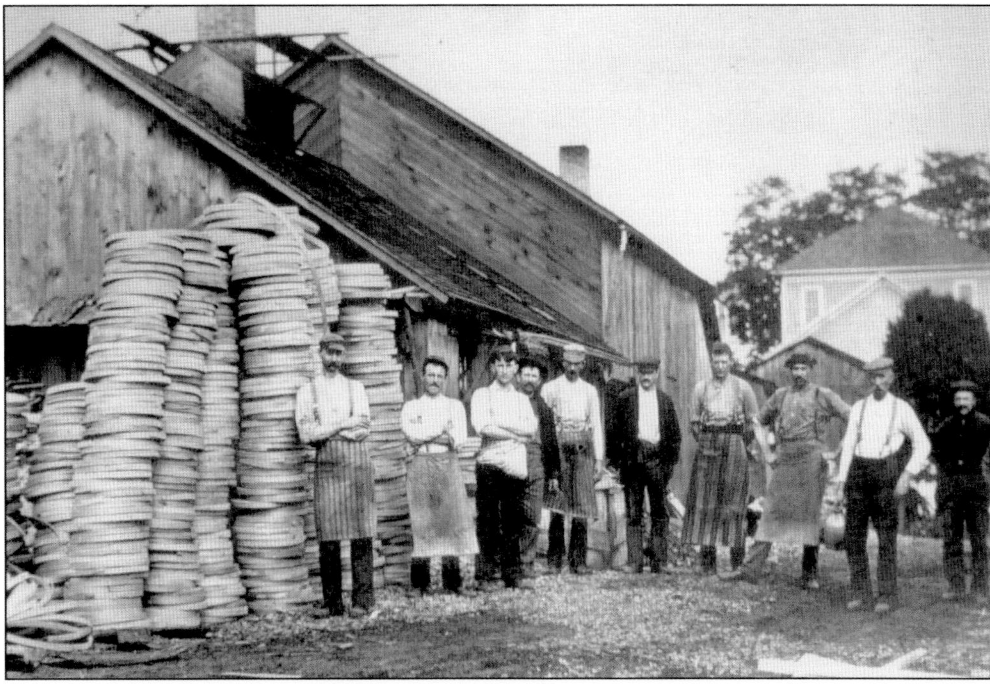

James Colwell and his family moved to Ontario in 1899 and opened a barrel-making (cooperage) shop in back of where the Masonic hall is today. The art of barrel making dates back to Biblical times and is still practiced today.

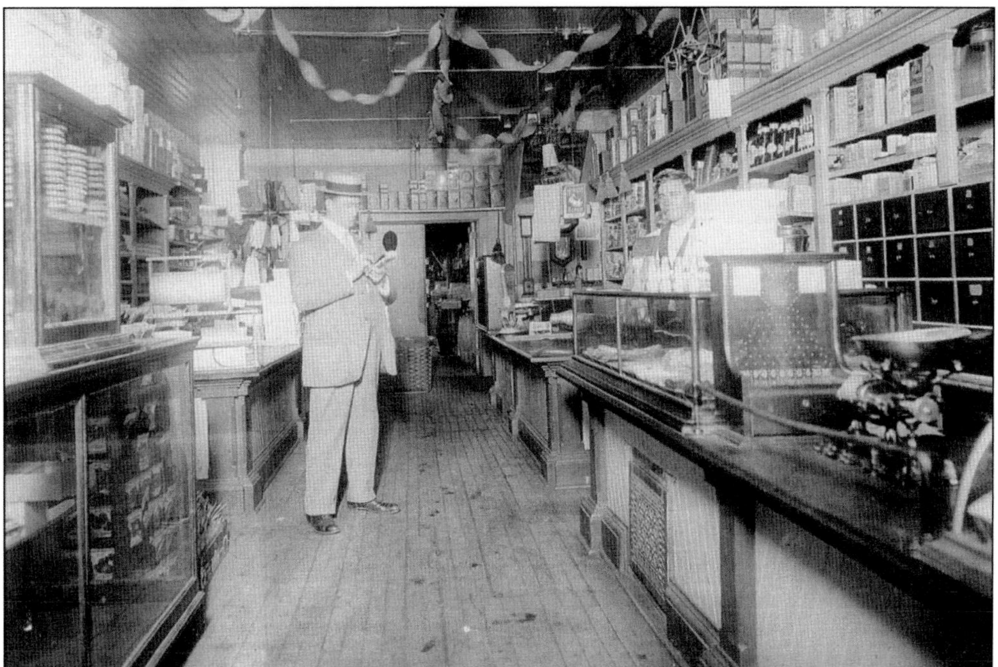

Grandin's store is just one of many little stores along Main Street of Ontario and Ontario Center. Today people have become used to quite a variety of each product sold in a store. Not so with these stores of yesteryear. If they sold a product, often there was only one brand.

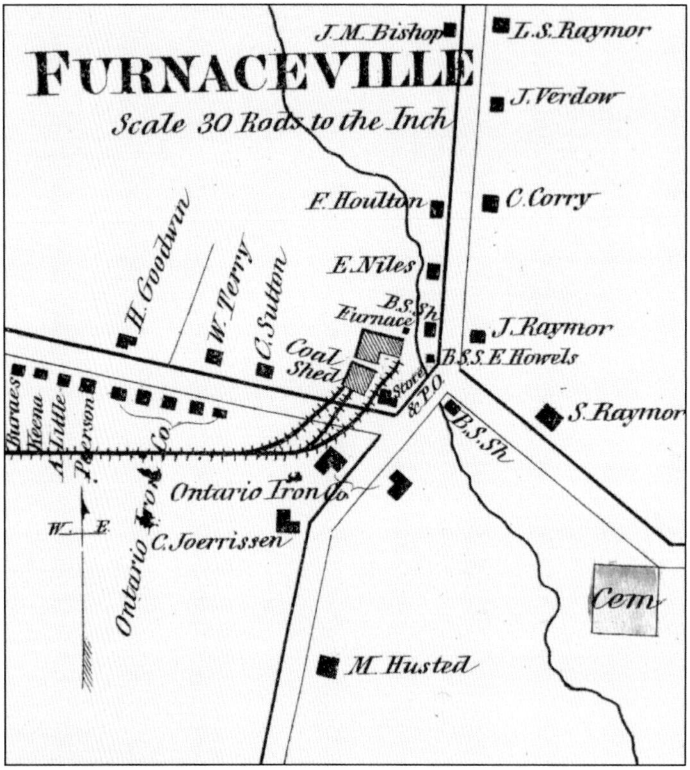

This map of Furnaceville is taken from D. G. Beer's and Company *Atlas of Wayne County New York, 1874*. Furnaceville was located near the lake on Furnace Road. The intersections seen are Bailey Road to the west and Trimble Road to the east.

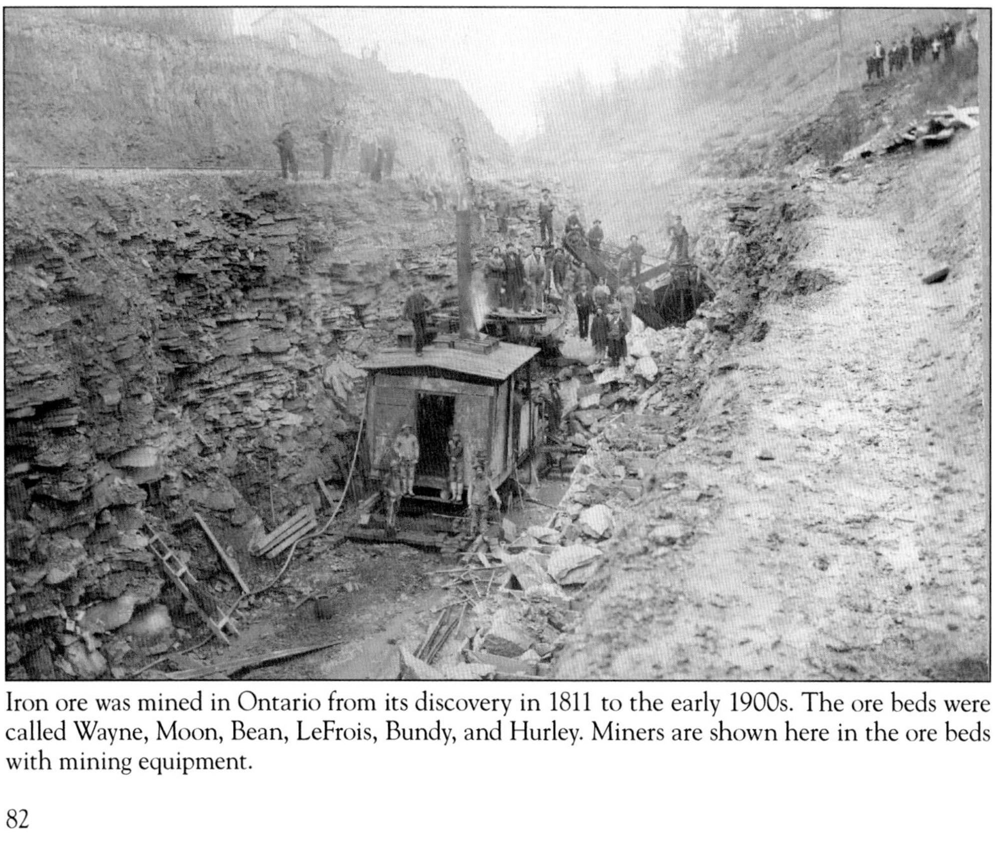

Iron ore was mined in Ontario from its discovery in 1811 to the early 1900s. The ore beds were called Wayne, Moon, Bean, LeFrois, Bundy, and Hurley. Miners are shown here in the ore beds with mining equipment.

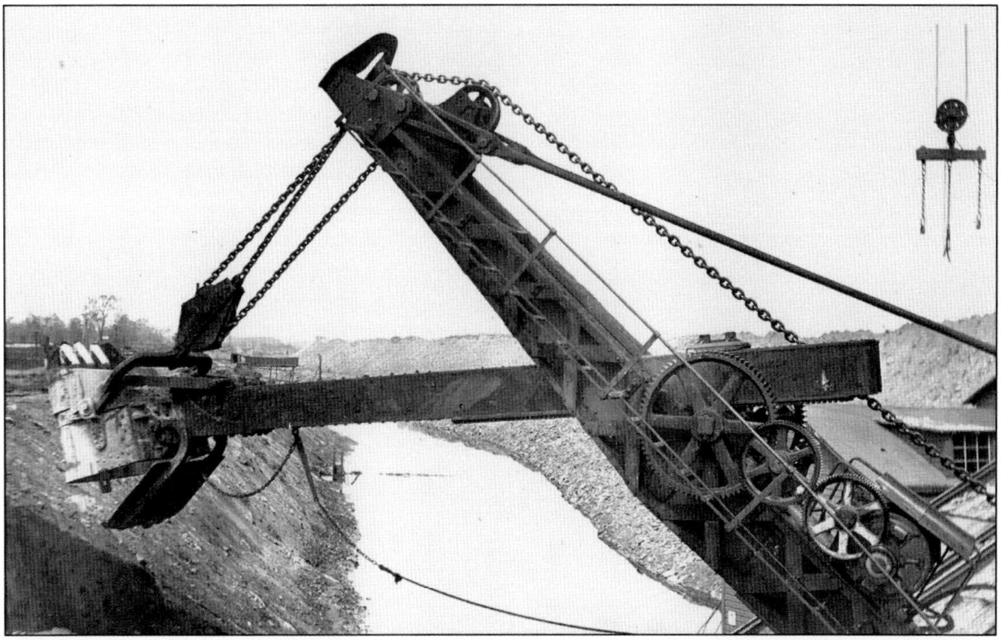

Early mining was done by digging with shovels and transporting with wheelbarrows and then with horses and dump carts. As the mining advanced, heavier equipment was used. The steam shovel is shown with the ore bed filled with water in the background. Later the small Marion steam shovel was replaced by the electrified Vulcan shovel.

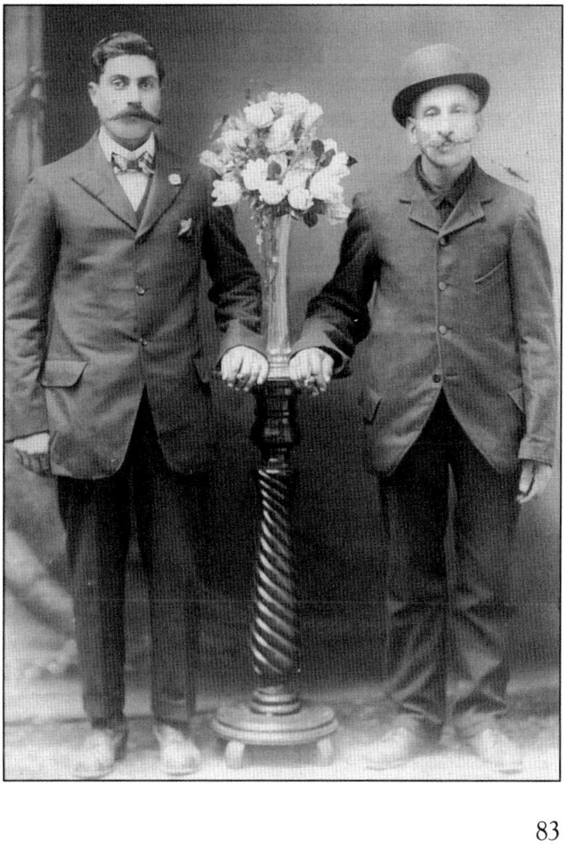

Mine workers like Carmen Garofli (left) and Joe Mitchell were easily identified when they traveled outside of Ontario, due to the red dust on their boots, clothing, and even mustaches. Immigrant workers came from England, Ireland, Italy, and then later from Holland and Belgium. The average wage for these early miners was $1 per day.

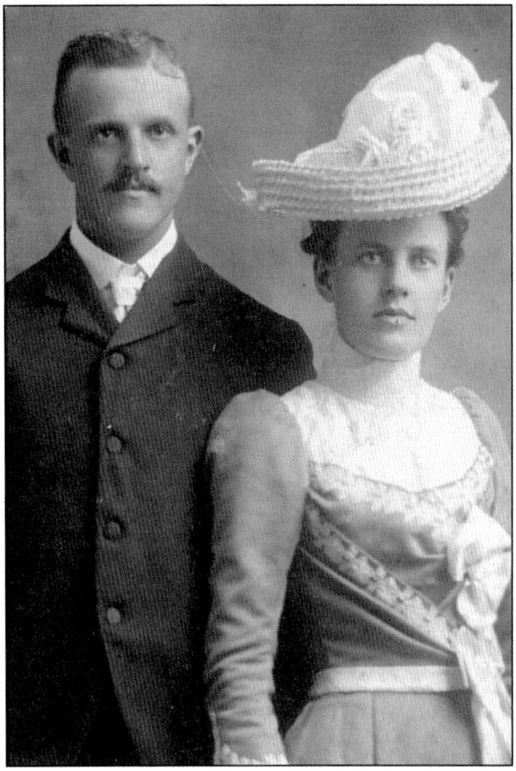

Lynn Watson (left) worked most of his life in the ore beds. He rode his bicycle to work each day and worked both the early steam shovel and the later electric shovel. His wife, Callie, raised chickens, sold berries, and did tatting and sewing.

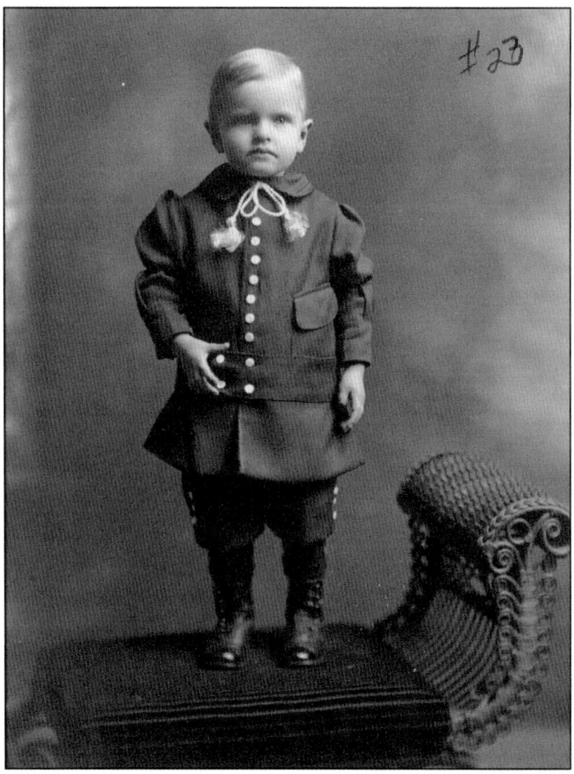

Lynn and Callie's son, Earl, was born in 1913 and spent his early years in the "little red house" that is now at Heritage Square Museum. He attended the Brick Church Schoolhouse. Later he worked nights at the Lloyd Williams' mink ranch and attended Rochester Institute of Technology. He served in World War II.

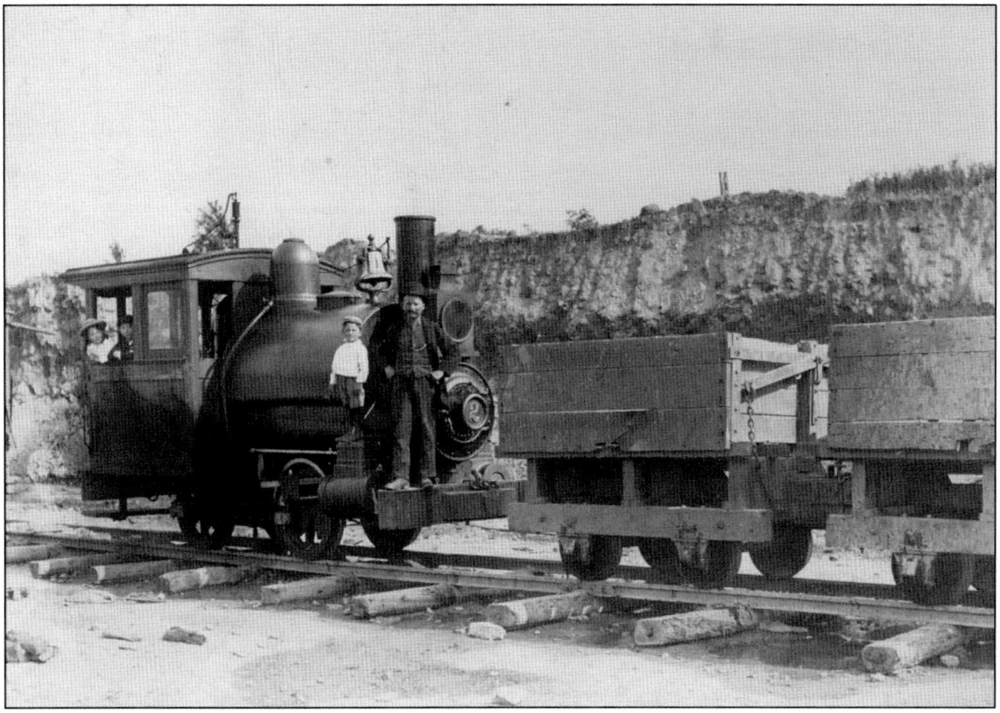

Equipment for the iron ore mining changed over time as technology increased. The first steam shovel was used in the late 1880s. Here are Harry Ruffell (left) and Ernest Ruffell in about 1900.

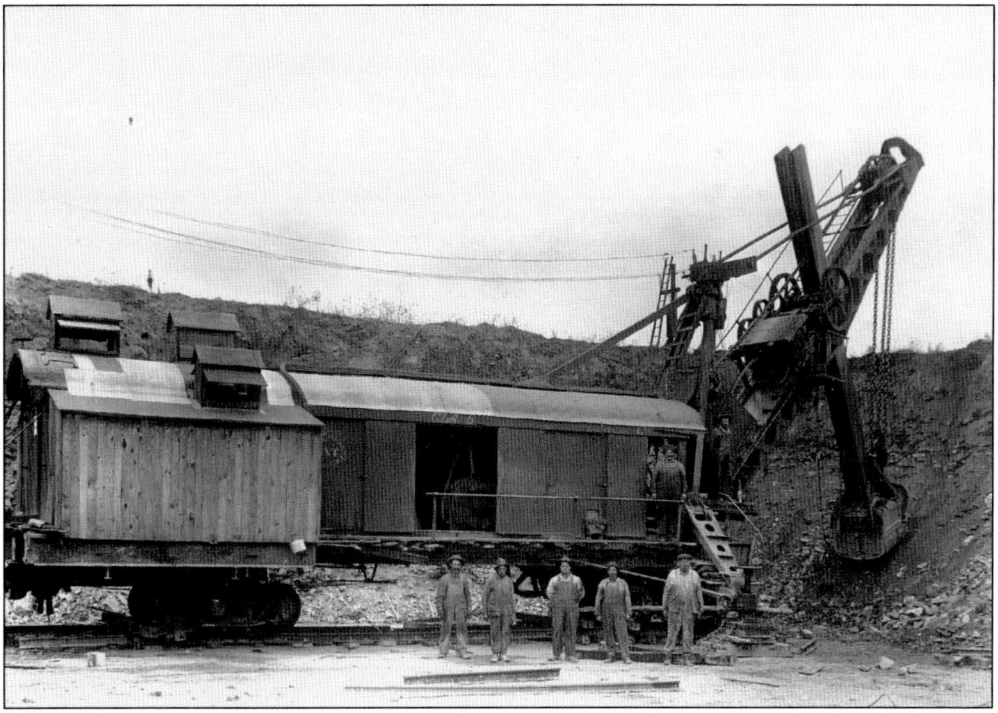

An electrified Vulcan shovel is shown here. Standing in front of the shovel is James E. Watson (far right). On the shovel are Lynn Watson (left) and Dr. Davis.

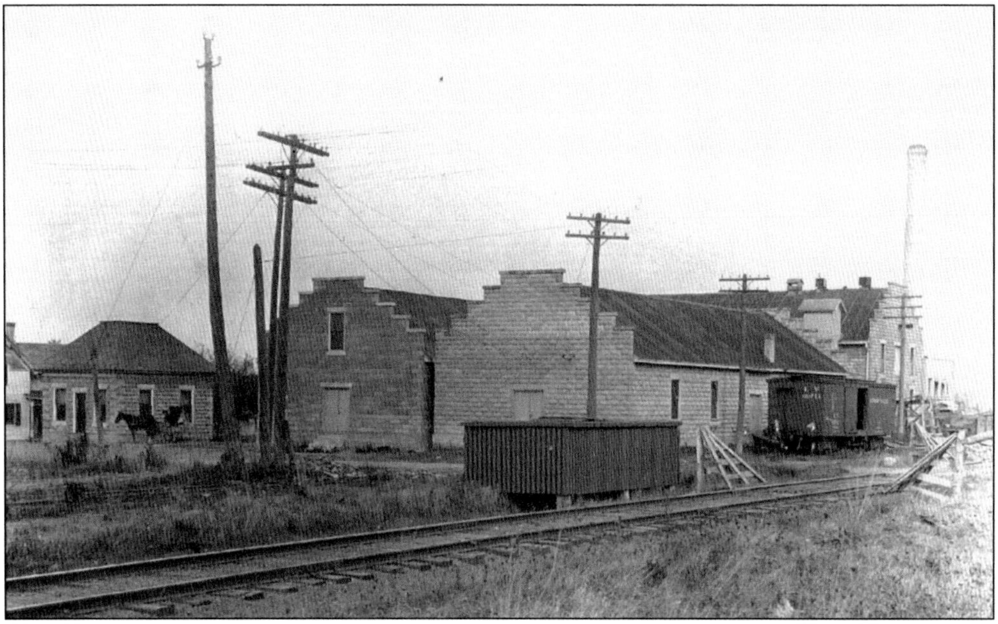

In addition to smelting the iron ore, it was found that the ore made good pigment for paint. In 1913, a paint mill was built along the railroad tracks, and the ground pigment was shipped all over the world. During World War I, the pigment made was used on warships for camouflage. Other uses included coloring mortar and rubber. The only visible signs of this once-thriving business are the remains of the foundation and chimney along Route 104.

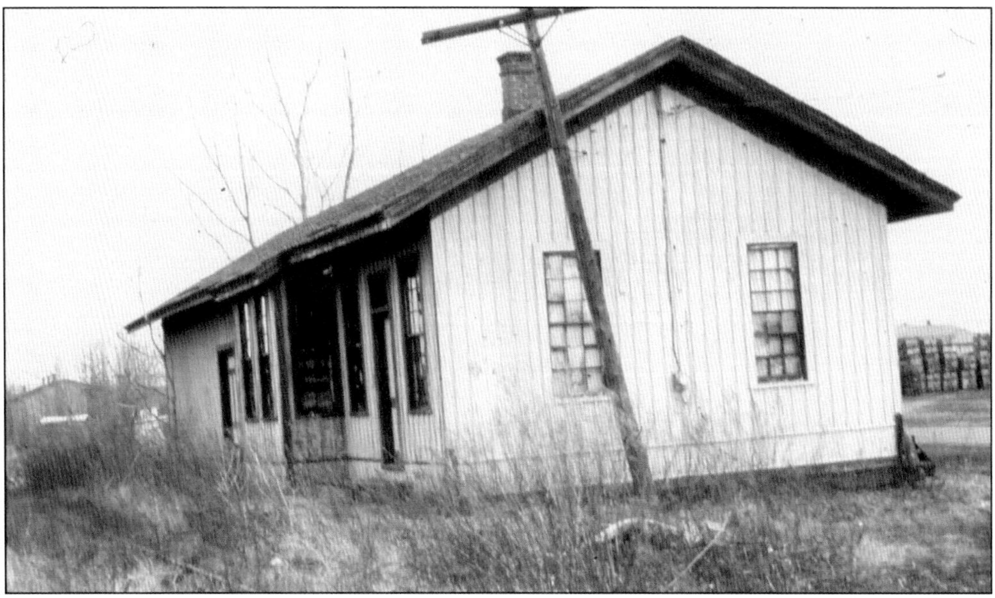

The Rome, Watertown and Ogdensburg Railroad was built in 1871 and created links to the ore mines and to the furnace in Furnaceville. The Ontario train depot became important as the train brought both trade goods and people to their destinations. Calvin Hubbard and Benjamin Green ran a bus service from the station to the local hotels and Furnaceville. This railroad was known as the "Hojack" line because, as the story goes, as a farmer was crossing the rails, his mule stopped and he kept yelling "Ho! Jack!" to get him moving again.

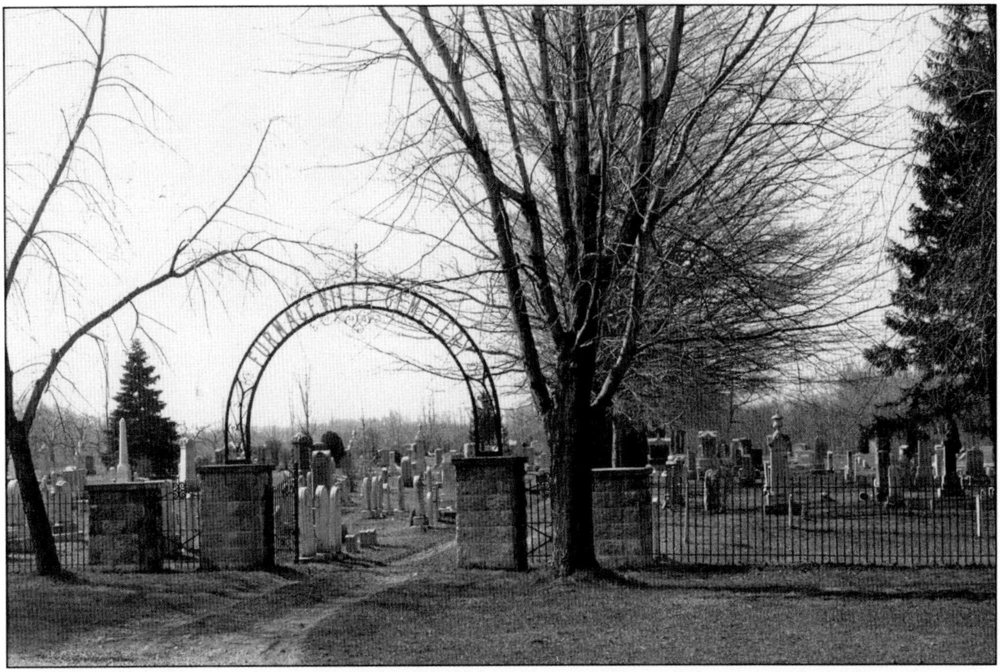

The Furnaceville Cemetery gates provide the only reminder of this once-flourishing business and community. This cemetery holds the remains of many pioneer families, including the first child born in Ontario—Melissa Hopkins. The cemetery has been enlarged several times.

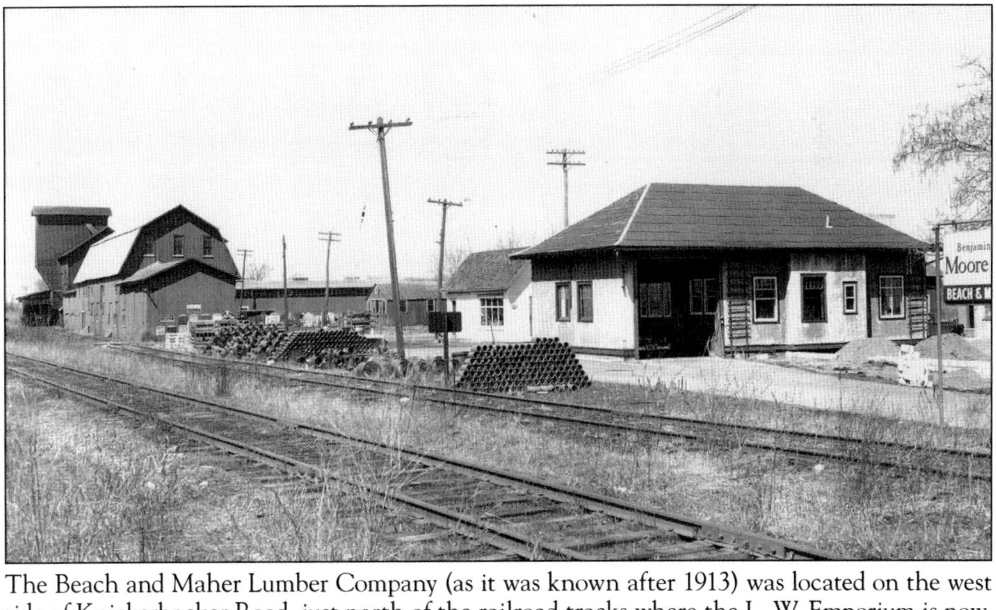

The Beach and Maher Lumber Company (as it was known after 1913) was located on the west side of Knickerbocker Road, just north of the railroad tracks where the L. W. Emporium is now. In the late 1890s, the predecessors of this company were important in the building of many homes and businesses in Ontario, including the Masonic lodge in 1903 and the State Bank of Ontario in 1913.

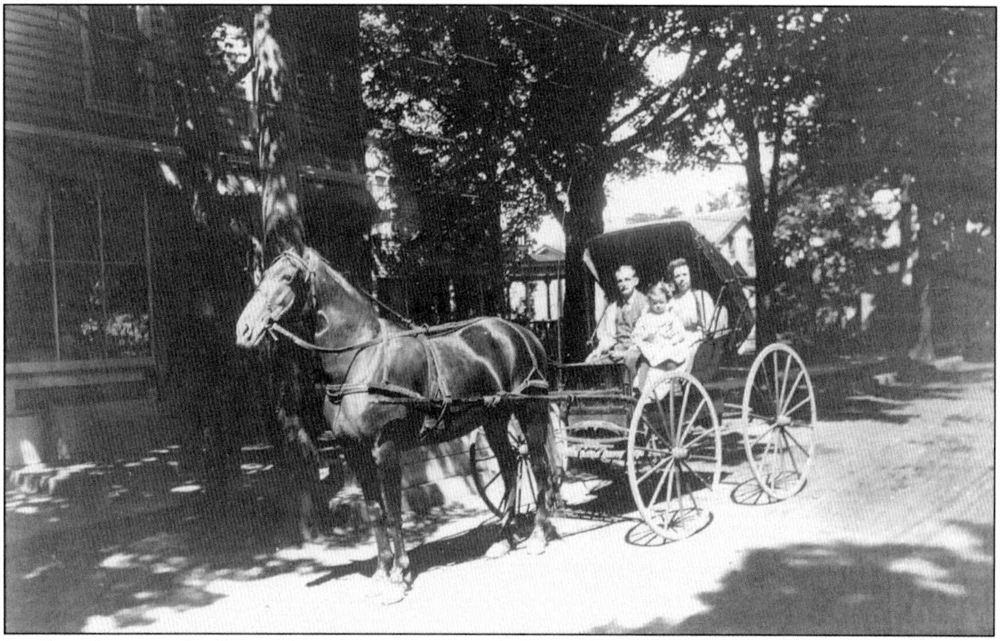

In the photograph above, A. W. Turner is with his wife and his daughter, Ruth, sitting in a horse-drawn wagon. They are in front of A. W. Turner's General Store on Main Street in 1909. In the photograph below, Turner and Ruth (posing with a dog) are standing in front of the same store. Today this store is Sullivan's Insurance at 1983 Main Street. In 1957, Ruth Turner Sheahen wrote her memories of the business district of Ontario. These memories have made it possible to glimpse into the past of the section of Main Street in Ontario from Knickerbocker Road to Walworth/Furnace Road. Ruth died in Florida in April 1962.

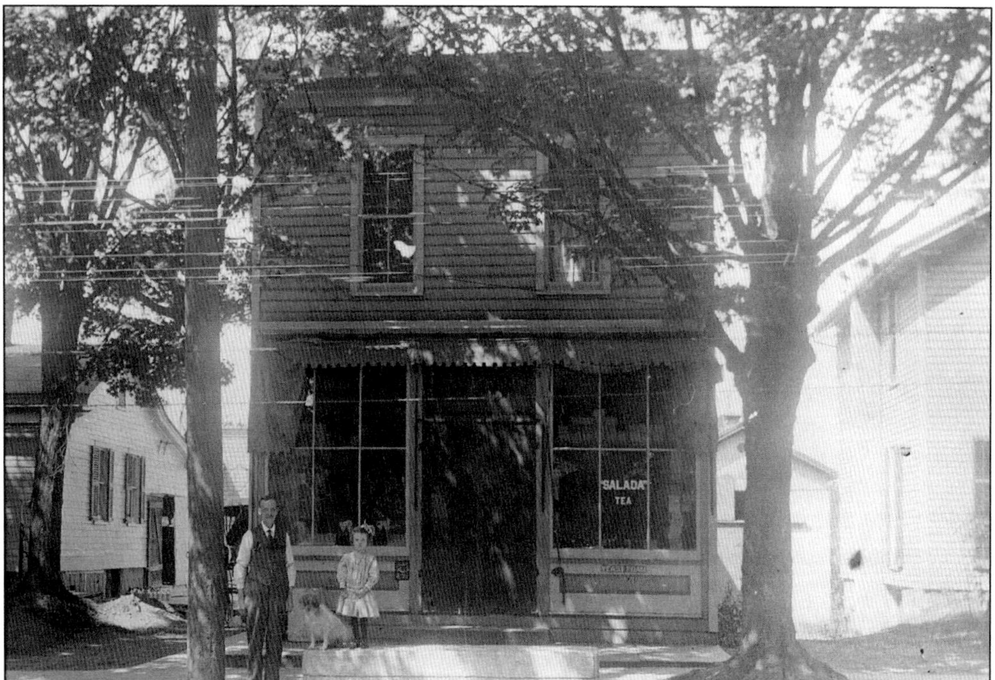

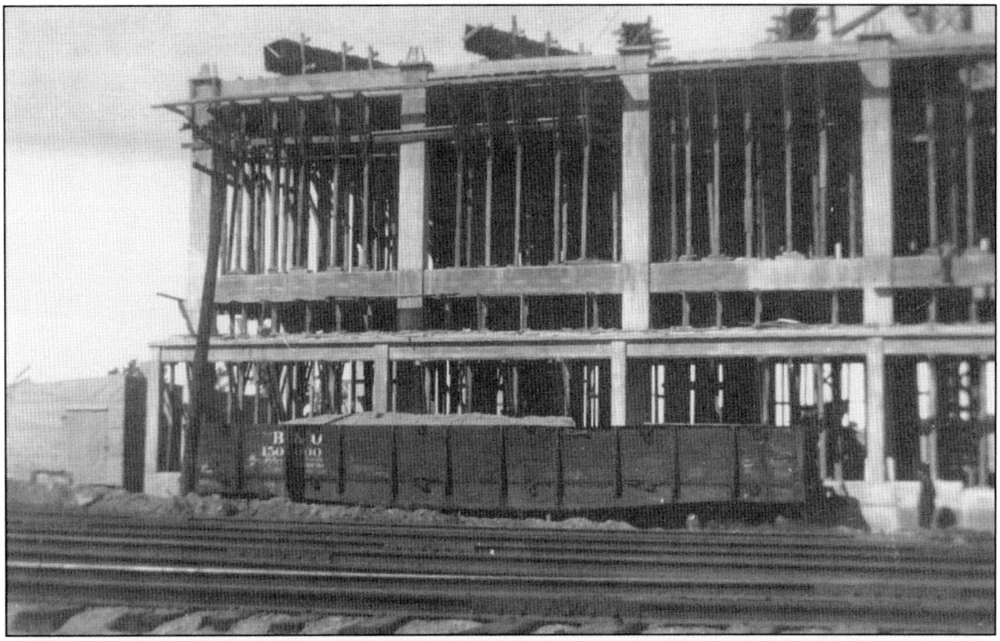

Located at the northwest corner of Railroad Avenue and Furnace Road, the Ontario Cold Storage was under construction in 1920. Because fruit and vegetables were grown in Ontario, there was a need to build a structure that would store the crops until there was a demand for them. Under the leadership of J. S. Albright, men gathered together in 1919 to create an organization to raise money for the building.

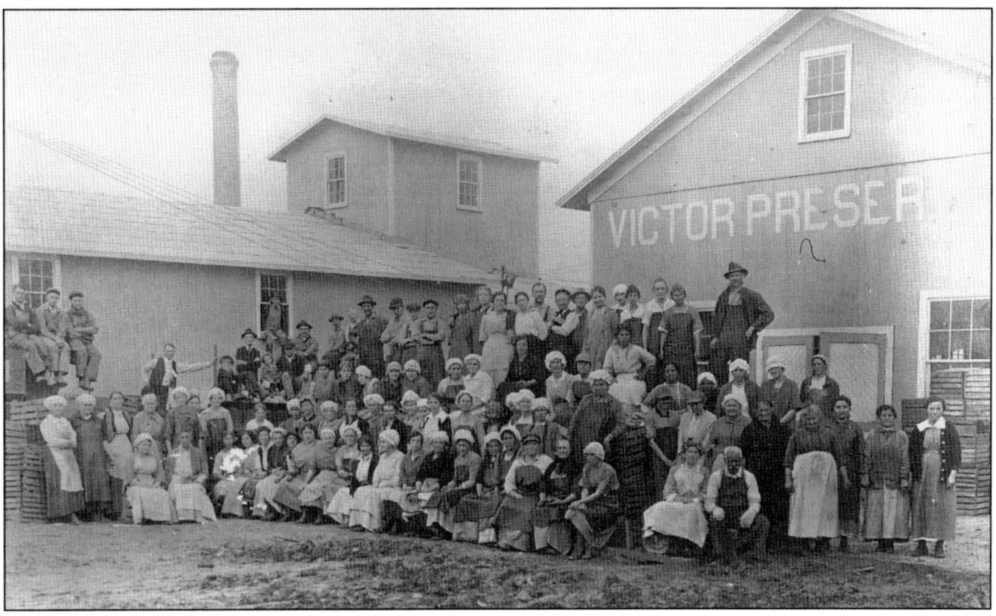

Victor Preserving Company expanded into Ontario. The owners wanted the canning plant to be closer to the source of the fruit being processed. Three directors, Edward J. Tobin, Eugene S. Berry, and Lee J. Wilbur, purchased land north of the railroad tracks on Ontario Center Road and built a brick building in 1912. Workers pose here in 1918. Tobin is leaning on a post on the left side of the photograph.

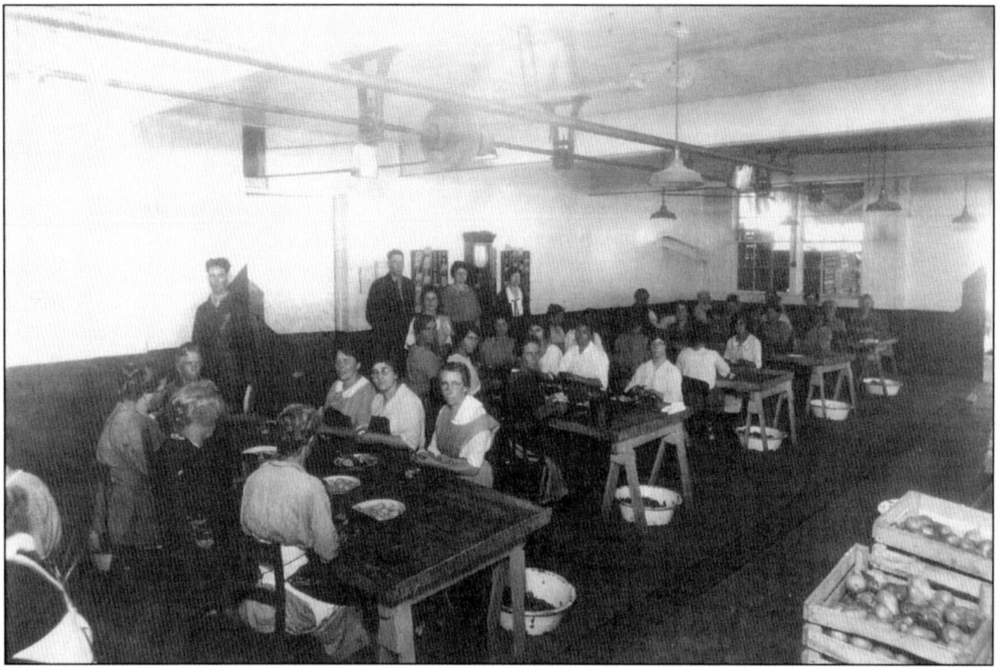

Ed Tobin bought land just south of the railroad tracks from Glen C. Cone in 1916. In 1918, workers prepared apples at Victor Preserving. The company provided an outlet for local farmers, helped with employment for local residents, and paid taxes to help support the town. This company is still there today.

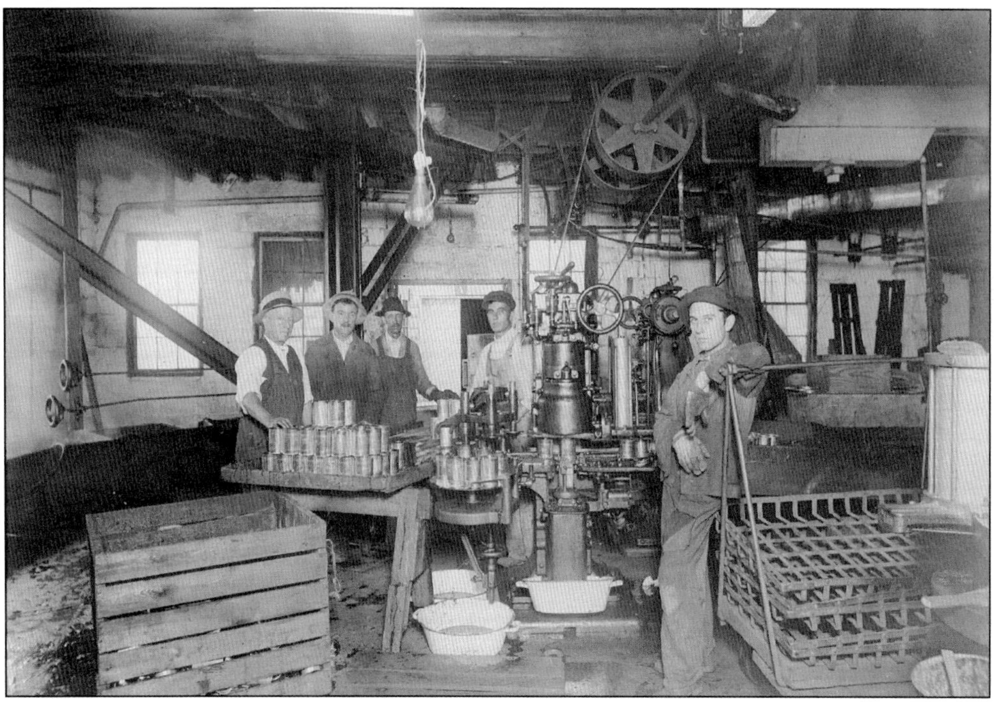

Inside the Victor Preserving Company, five workers are, from left to right, Bob Stone (the boss), Frank Leonard (the sealer), George McCrea, Frank ?, and Ernest Ruffell.

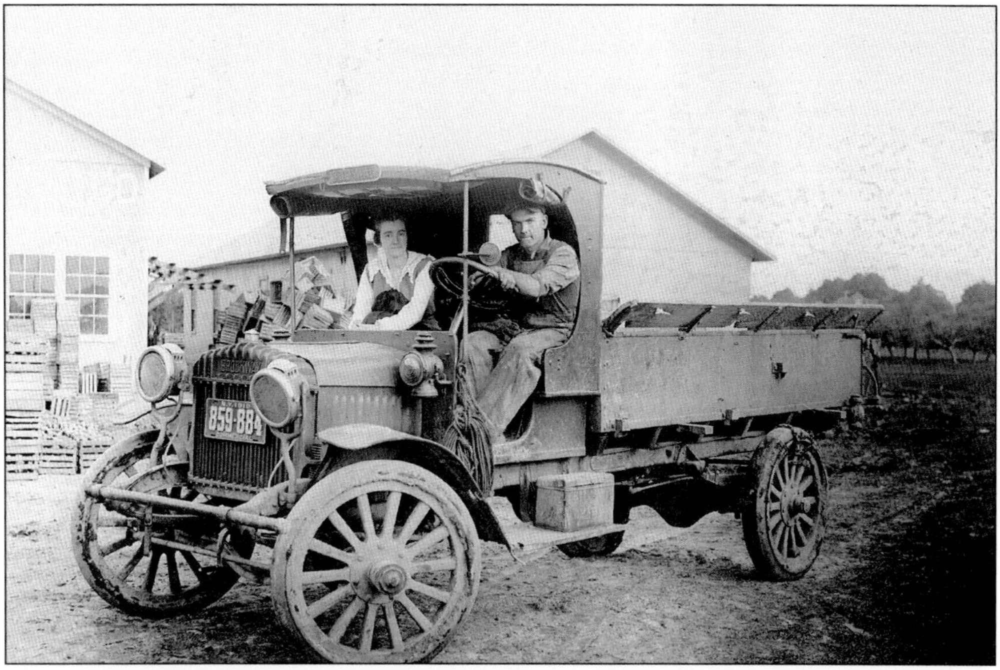

This truck, at Victor Preserving, is driven by Ed Bly in 1918. Pauline Fitzgerald is his passenger.

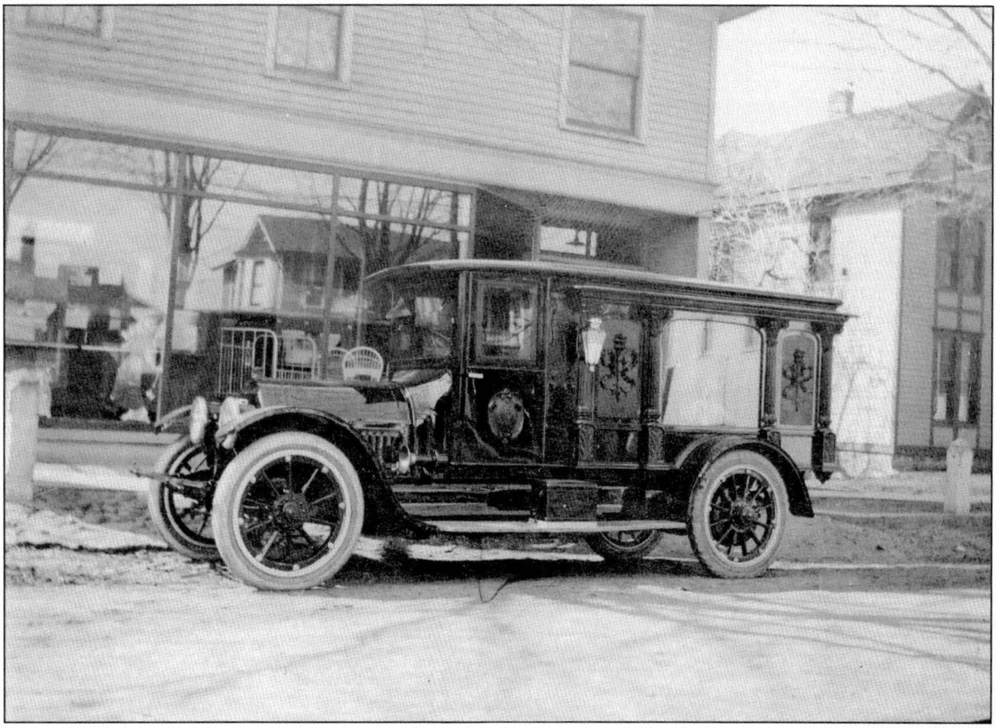

This fancy early vehicle is the Howk-Mepham funeral hearse. Ed Howk purchased the funeral business in 1890 from Peter Freer. Walter Mepham, who had lived with the Howks, died in 1945. In November 1945, Robert Laushey came to work as an assistant, and in April 1946, the business was sold to him and Allen E. Dye. Laushey took over from Dye in 1951.

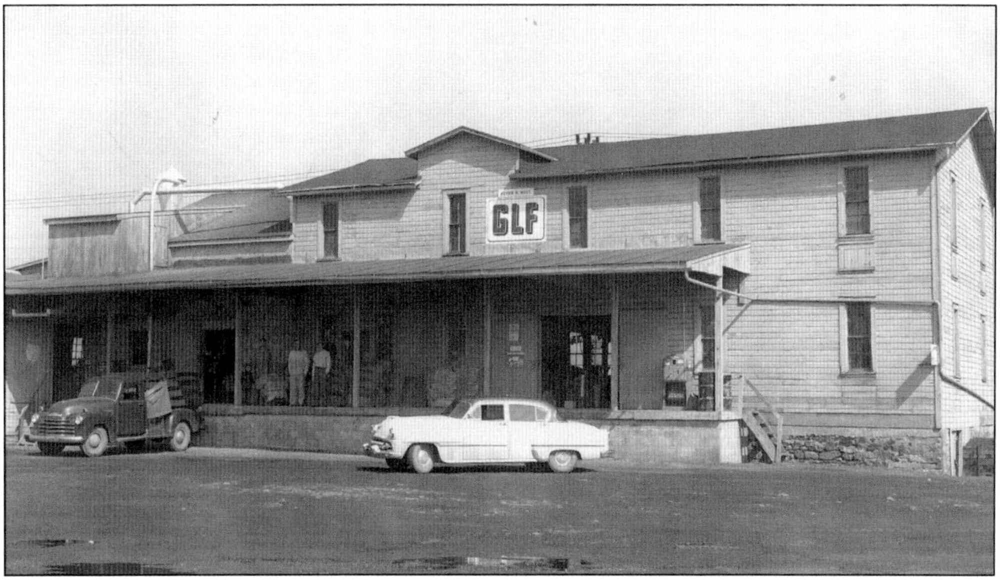

In 1899, Peter DeLass bought a coal business on the north side of the railroad tracks from Andrew Graham. When he bought the warehouse to the south from Pease and VerDow, he moved his coal business there. DeLass sold his business in 1931 to Peter Moll. Peter Moll's Feed and Coal is shown here in 1957. In 1960, it was purchased by Roy E. Herrmann and was known as Herrmann's Agway. The building burned on June 3, 1998.

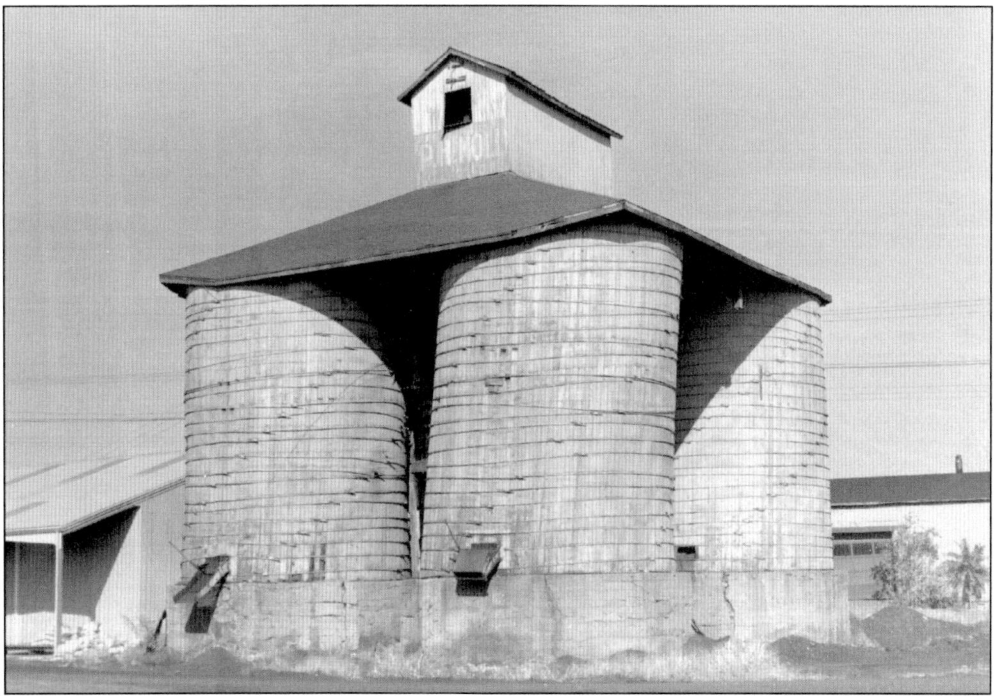

This is a close-up of the coal towers at Peter Moll's Feed and Coal. There are four masonry bases housing three-story-tall silos. Each silo is made of vertical staves bound together with closely spaced wires fastened in a spiral pattern. In 1975, these silos were torn down to make room for expansion by Agway.

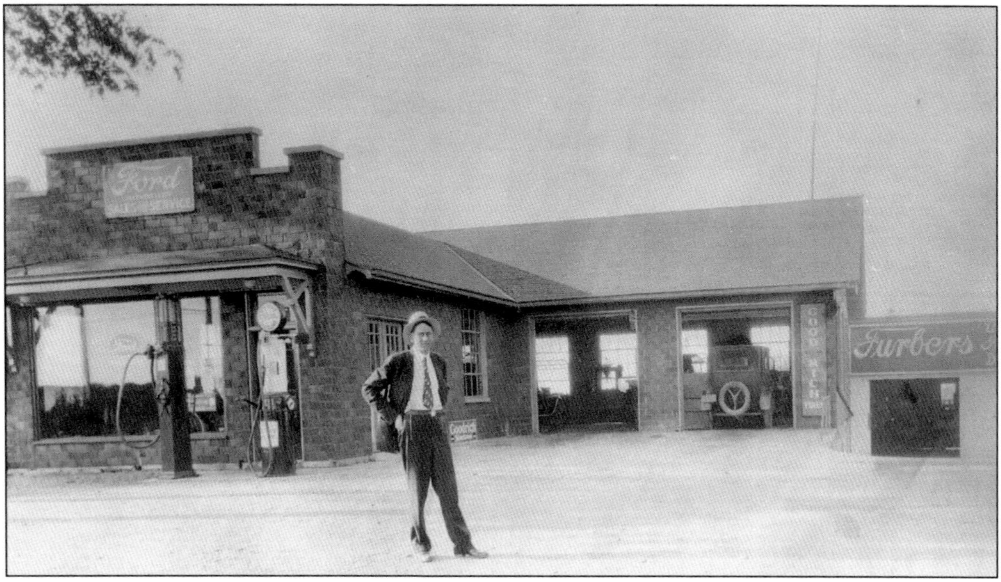

Furber's Ford Sales and Service is seen here in 1928 on the north side of Ridge Road, west of Ontario Center Road. Herbert J. Furber Jr., the owner, was one of the earliest automobile dealers in the town in 1915. Ford shipped unfinished cars by railroad boxcar to Ontario, where they were unloaded and hauled by wagon or bobsled to the garage for assembly.

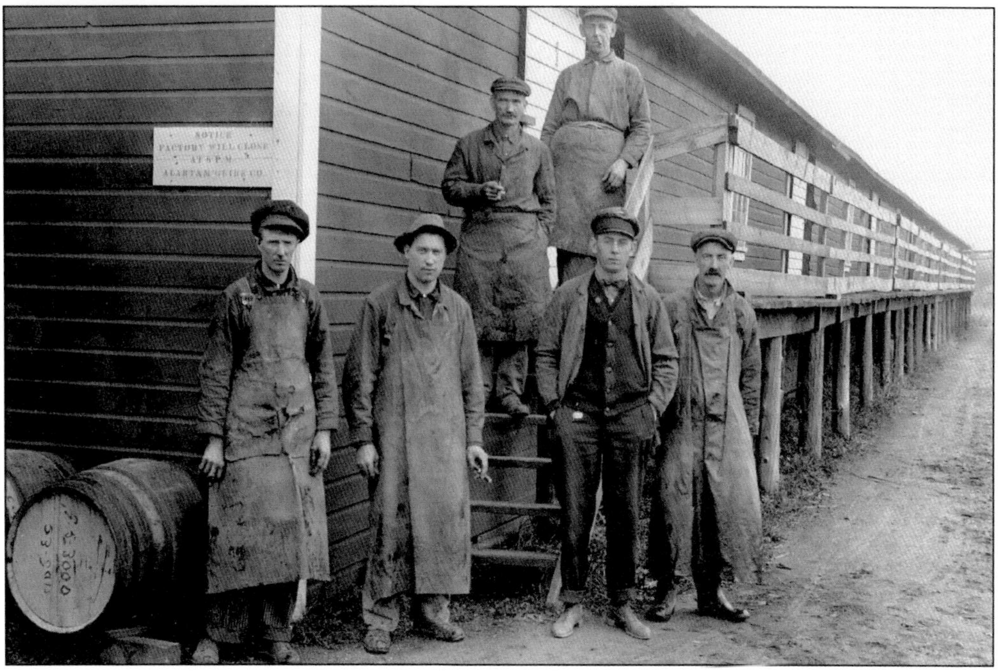

The first canning business in Ontario was located on Railroad Avenue. L. R. McGuire, a wealthy pickle packer, bought the buildings and operated a successful pickle factory, managed by Arthur Bowerman. Shown here in the 1930s from left to right are (in the front) Henry Covey, Andrew Hubright, Arthur Bowerman (George's son), and Alfred Watson. Behind them are Abe Seen (lower step) and George Bowerman (top step). Later the buildings were purchased by the R. and R. Empire Pickle Works, managed by J. Marion Biviano.

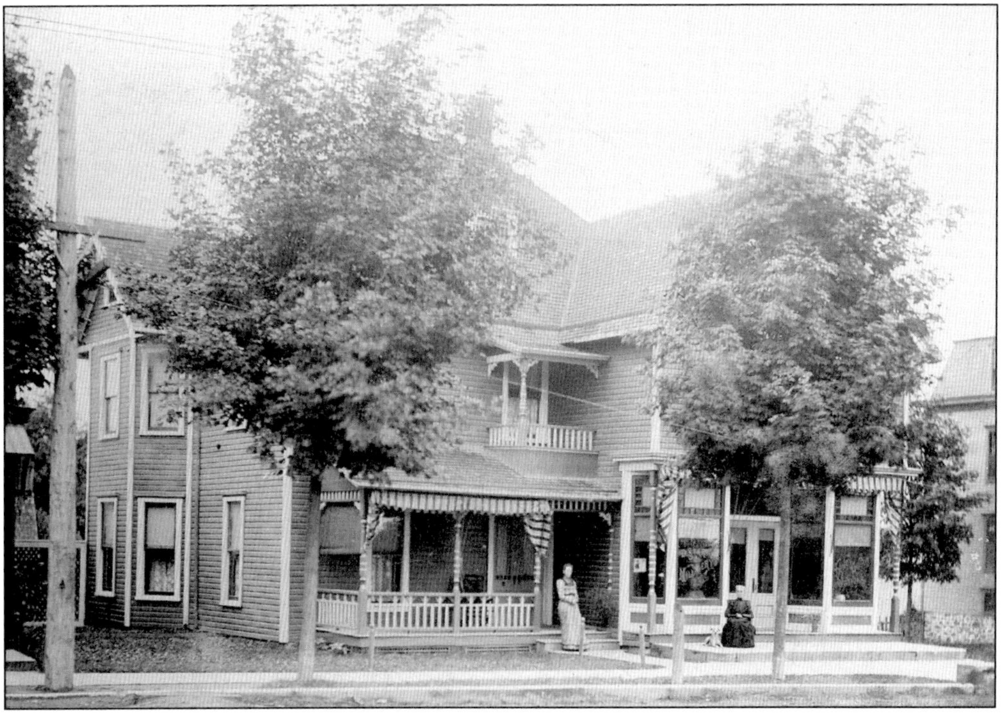

Dora Stark's millinery store was located at the northwest corner of Main Street. In 1904, Stark sold some of her hats for 25¢. Stark learned the millinery trade from Anna Grant.

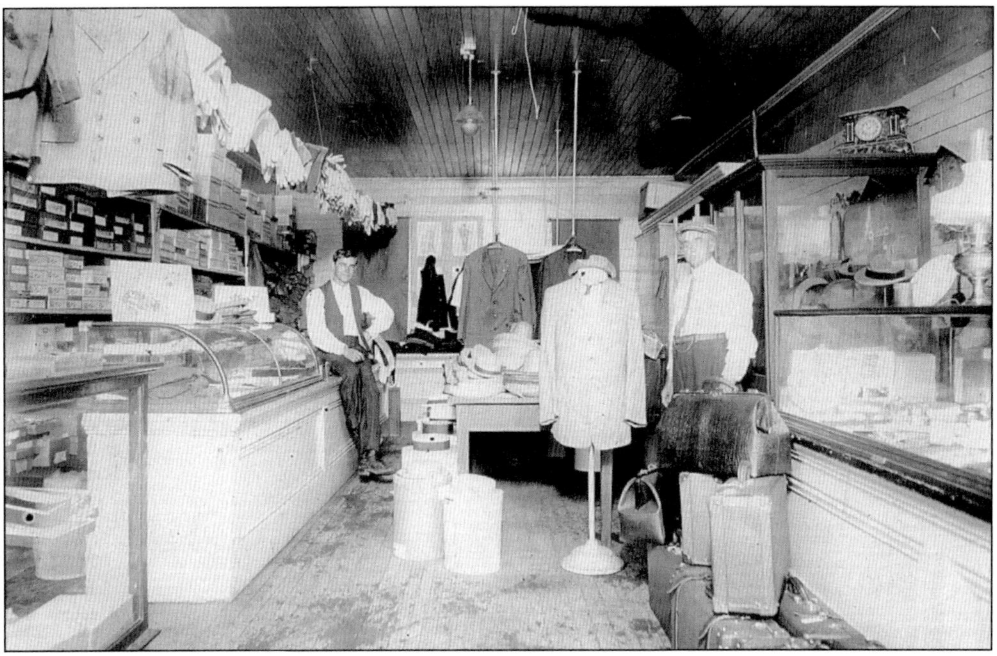

Allison McCowan (right) owned a men's clothing store, which was located on the south side of Main Street on the west side of the hotel. Shown here with Clayton Beach, McCowan sold his clothing interest and concentrated on selling shoes until he, in turn, sold his stock to Tony Noto in 1923.

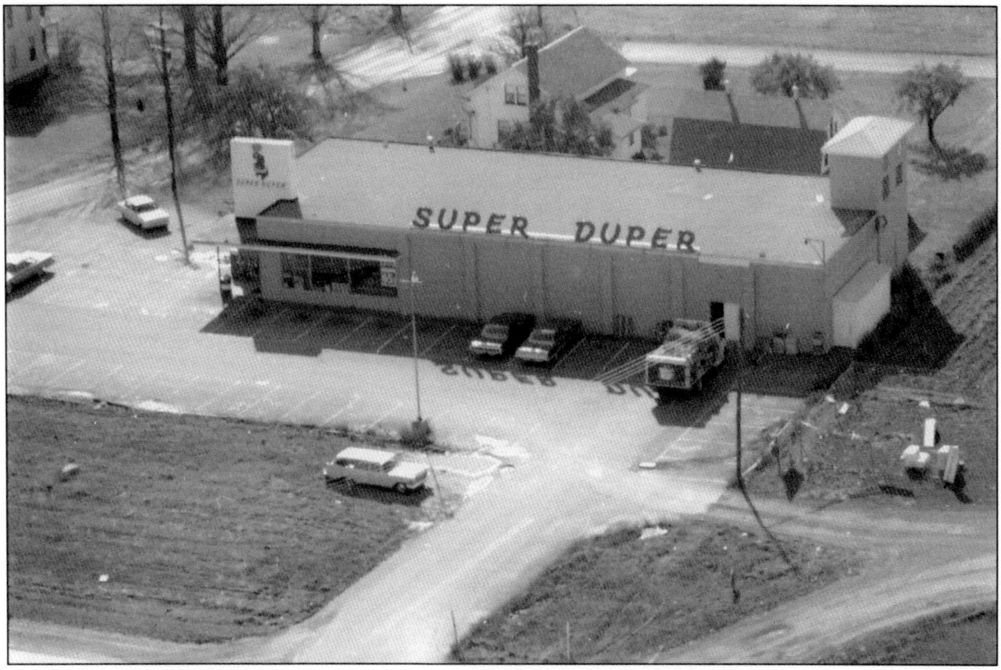

In 1960, John Almekinder's Red and White store was once known as the "Biggest Little Store" in Ontario. The store was moved to Route 104 and Furnace Road (now Konstantinou's Restaurant) from its former location on Main Street. The store was moved again to the old Ames Plaza as Almekinder's Super Duper where it remained until it closed in June 1998.

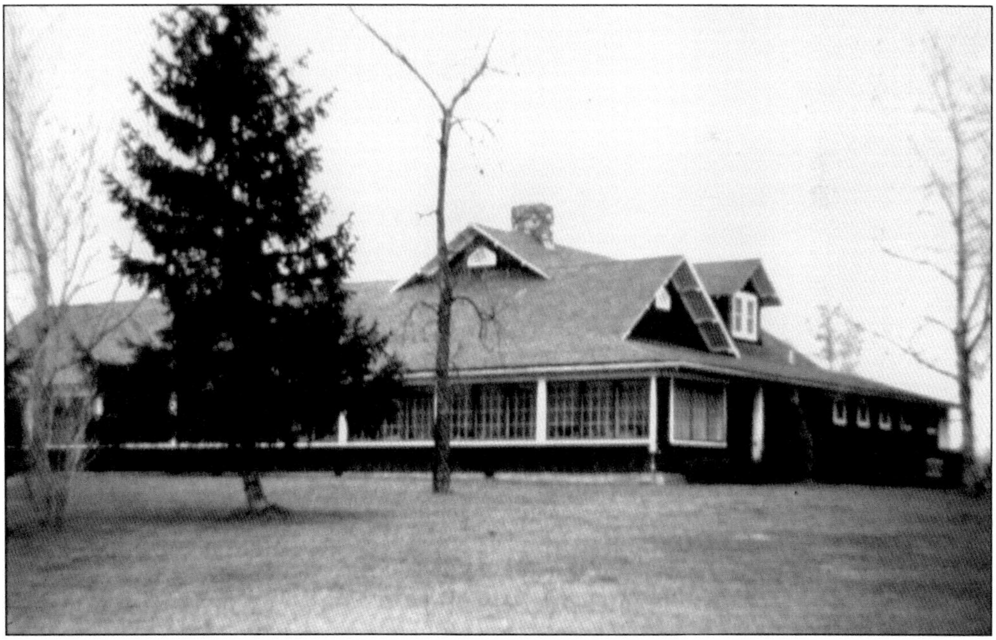

In 1928, the Ontario Entertainment Corporation purchased 100 acres for the firemen to hold their field days. In the 1880s and 1890s, the land was used as a racetrack for bicycles and horses. It then became the Ontario Golf Club. During the 1930s and 1940s, the golf club ran illegal slot machines. When news of a raid was heard, the machines were dumped in the local ore beds.

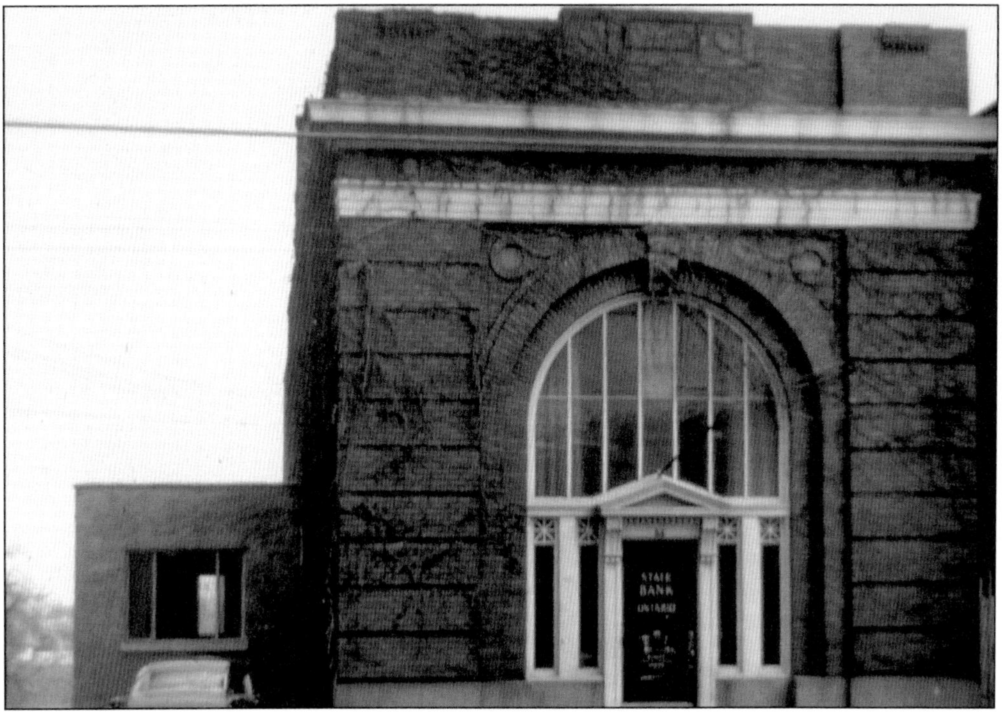

The State Bank of Ontario was built in 1913 and opened for business in February 1914. Over the years the building has been remodeled, has had additions made, and has changed names many times.

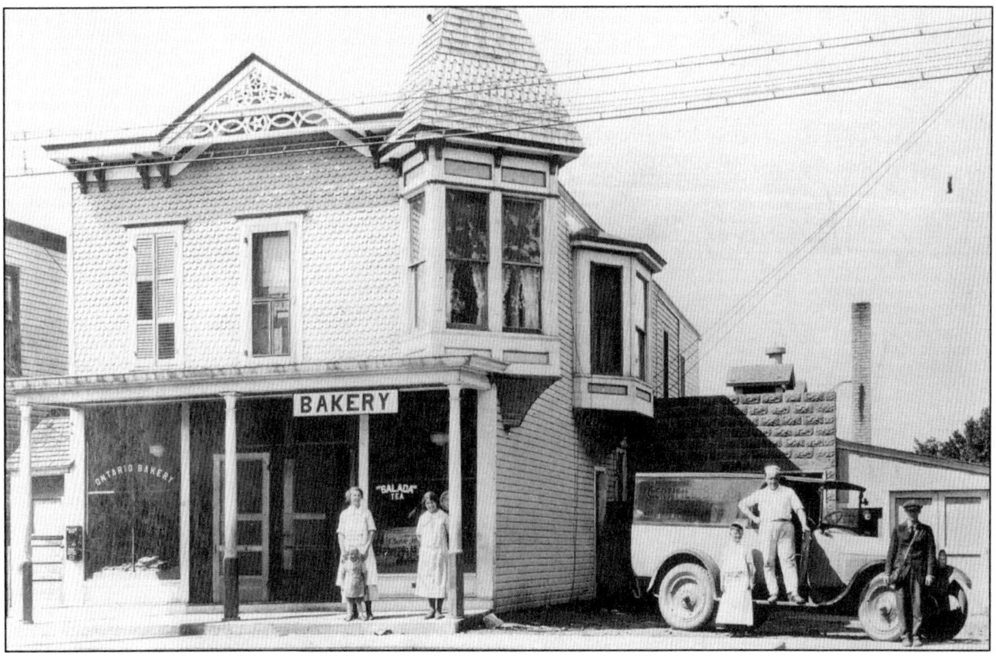

Lammes Bakery, shown as it was in 1926, was located on the north side of Main Street. Shown here, from left to right are Hellen Lammes, Hilda, Jane, and Reindert Jr., Reindert (Hellen's husband), and Howard Robie. Built in the 1880s, this building also housed a casket and millinery shop, a post office, a pool hall, a restaurant and a coffee shop.

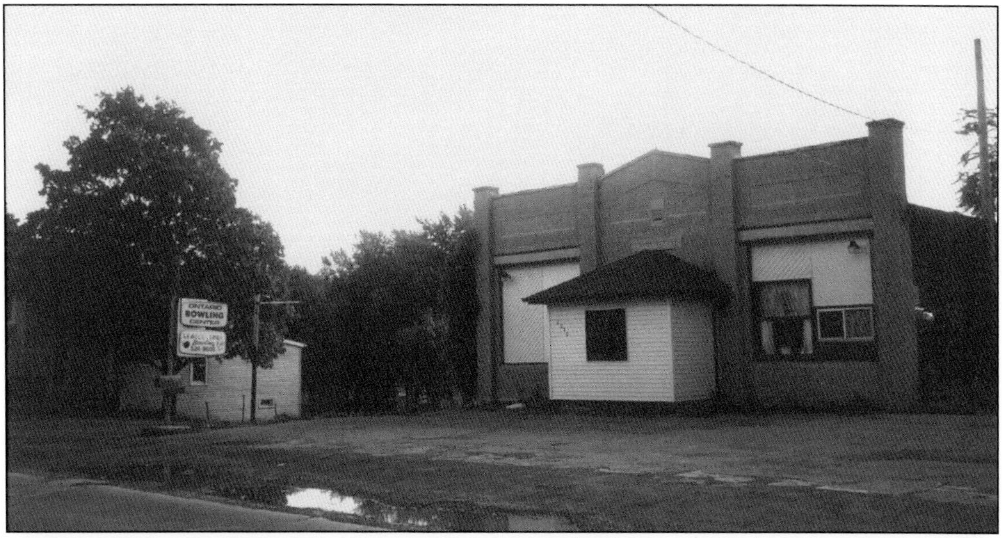

In 1921, Charles Bartl opened a vest factory on the third floor of the hotel building. In 1924, he built a factory on East Main Street. When the factory closed, the building was sold to the Ontario Fire Company for a fire hall. It was later sold to Ed Goetzman, who opened the Ontario Bowling Hall.

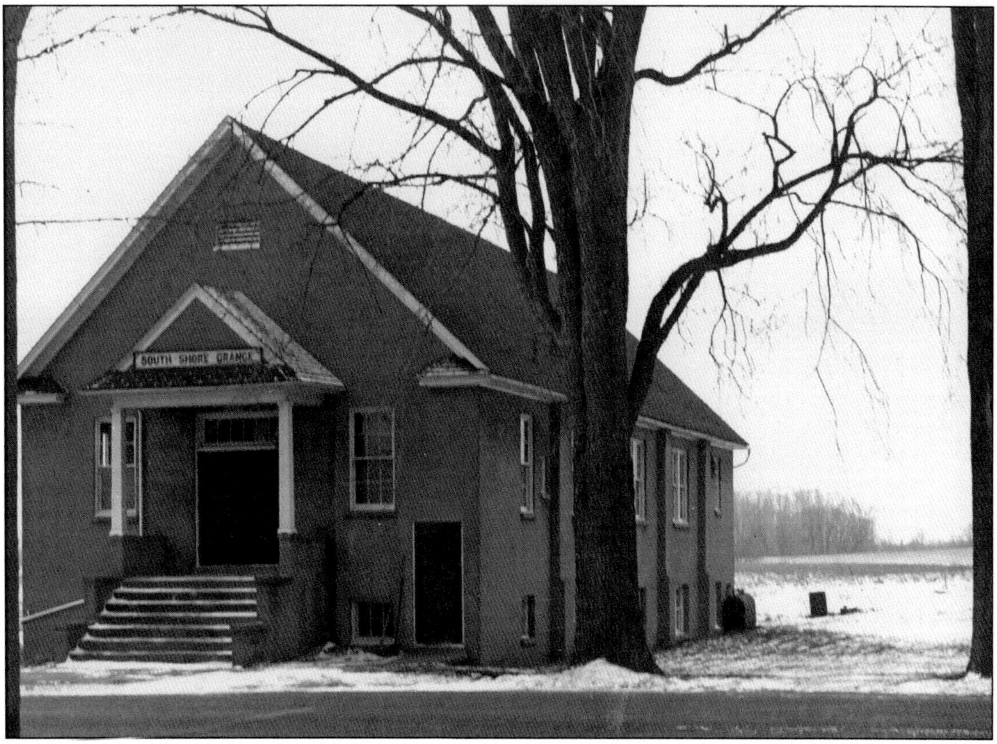

This stucco building, known as Palmer Hall, has undergone many changes in ownership. In 1932, South Shore Grange constructed this building as its meeting hall. In April 1964, members voted to give the building to Ontario for use as a town hall. It was used for the town's library and meeting hall as well as town offices until the new town hall was built in the early 1980s. Now it houses justice offices.

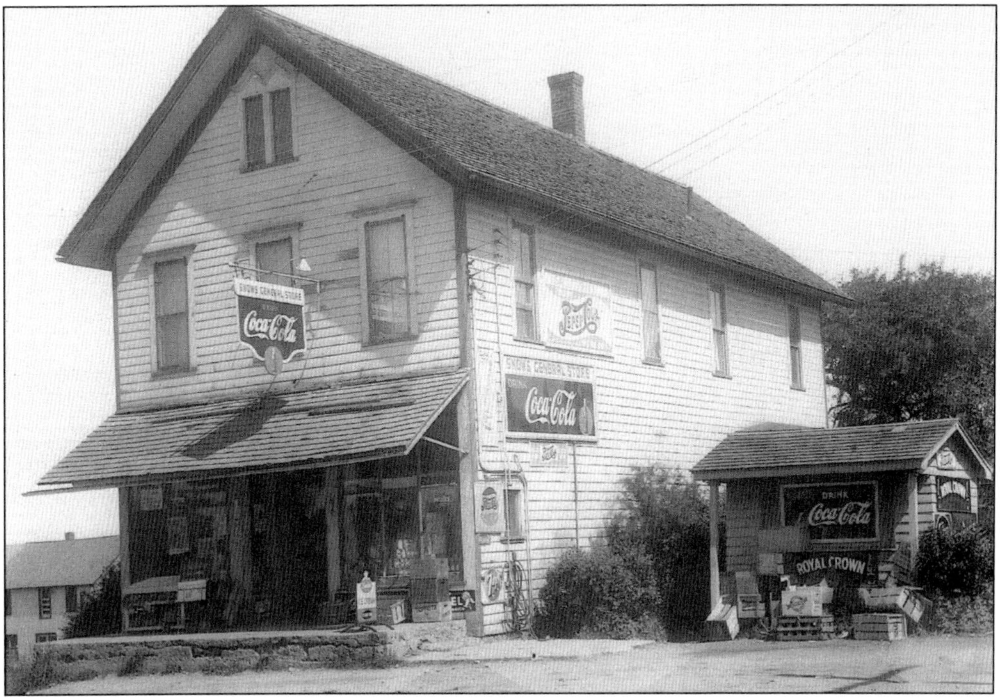

Snow's General Store was located on the corner of Lakeside Road and Ridge Road in 1940. It was purchased by Henry Snow in 1938. The Williams' mink ranch was next door.

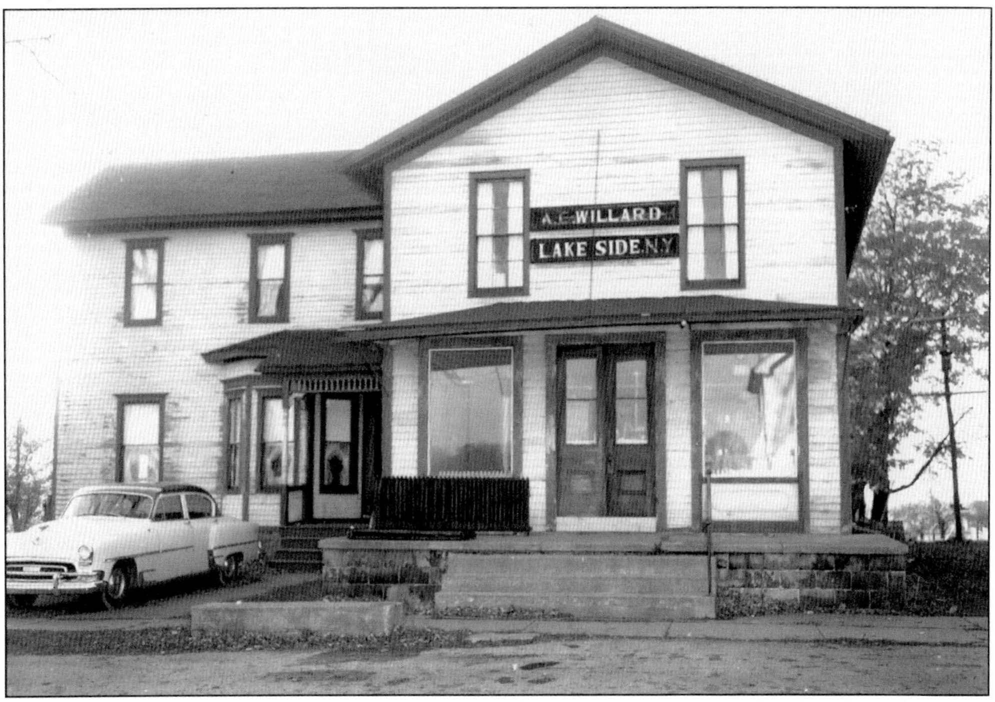

Willard's General Store and Post Office was on the southwest corner of Lakeside and Boston Roads. It was once the scene of a robbery that involved a manhunt by the Rochester police. The thief was captured nearby in the woods.

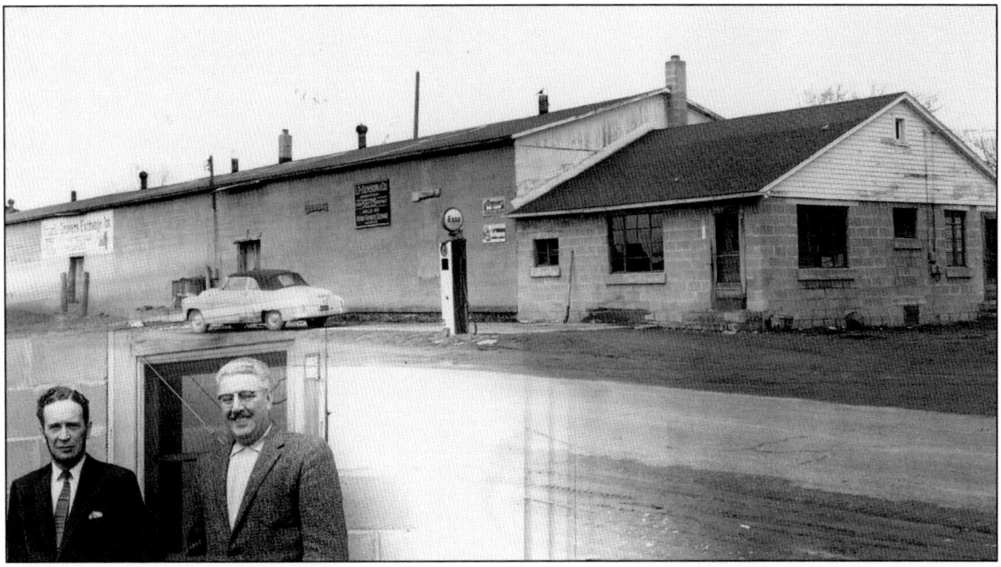

The Ontario Growers Exchange, shown here in 1957, was located on the north side of Railroad Avenue. Elwyn W. Leaty (right), also known as "Al," established the Ontario Growers Exchange in 1947. He added to the business in 1950 by buying the Huxley Farm on Ridge Road in Williamson and again in 1953 by buying the T. H. Sheahen Warehouse. Robert Robertson (left) was the office and sales manager.

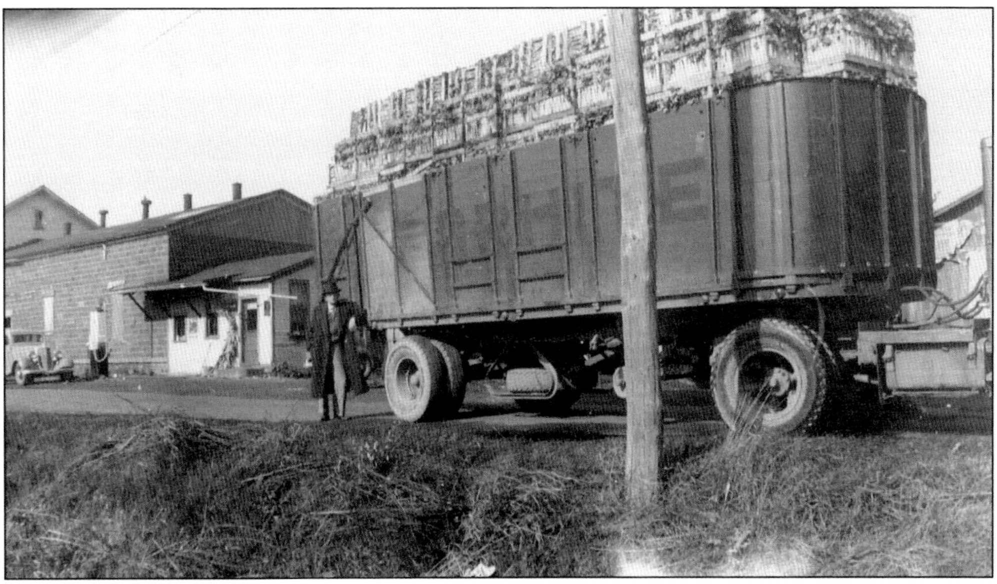

Shown here in 1938, the T. H. Sheahen and Sons wagon is loaded with celery. Thomas H. Sheahen entered the produce business in 1918. He purchased the building on the corner of Furnace Road and Railroad Avenue on the south side of the railroad tracks. The warehouse was originally built by Frank Tassel about 1910.

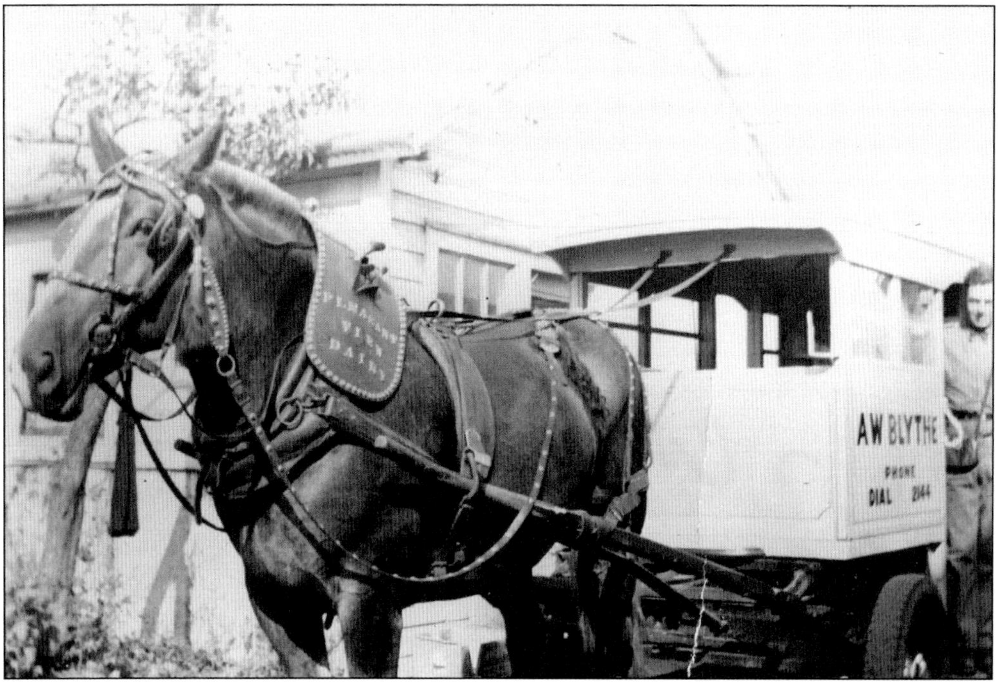

In 1919, Albert Blythe bought a milk route from Ben Hoag and delivered milk, very successfully, for many years. The man in the photograph is Milton Vane, who worked for Blythe and later married his daughter Ruth Blythe.

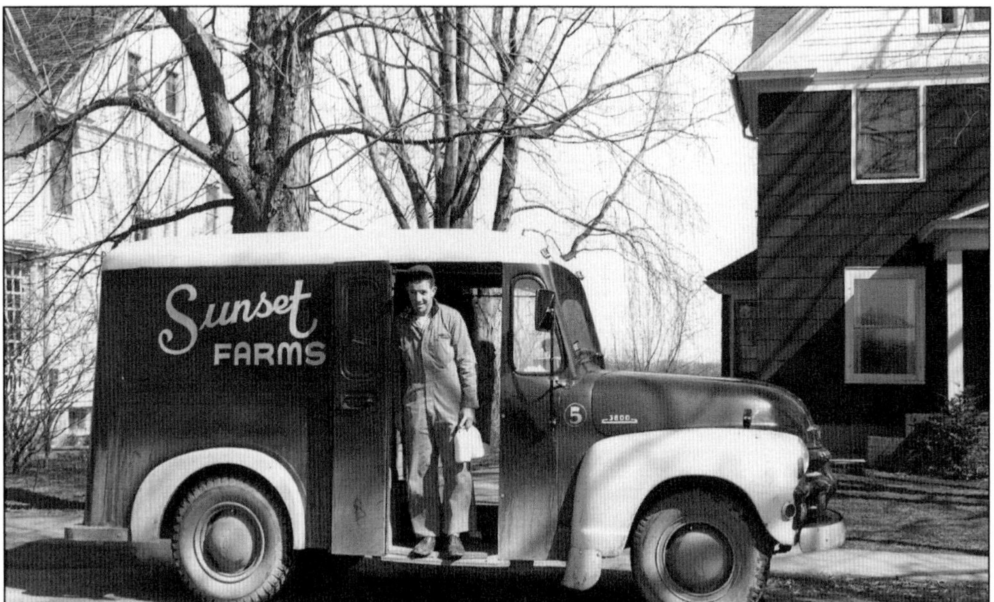

Blythe sold his business to Peter Leenhouts in 1943. Peter died in 1944. His widowed wife, Myrna, married Karl Raup. They built the Leenhouts Dairy on Ridge Road across from the elementary school. In 1955, the business was sold to Sunset Farms. Milk was delivered to rural and village families by truck. Don Pender is shown here in 1957.

The Ontario Free Library opened on January 5, 1915, with Anna Colwell as the first librarian. At one time it was located here in this tiny building where the Ontario Volunteer Emergency Service is now. In 1951, the Friends of the Ontario Public Library was formed to support the library's role in the community. James Switzer was elected the first president of the organization.

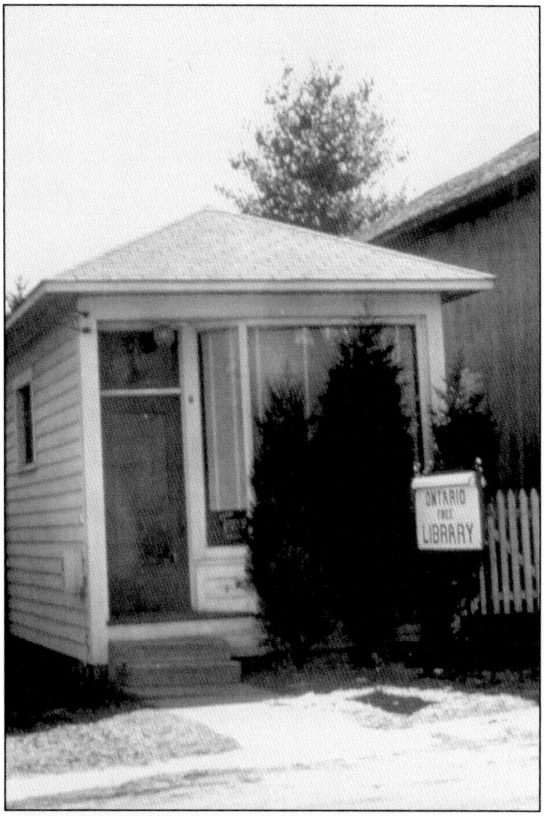

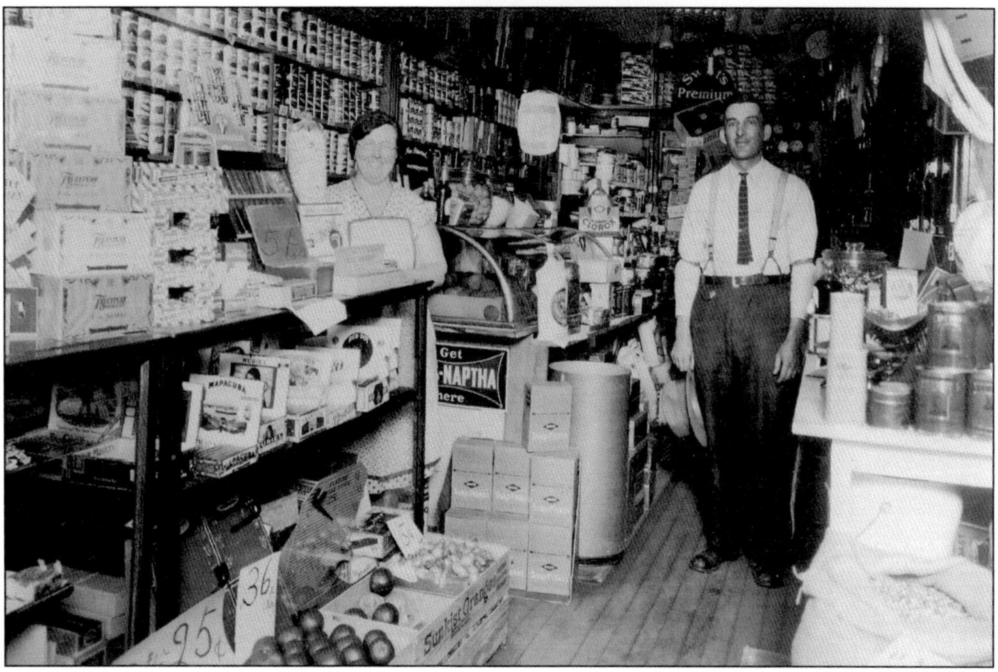

Lloyd Williams and his wife, Ruth, owned a general store on Ridge Road at the corner of Lakeside Road in an area known as Fruitland.

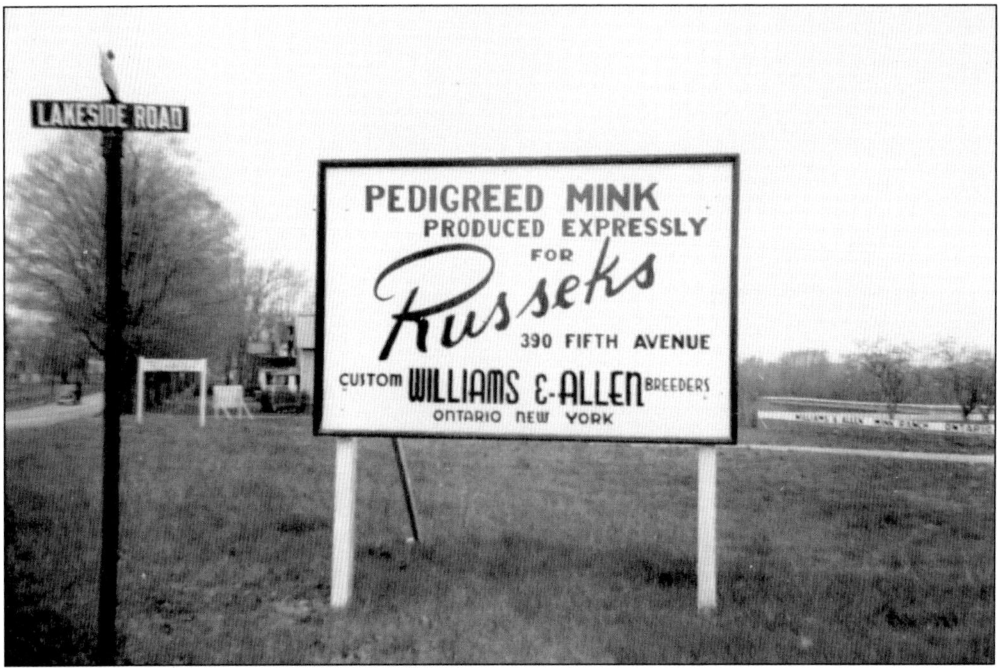

In 1931, the Williamses started a mink ranch with five female and two male mink. By 1941, it was known as one of the largest mink ranches in the world. Lloyd Williams was joined by Gordon J. Allen in 1936. Williams and Allen sold the business to H. W. Patterson in 1938. By 1944, there were 10,000 pens on the north side of the Ridge Road and 6,000 pens on the south side. In 1951, Patterson sold the enterprise to Howard and Dorothy Huckle. Bred to get the darkest fur, the Eastern mink were purposely kept in cages outside so their fur grew thick. The mink were bred in March, weaned in July, and were ready for pelting in December. It took between 80 and 120 pelts to make one mink coat.

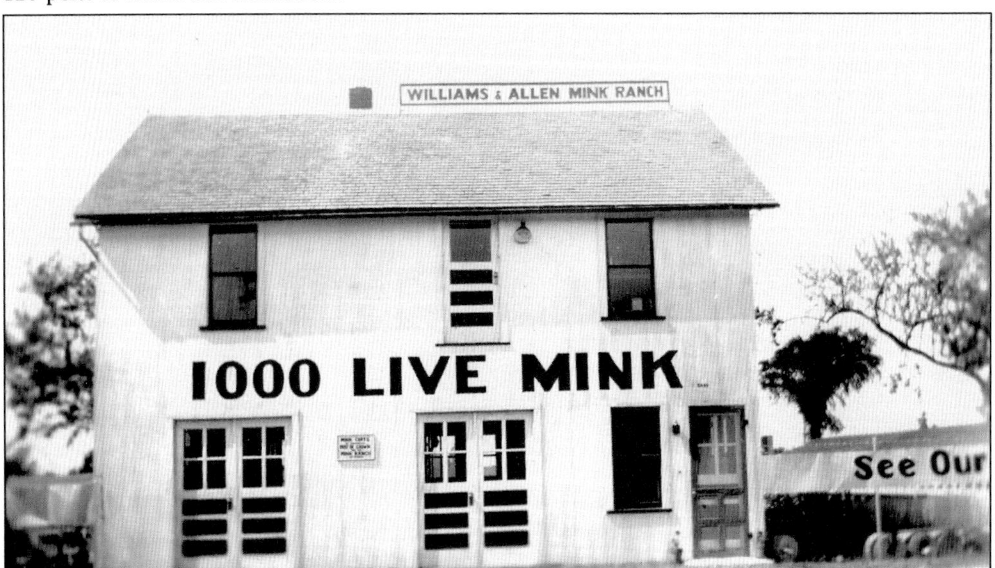

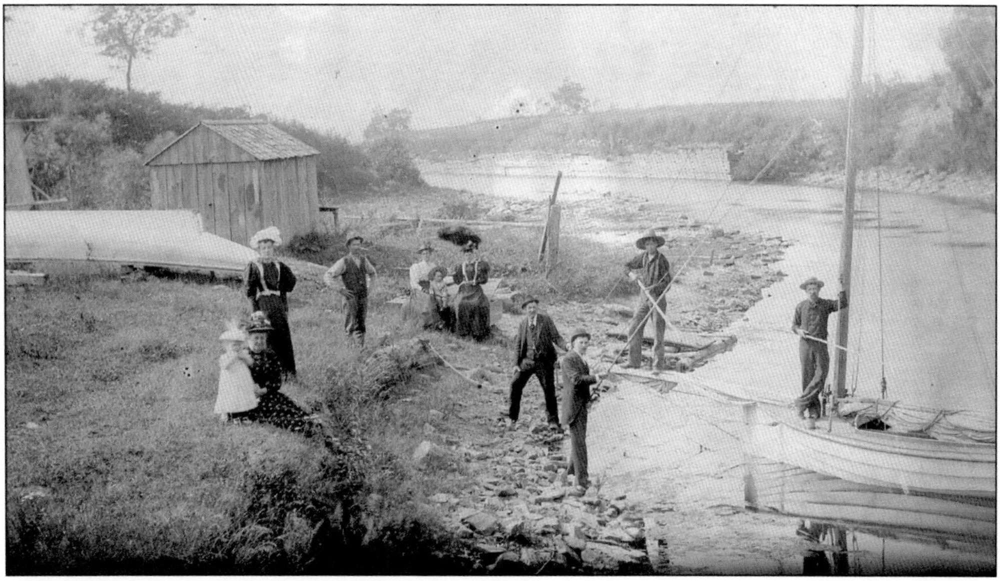

Bear Creek Harbor, shown here in the late 1800s, was once a fishing center and then a shipping port for iron ore. Today it is owned by the town and is used as a public park and boat launch.

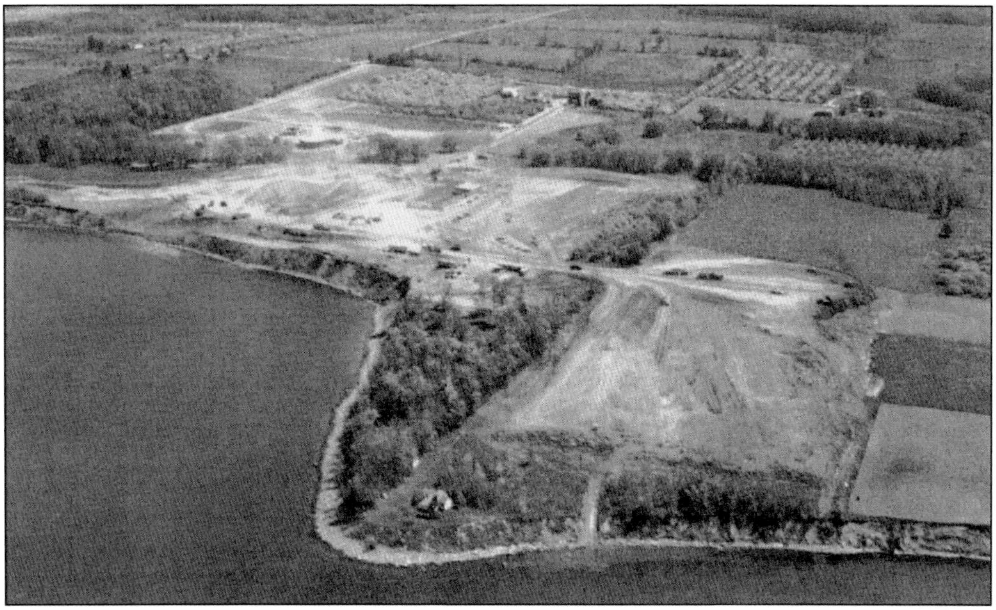

Smokey Point Farm was originally owned by Zebedee Hodges II and his wife, Sarah Ann Wilkins. In the early 1960s, Rochester Gas and Electric was looking for a place for a new electric power plant and settled on the Ellwanger and Bailey farms. Groundbreaking for the plant was in April 1966. This is a view of the building of the Ginna plant taken from the lake.

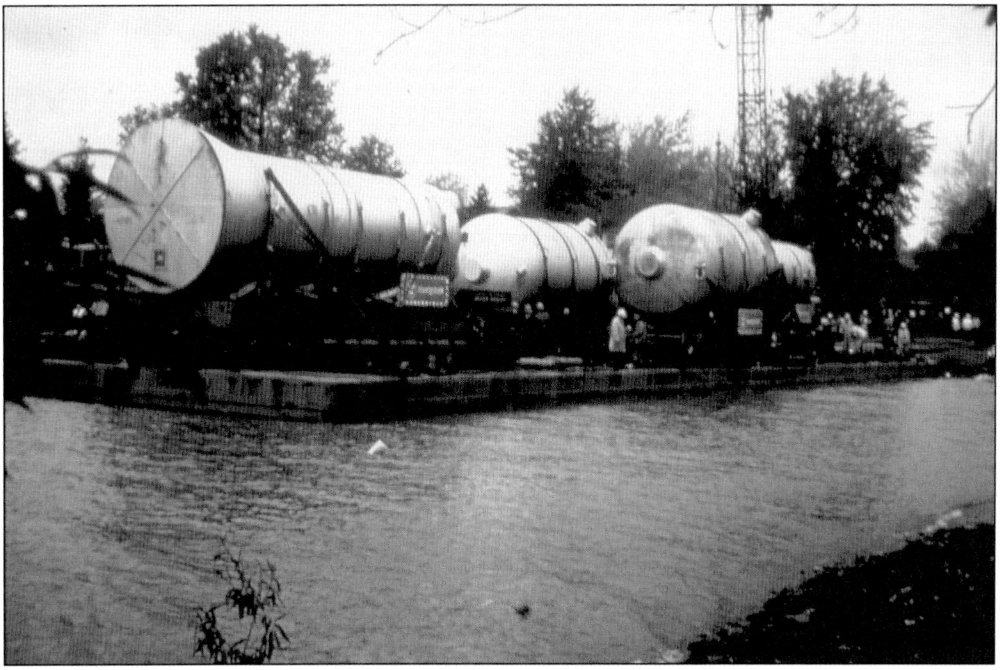

Bear Creek Harbor was dredged by Rochester Gas and Electric in 1966 to accept the reactor core for the nuclear power plant. This same little harbor was dredged again in 1996, when the replacement steam generators were delivered.

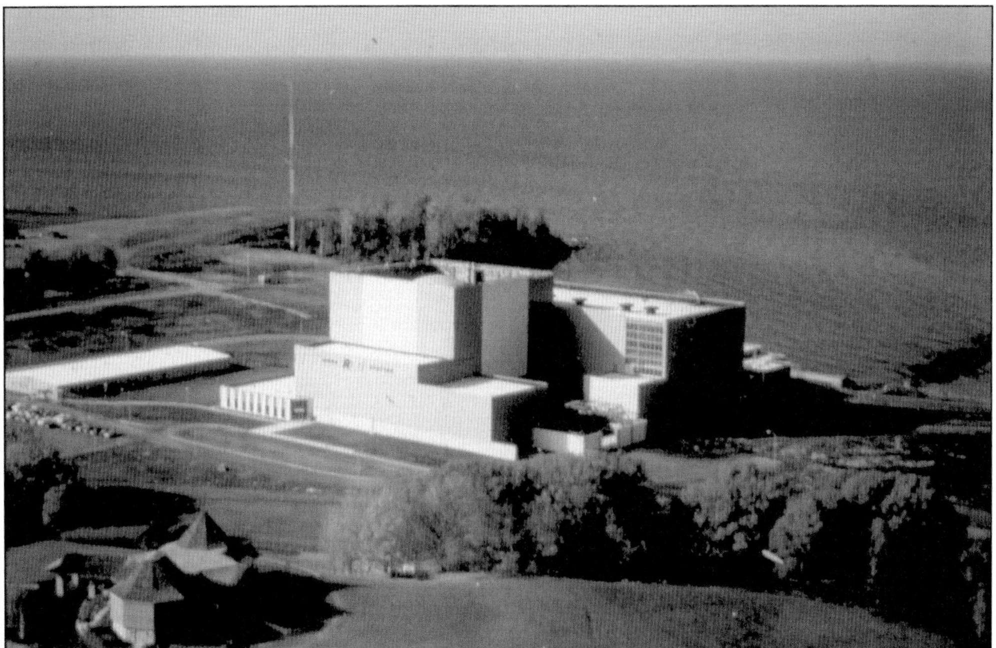

The Ginna Nuclear Power Plant went into full commercial operation on July 1, 1970. The plant's original 40-year license was recently renewed. In 2004, the plant was sold to the Constellation Energy Group. During the recent outage, the plant was upgraded to increase electrical output.

Seven

A Community of Good Neighbors

People gather together in groups for a variety of reasons—social, civic, religious, political, and entertainment. Over the years, many community volunteers donated time and money to have pieces of the town's history preserved. Heritage Square Museum is the historic jewel of the town of Ontario. It is located at the intersection of Brick Church and Ontario Center Roads. The museum is owned and operated by the Town of Ontario Historical and Landmark Preservation Society. Visitors can catch a glimpse of what life was like in the mid-1800s. Organizations have also banded together to celebrate. This chapter contains a sampling of the town's organizations. Some have long since dissolved; some are still active today.

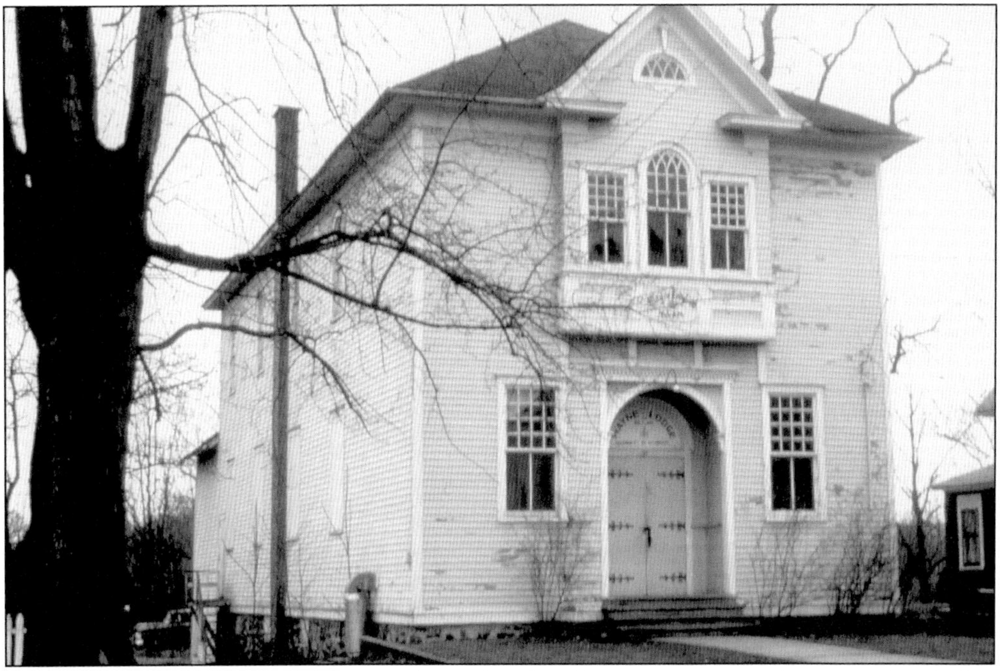

Built in 1903, the Masonic lodge has a hipped roof with projecting gable dormer and a Gothic sash. The congregation of the Calvary Baptist Church once held weekly services here. Movies were also shown in the building.

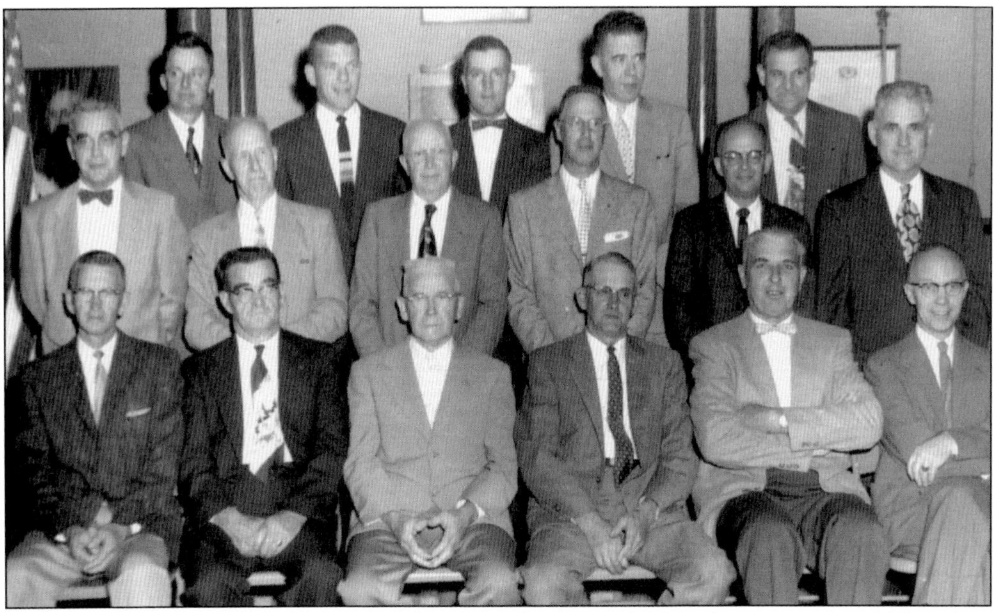

Wayne Lodge No. 416 of the Free and Accepted Masons had its beginning in 1856 and its charter granted in June 1857. Photographed in 1957, the past masters from left to right are (first row) Melville Sheahen, John VanHoover, Edward Sheahen, Floyd Gage, Harold Payne, and Carlton Cone; (second row) George Closs, Reno Merhoff, Eugene Wood, Parker Bridges, Rex Ransley, and Irving Armstrong; (third row) Bill Bauer, Don Merhoff, John VanderBrook, Harold Burden, and Maylon Riker.

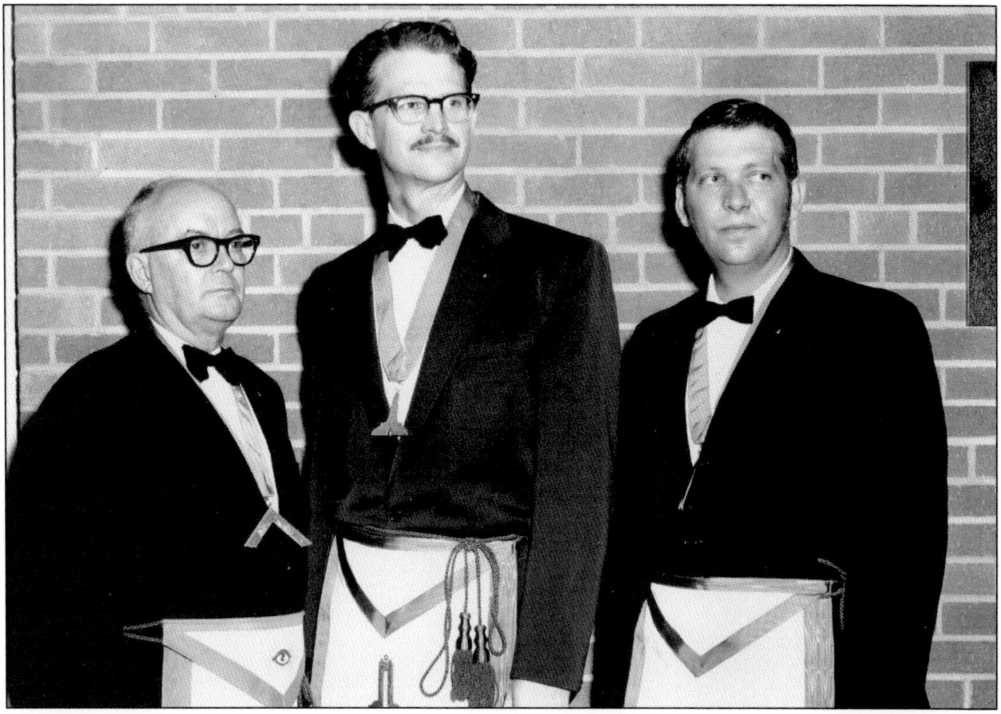

The Wayne Lodge No. 416 officers in 1971 were, from left to right, Rex Ransley, Robert Schneider, and William Cuppernell.

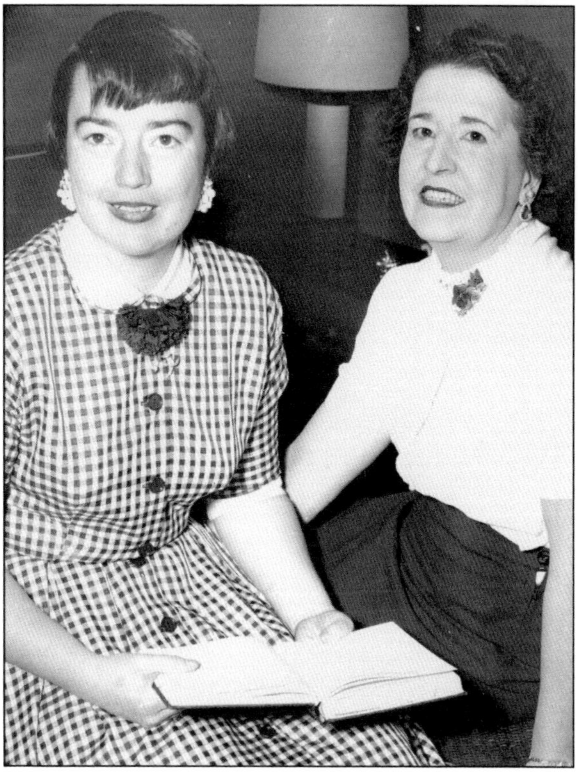

The Order of the Amaranth, a fraternal organization closely connected with the Masons, began in Ontario in January 1921. Meetings were held on the third Monday of each month in the Masonic temple on Ridge Road. Pictured here are, from left to right, Phyllis Waterman (district deputy) and Cornelia Verdine (royal matron) in 1954.

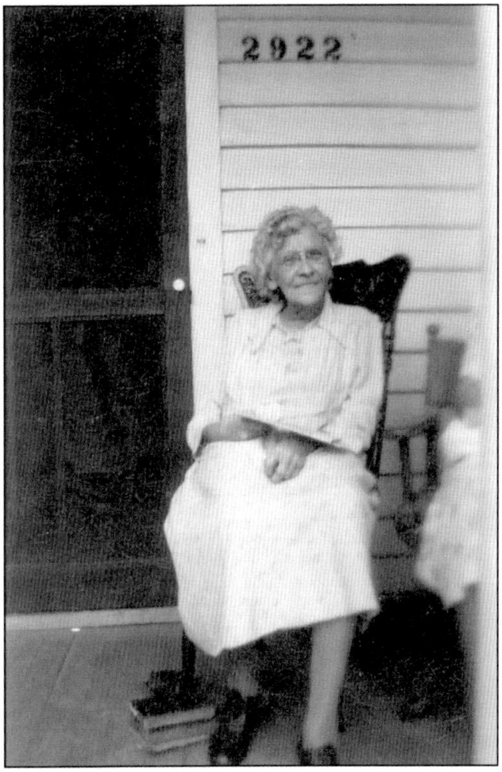

Hattie Fries founded the Ontario Chapter No. 296 of the Order of the Eastern Star in 1903 and served as its first worthy matron.

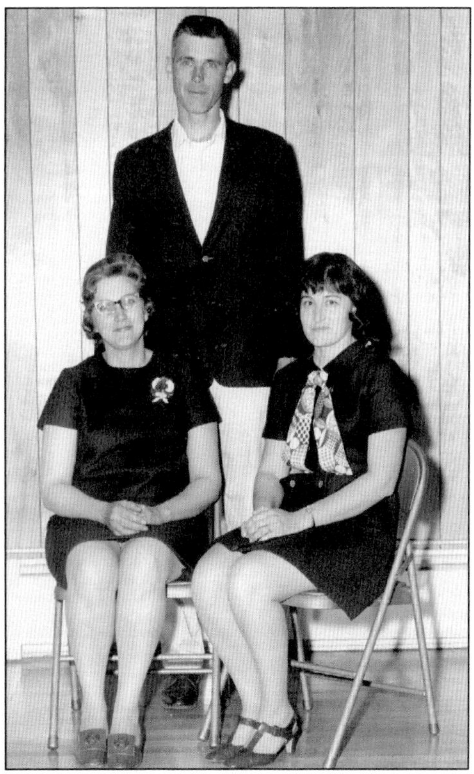

The Order of the Eastern Star is the largest fraternal organization with ties to the Masons. Shown here are, from left to right, Brenda Keisinger, Lyndon Keisinger, and Natalie Slocum in 1971.

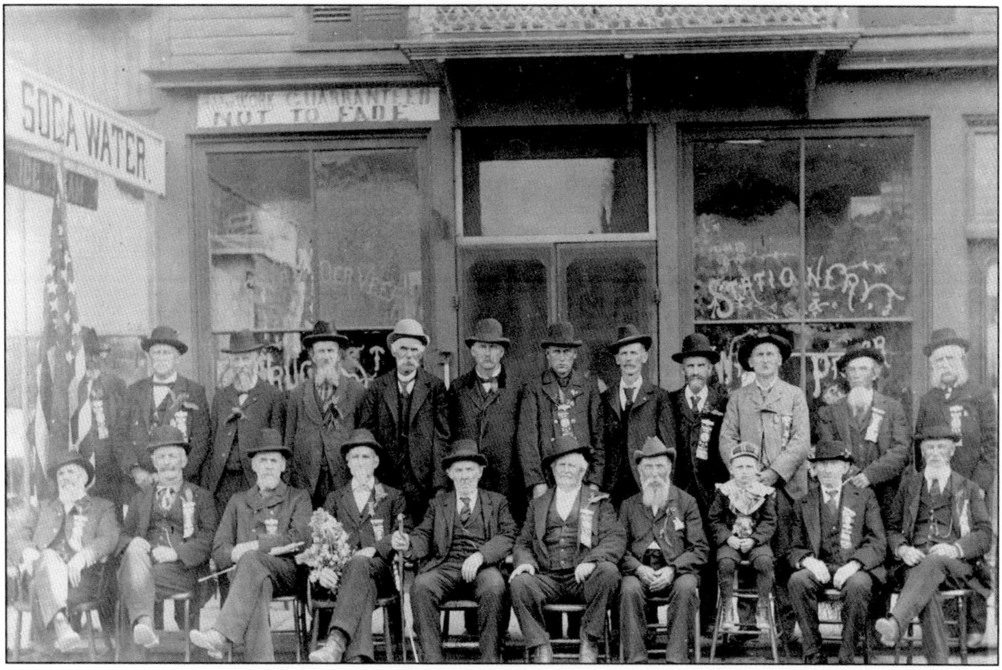

Myron M. Fish Post GAR No. 406 was formed to honor the son of Capt. Chauncey Fish who died in the battle of Winchester on September 19, 1864. This photograph, taken in 1885, shows, from left to right, (first row) Judson Grippen, Edgar Perrin, James Speller, Thomas Dodswell, John Hall, Charles Whitcomb, Loren Denney, James Prentiss's grandson, Pat Kiel, and William Birdsall; (second row) Sam Vande, Levi Allen, Eugene Sanders, Chester Stanford, Ike Warren, Charles Sanders, Dan Russell, Alfred Esley, Orin Casey, James Prentiss, Benjamin Mepham, and William Sinsabaugh.

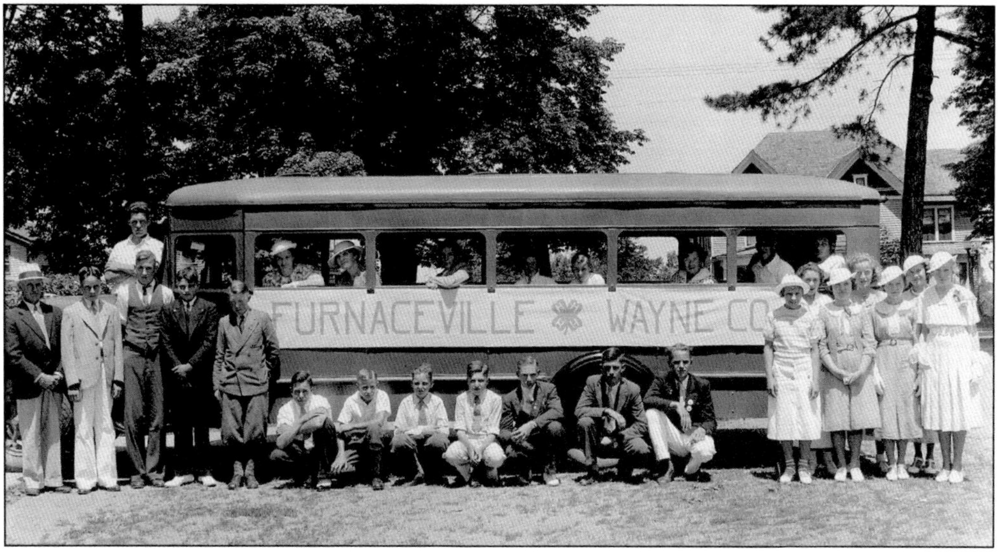

The Furnaceville 4-H group took a trip to Ithaca in 1934. The group was organized under the leadership of Frank Beneway and his wife at the beginning of the Depression when farmers were among the first to receive lower incomes. To raise money for the trip, they put on plays at the high school. Helen Beneway was awarded free trips to Chicago for her outstanding leadership work.

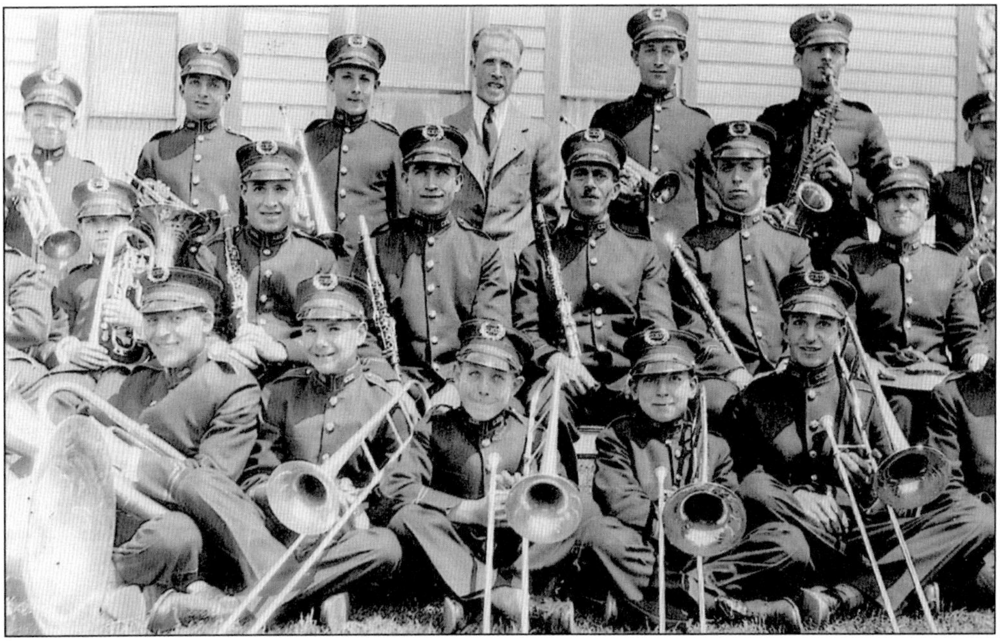

Tom Guggino was the leader of the Ontario Italian Band, a group that existed from 1929 through the 1930s. From left to right are (first row) Angelo Catalano, Carmen Arrigo, Frank Gabriel, unknown, and Jim Ademaro; (second row) unidentified, Tony DiRose, Alfred Ziccaro, Carmen Garifolo, Joe Catalano, and Charles Cimino; (third row) three unidentified men, Tom Guggino, Angelo Gabriel, and Pete Mitchell.

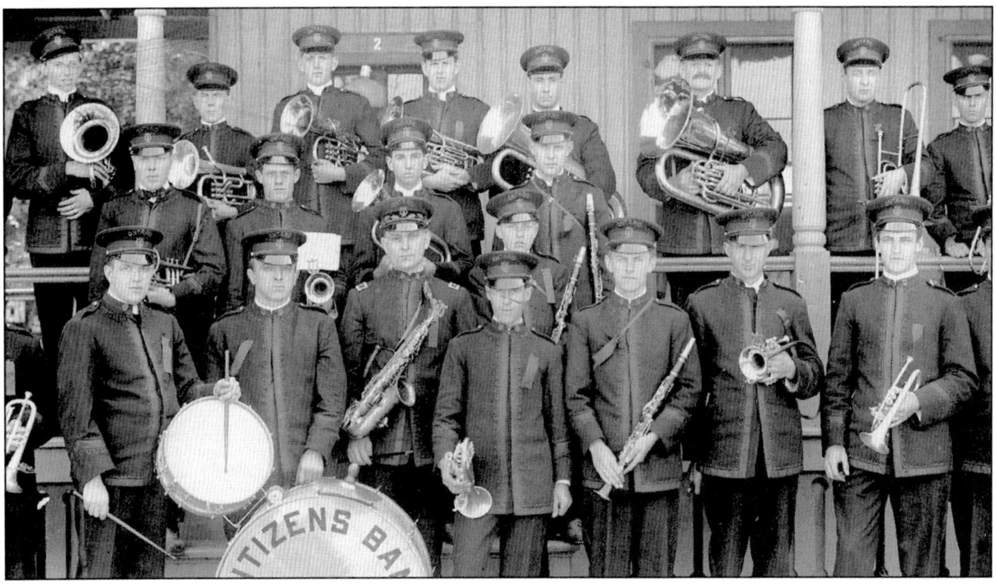

The Ontario Band was created in 1911 by Lew Clark. It held weekly Saturday night concerts, which drew audience members from miles around. Shown here are, from left to right, (first row) Elmer Toussaint, James Maher, Lew Clark, Perry Manktelow, Ike DeNeef, Charles Mitchell, and Burt Weeks; (second row, in the center on the steps) Arnold Flowers, Richard Whitbourne, Gordon Trimble, and Bun Whitbourne; (third row) Luther Howk, Floyd Peer, Carl Mepham, Floyd Mepham, Bill Perrin, Joe Whitbourne, Gordon DeVille, and Hun Albright.

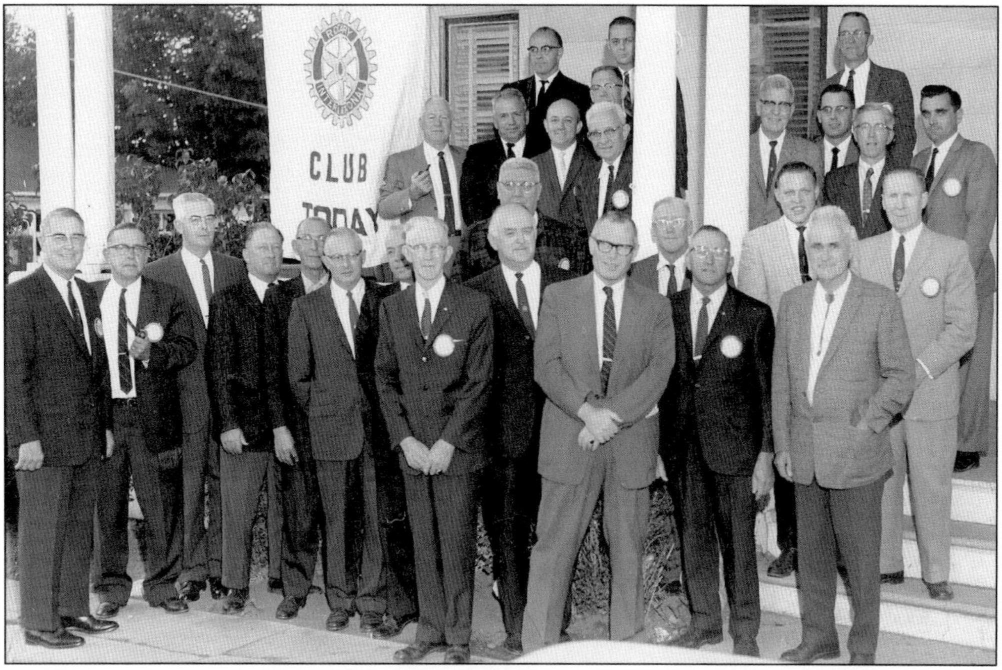

The Ontario-Walworth Rotary Club is a part of the Rotary International, a worldwide service organization. In Ontario, it began on May 14, 1945. The first meeting was held at the First Baptist Church, then in various places around town. The organization helps raise money for Camp Onseyawa for handicapped children and does other community service projects. It has sponsored the Boy Scouts and Cub Scouts since 1947, awarded selected high school students with the Student of the Month award, and participated in the student exchange program. Although it began as an all-male organization, more recently it has opened to women. Helene Saxman was the first woman member in 1989.

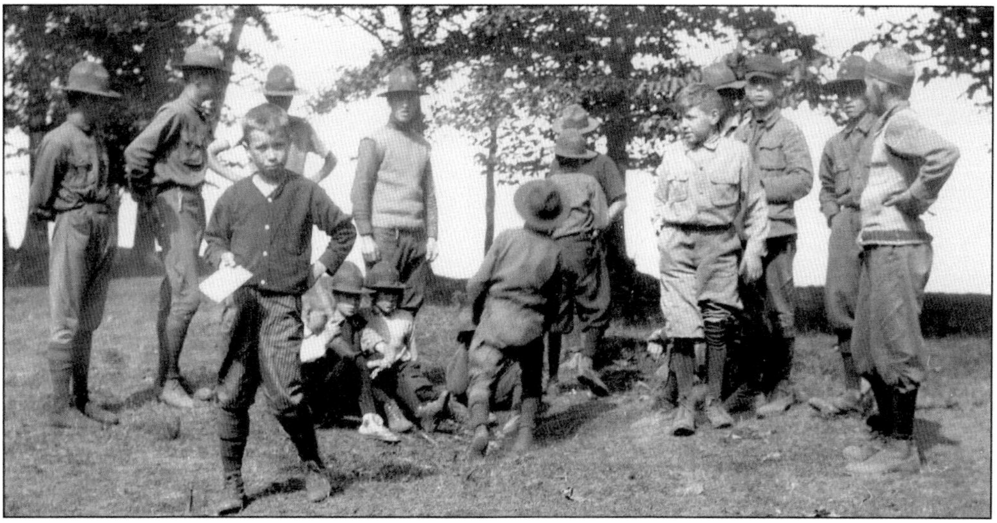

Scouting in Ontario has been around for a long time. The first Boy Scout troop began here in 1912. The first troop of Girl Scouts organized in 1919. Both boys and girls enjoyed camping in area camps—the boys at Smoky Point Farm (now Ginna Nuclear Power Plant) and the girls at Beneway's Woods. This photograph shows a group of boys in the early 1900s.

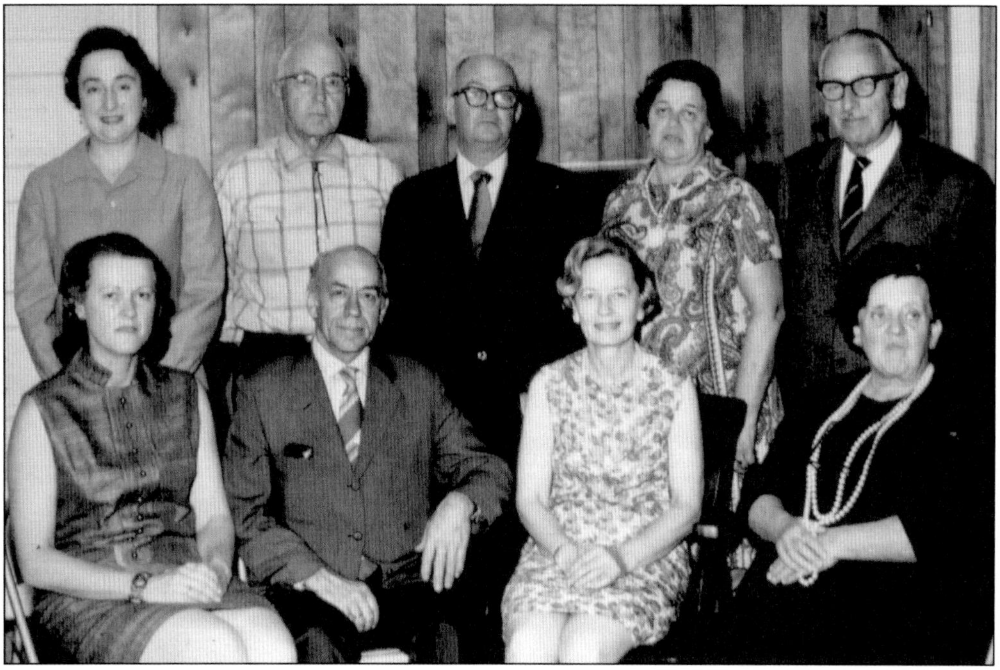

In 1969, concerned townspeople organized the Town of Ontario Historical Society and received a temporary charter in 1971. Shown here are the first officers, from left to right, (first row) Dorothy Huxley Cantin, Wilson Johncox, Ruth Faas, and Lucille Thompson Twitchell; (second row) Virginia Scully Hill, Howard VerDow, Rex Ransley, Fern Huxley Palmer, and Ray VandeVate.

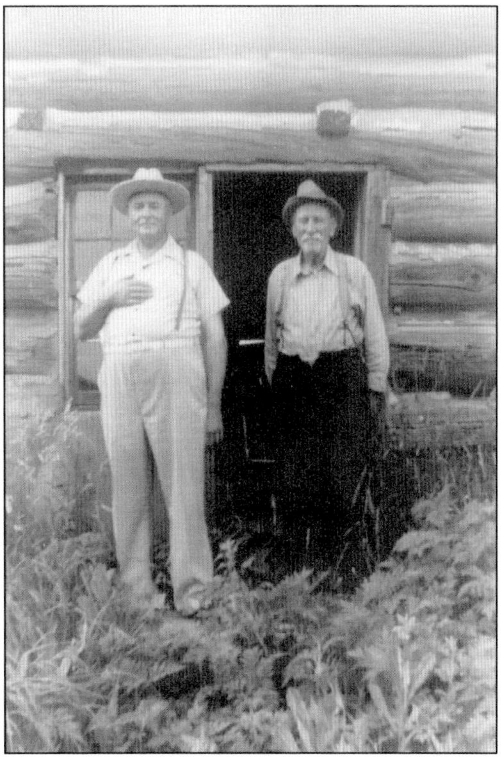

Lewis Ruffell and his father, Samuel Ruffell, are in front of their log cabin at its original location. In the early 1800s, a 25-square-foot home cost only $50 to build. A good log cabin, if built by someone else other than the homeowner, would cost $100.

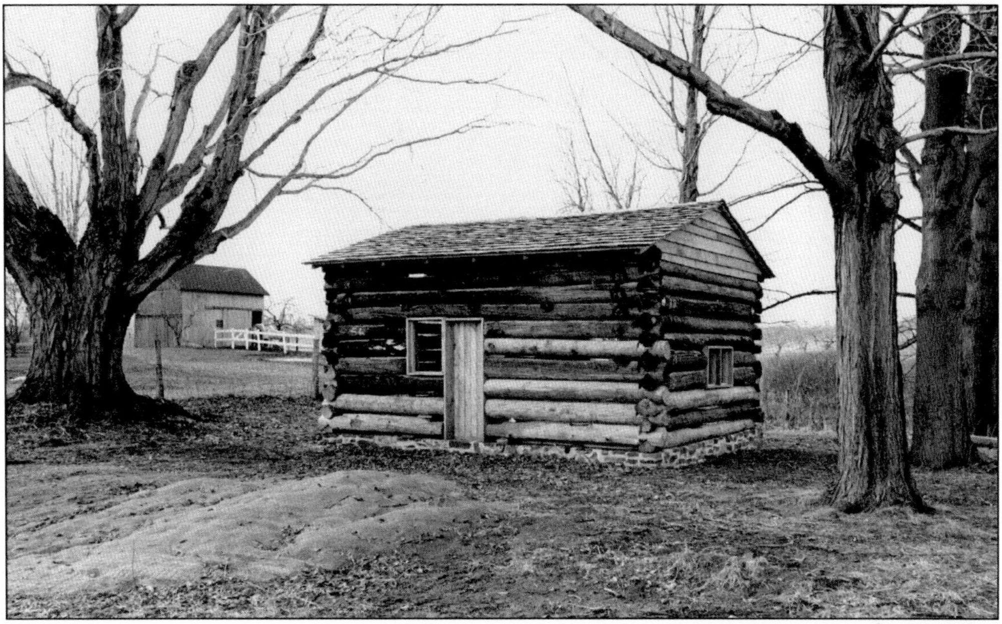

James Ruffell built this log cabin on Orebed Road (Kenyon Road) during the Civil War. It was a replacement for an earlier one built further back in the woods. In an 1894 Williamson newspaper there is a story about the owner. On his deathbed, Ruffell pointed toward the clock and struggled to tell his family something, but he died before he could deliver his message. Years later his grandchildren were playing "hide the marbles" and found $200 in gold and $133 in silver hidden in the logs behind the clock. In 1970, the log cabin was donated to the Ontario Historical Society by Michael Robusto with the stipulation that it be moved. The move involved dismantling the logs one by one (seen below). The logs were carefully numbered with tin plates that came from the canning factory.

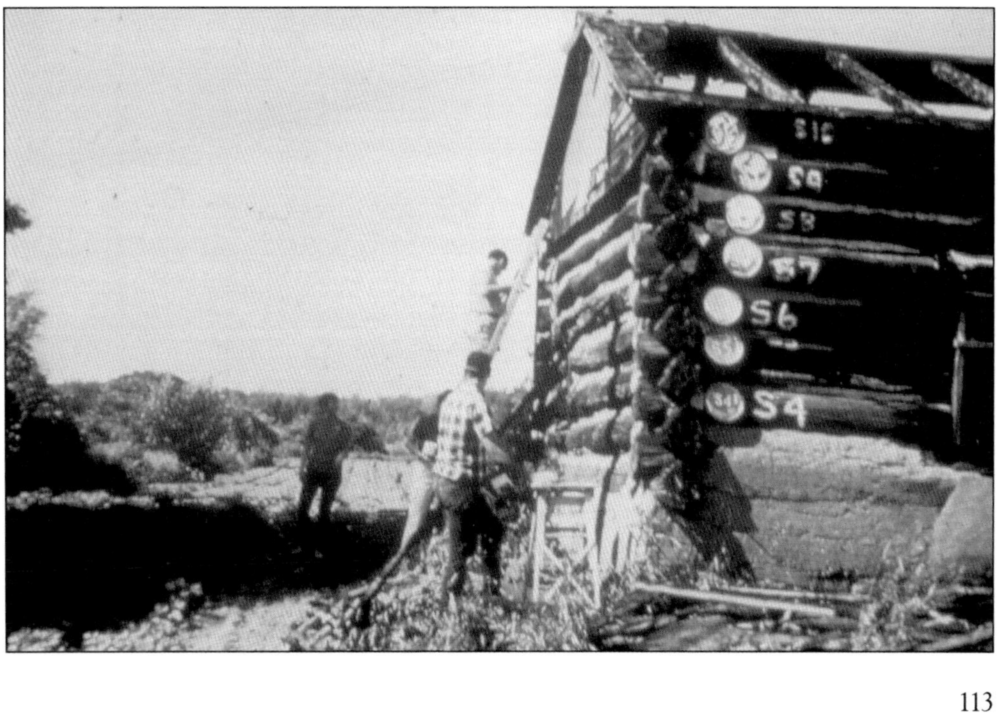

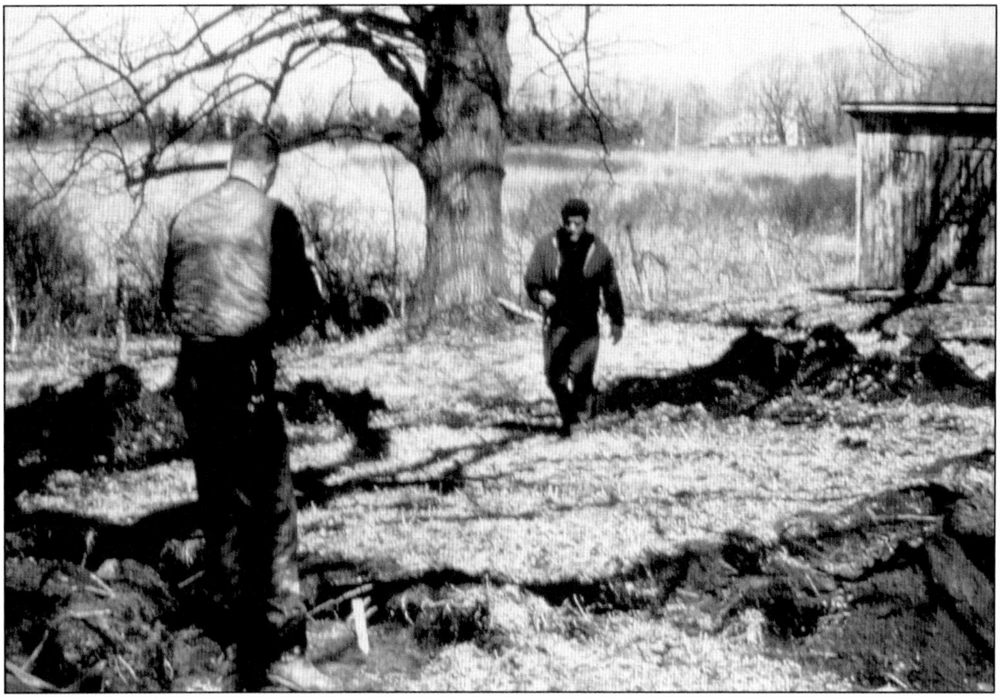

The logs were moved and stored on the Ruth Faas property until funds could be raised to reassemble the cabin at its new location. Extra logs to replace the ones burned in an earlier kitchen fire were donated by Rochester Gas and Electric Company. The log cabin's new foundation of red medina sandstone was prepared at the new site at Heritage Square.

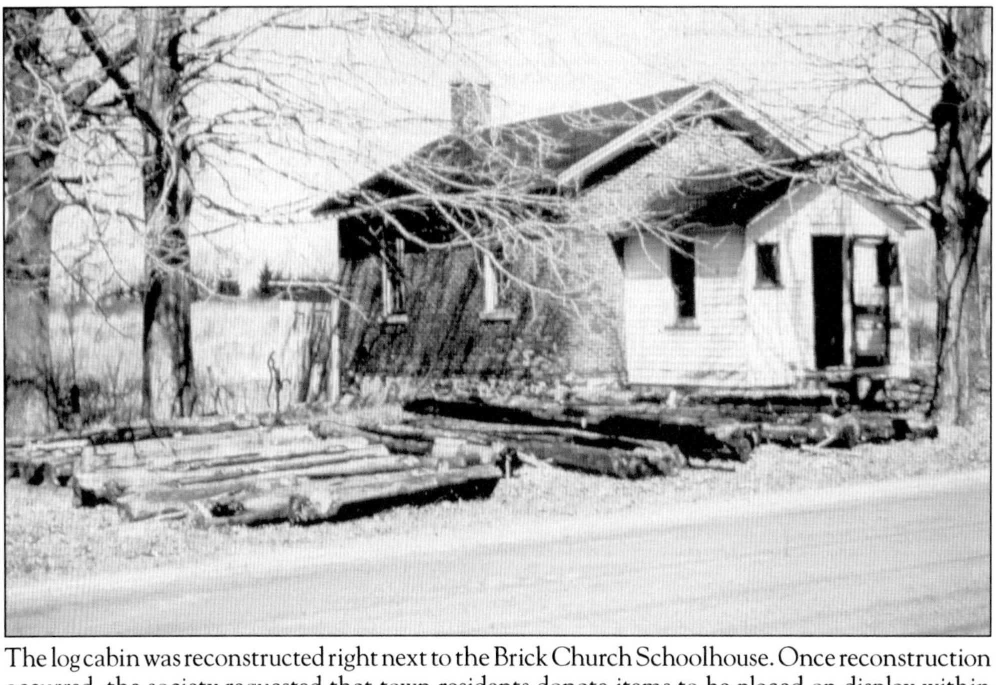

The log cabin was reconstructed right next to the Brick Church Schoolhouse. Once reconstruction occurred, the society requested that town residents donate items to be placed on display within the cabin. Visiting this building takes one back to a time when the town was first started.

Just to the east and south of the log cabin, Fred Micha is standing by the largest sugar maple tree in New York State. The tree was carefully measured, and the designation was made in 1997.

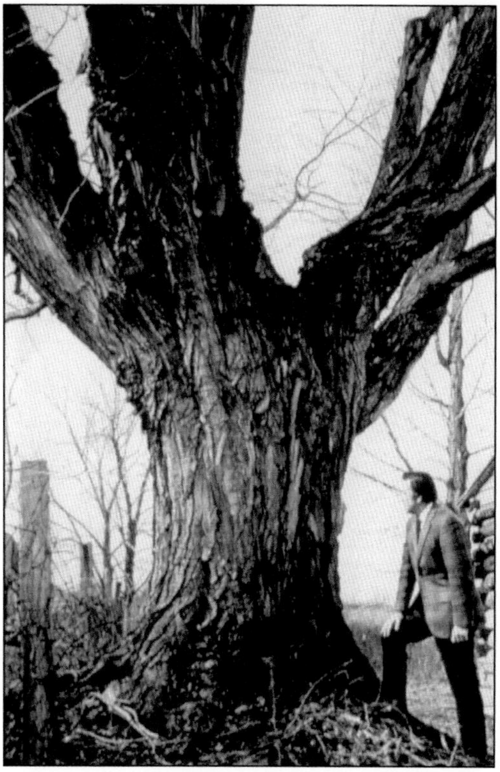

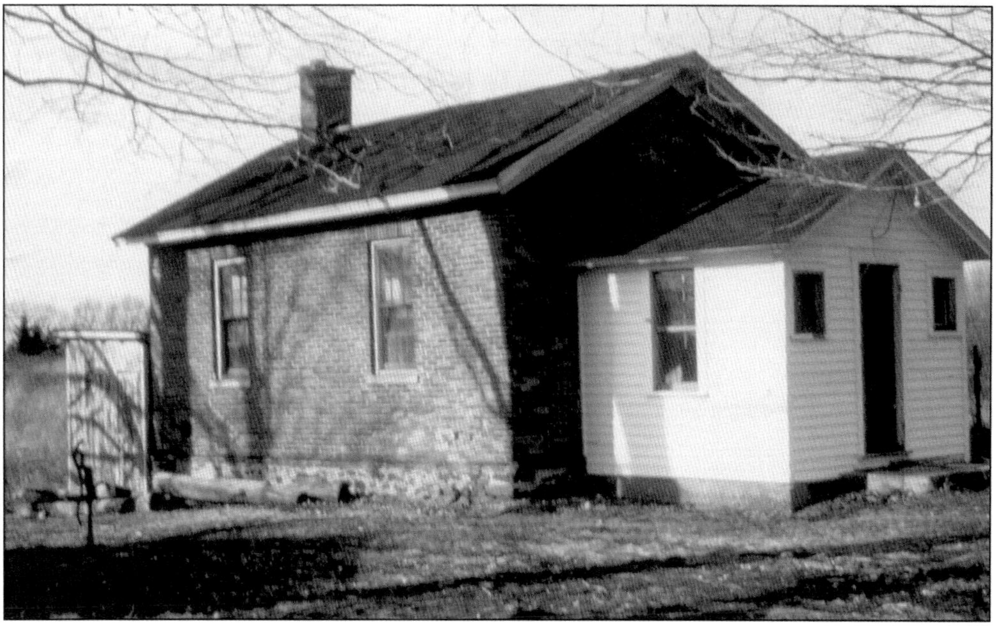

The Brick Church Schoolhouse, District No. 4, is the only one-room schoolhouse left in Ontario that remains as it was when it was built in 1868. In 1949, after becoming decentralized, the school was bought at auction by Elwyn Harris. In 1971, at the time of Harris's death, the Town of Ontario Historical Society purchased the building from his estate for $1,000. Land at the site was generously deeded to the society.

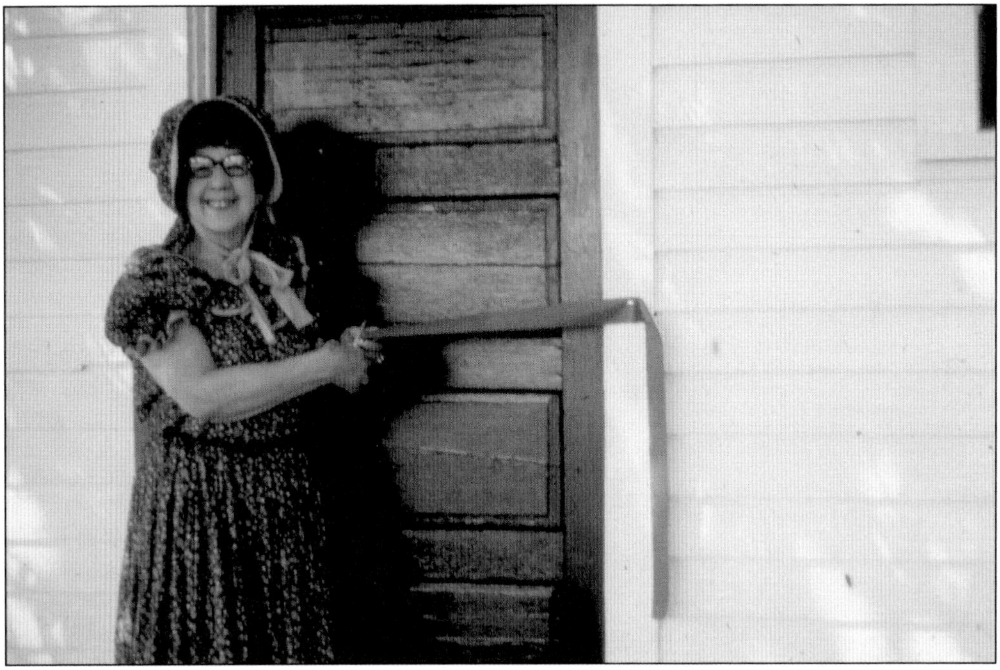

Augusta Trimble, town historian at the time, cuts the ribbon to open the newly restored Brick Church Schoolhouse at Heritage Square on September 8, 1973. Carefully restored and preserved, the school is a fascinating place for visiting schoolchildren to get a glimpse at what school was like years ago.

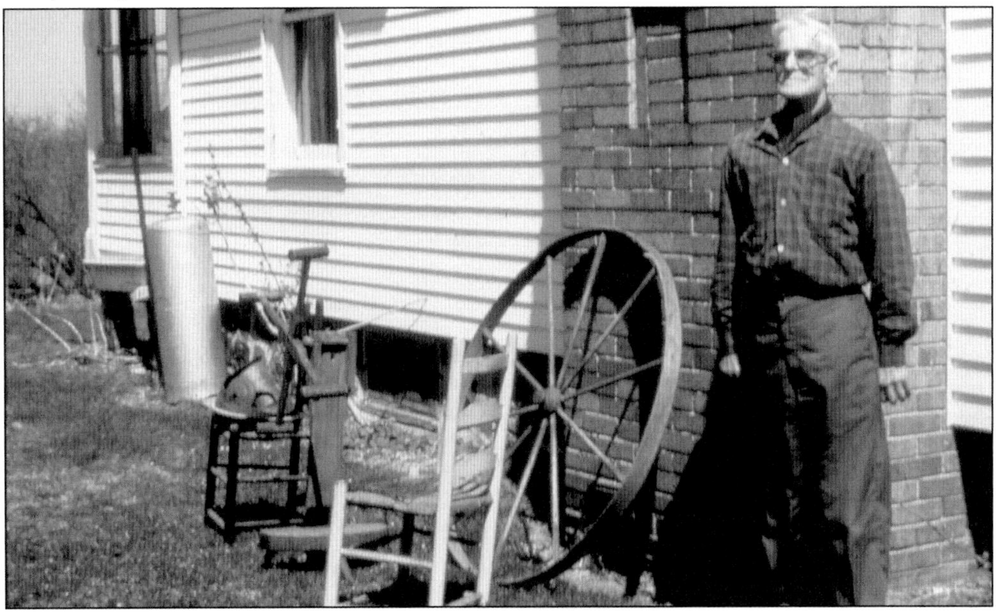

Ross Gates is shown here standing by the items he donated to the historical society to put on display in the buildings at Heritage Square. Ross was a member of the Masons, the South Shore Grange, and the Town of Ontario Historical Society. He was born in 1887, attended the Albright Schoolhouse, and lived on the family farm of 230 acres. This farm was eventually bought by Rochester Gas and Electric in order to build the Ginna Nuclear Power Plant.

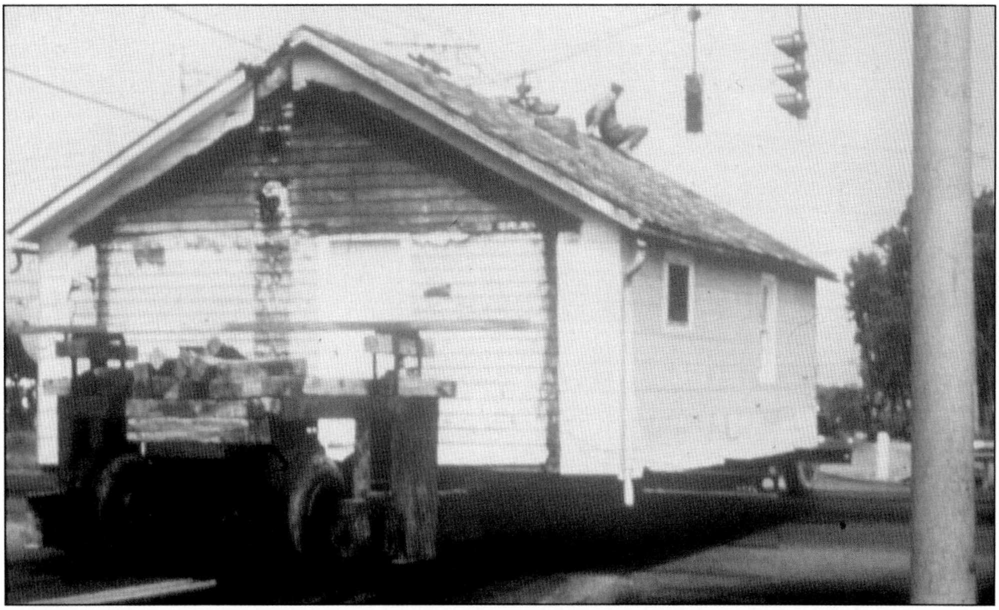

In 1974, the Baptist Meeting House, having been donated to the historical society, was moved to Heritage Square. The Baptist congregation met for the first time on July 3, 1834. Its first meetinghouse was on the southwest corner of Ontario Center. The congregation later built a larger church, and it is believed that it used this earlier church building as a parsonage. The 1834 *Wayne County New York Atlas* shows these two buildings side by side.

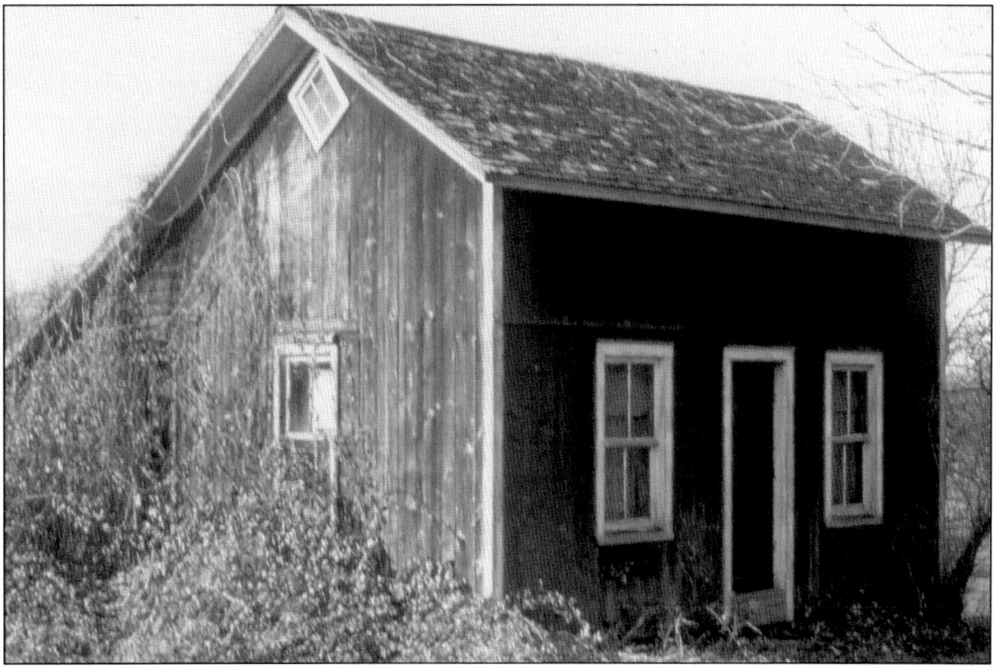

The Ore Miner's House, once owned by Callie and Lynn Watson, was built in 1860. It was the third building moved to Heritage Square. This home was donated to the historical society by Earl and Bernice Watson in 1977. As with the cabin and the meetinghouse, it had to be removed from the donor's land and brought to Heritage Square. The move was one-eighth of a mile due north.

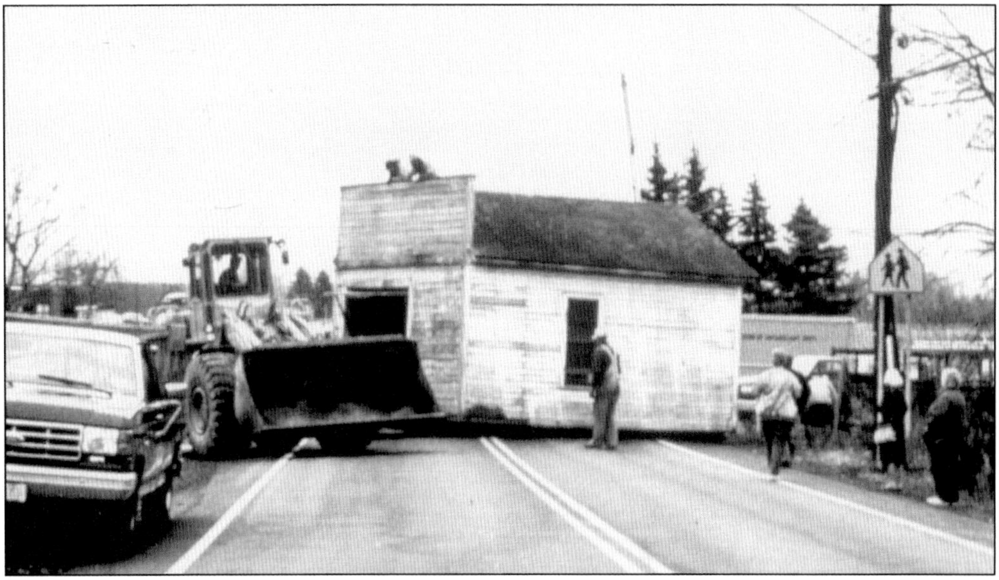

This building has served many uses. In 1895, it was the site of the Freeh Cobbler Shoppe. When John Freeh was appointed postmaster in 1897, he had his post office here as well. It was a barbershop owned by George Miller in 1903. In 1909, it was the Ontario Center Boot and Shoe Store operated by George Brown. In 1919, it was moved from Ridge Road to Ontario Center Road and turned into the town lockup (jail). Donated by Willis and Christine Butler, it was moved to Heritage Square in 1992.

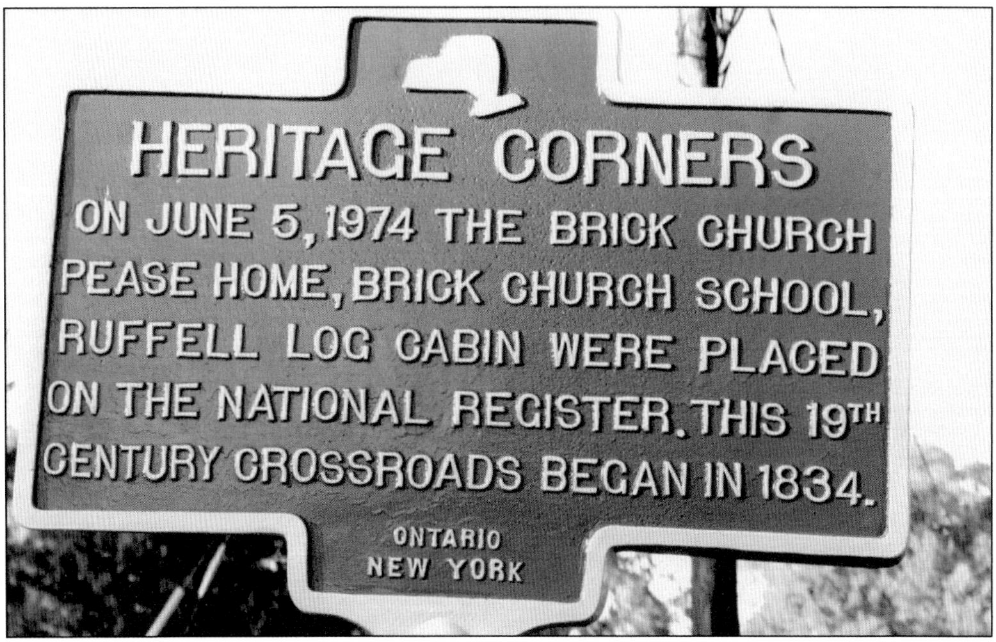

The Heritage Corners landmark sign marks the corner where Heritage Square Museum, the Brick Church Schoolhouse, and the Pease Homestead are located. It was placed on the National Register of Historic Places on June 5, 1974. Additions to the museum grounds include the Warner Farm House, the apple dry house, the exhibit barn, two outhouses, a corncrib, and, just recently, the Ontario Train Depot.

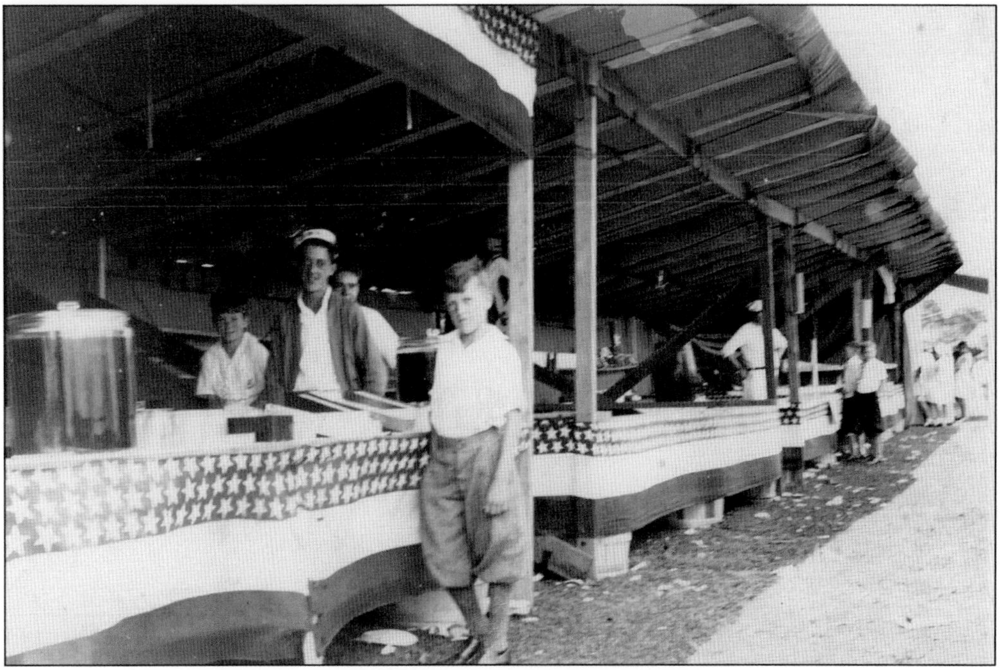

Through the years, the residents of Ontario celebrated events in many ways. Beginning in 1924, the Ontario Firemen's Field Days was a much-awaited event each summer. After the first year, it was held at the land the firemen had purchased on Walworth Road (now the Ontario Golf Club) until 1941. This photograph was taken in 1933.

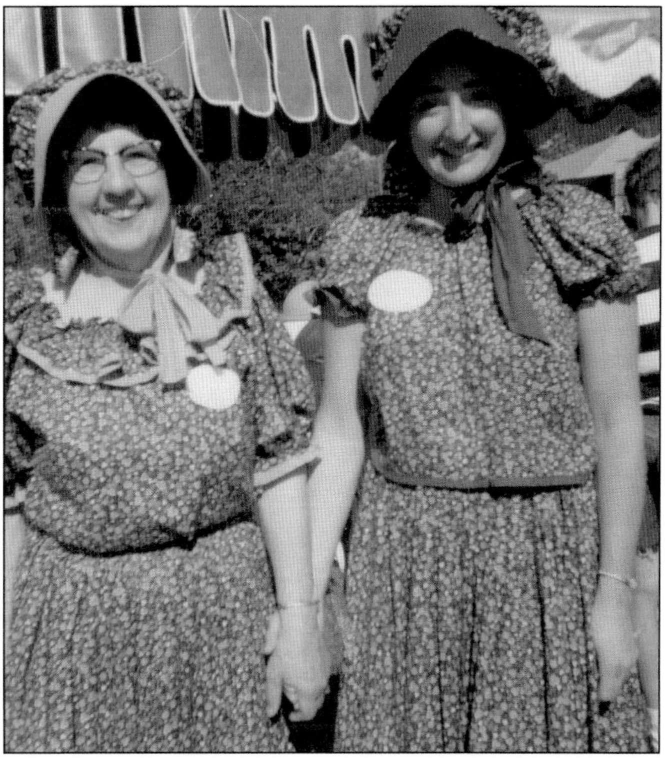

Town historians Augusta Trimble and Virginia Scully Hill are at Casey Park on October 2, 1971, at an event called Get Together Ontario Days. More recently, yearly similar events have been called Summerfest and Village Days.

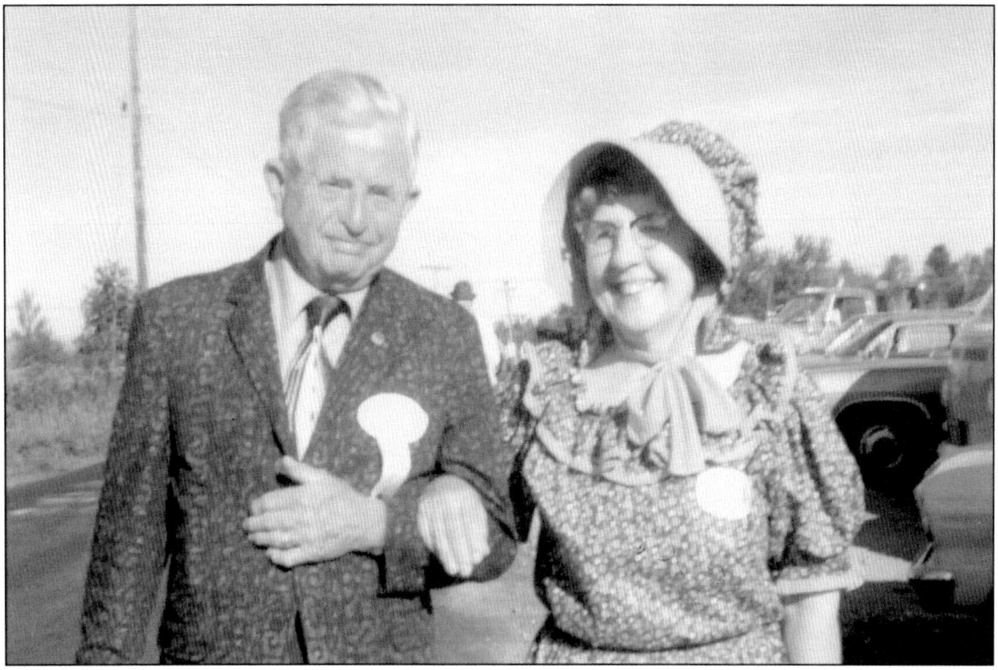

Casey Park, the town's public park, which encompasses an old iron ore bed, began in 1964. The park was first used for swimming, and in 1967, land was cleared for baseball diamonds. The park is named for Earl Casey. Casey, shown here on October 2, 1971, with Augusta Trimble, was supervisor of the town from 1958 to 1963.

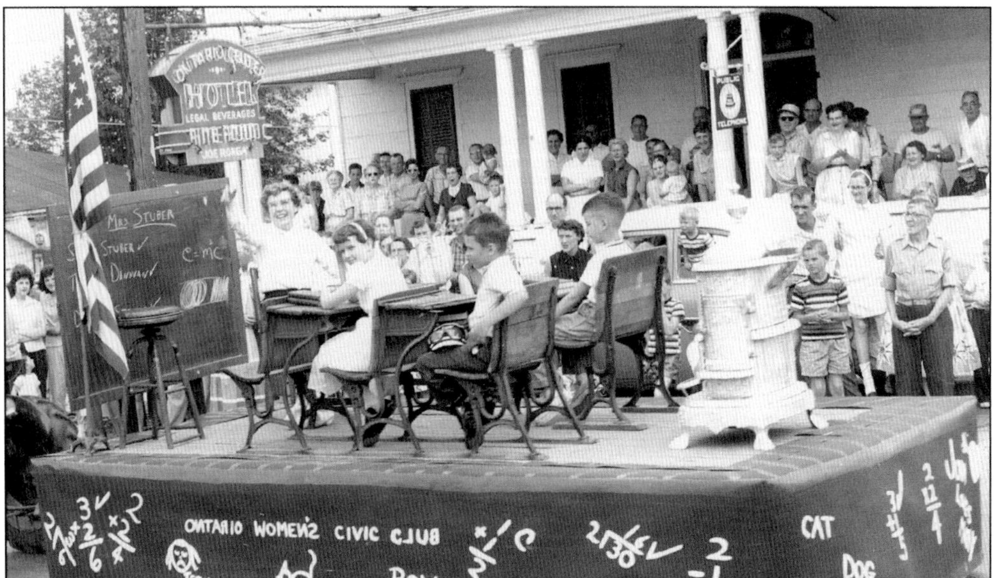

Ontario celebrated its sesquicentennial in 1957. One of the events was a huge parade down Main Street on the Fourth of July. It drew an audience of between 15,000 and 20,000 people and had about 50 parade units. One of the floats was created by the Ontraio Women's Civic Club. Organized in 1947, this group's purpose is to make Ontario a better community by enhancing the cultural, social, and civic development.

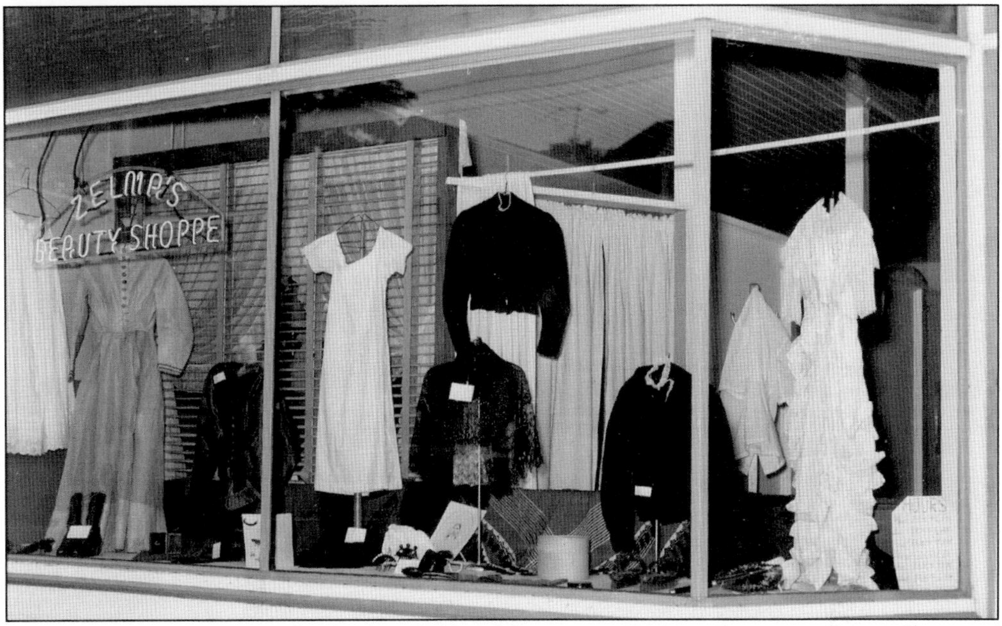

Local businesses were involved. Here Zelma Liljenguist's Beauty Shoppe is shown decorated with old-fashioned clothing. The Ontario Chamber of Commerce has been actively involved in the town since 1928. Some of the achievements of this group are the renumbering of the homes and lots in town, the purchasing of the "Welcome to Ontario" signs, and Christmas street decorations and banners.

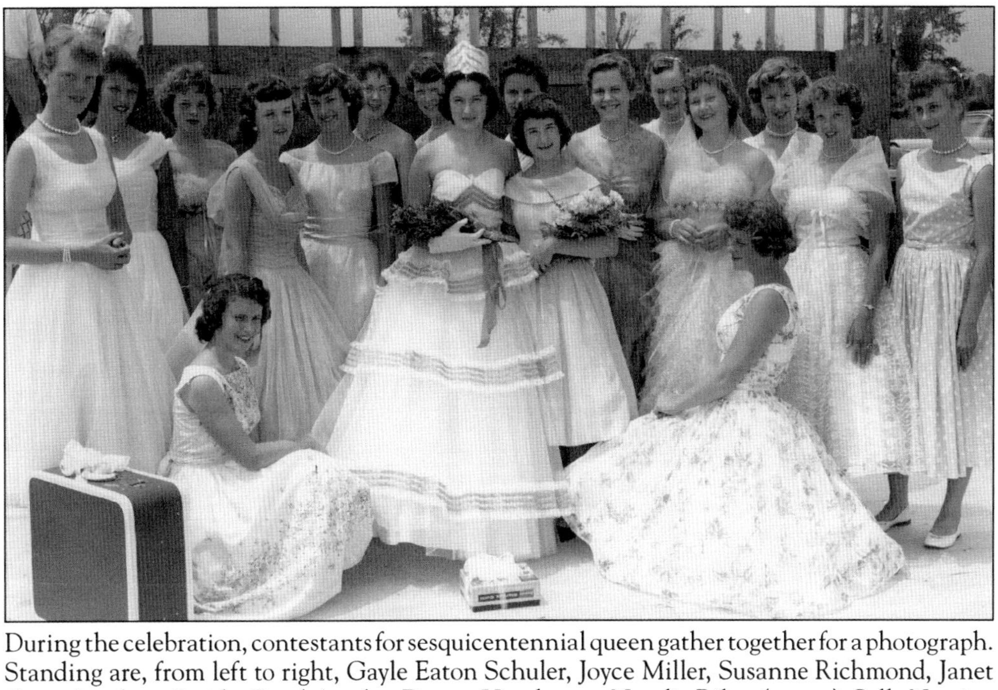

During the celebration, contestants for sesquicentennial queen gather together for a photograph. Standing are, from left to right, Gayle Eaton Schuler, Joyce Miller, Susanne Richmond, Janet Cone, Marlene Smith, Carol Amsler, Donna Henderson, Natalie Riker (queen), Sally Nortier, Joan Thompson, Phillis Serafine, Nancy Williams, Judy Clark, Diane Lancy, Beverly Miller, and unidentified. The two who are kneeling are Karen Hack and Michele Carey.

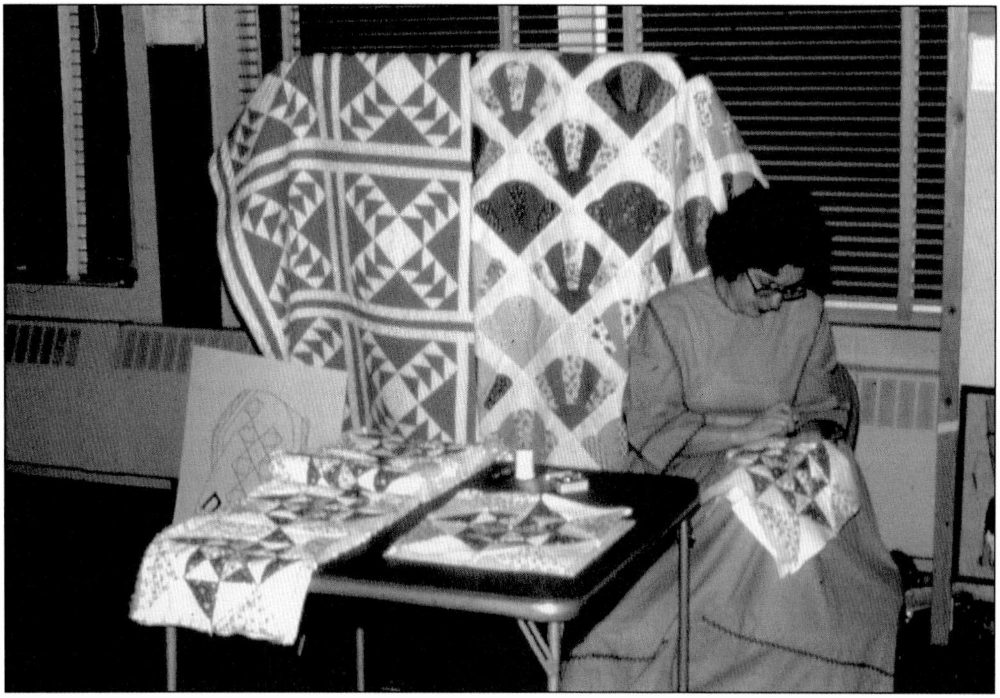

Quilters demonstrated how to piece together and sew a quilt. Quilting, in various forms, has been done since Egyptian times. There are many ways to create a quilt, with piecework only one form.

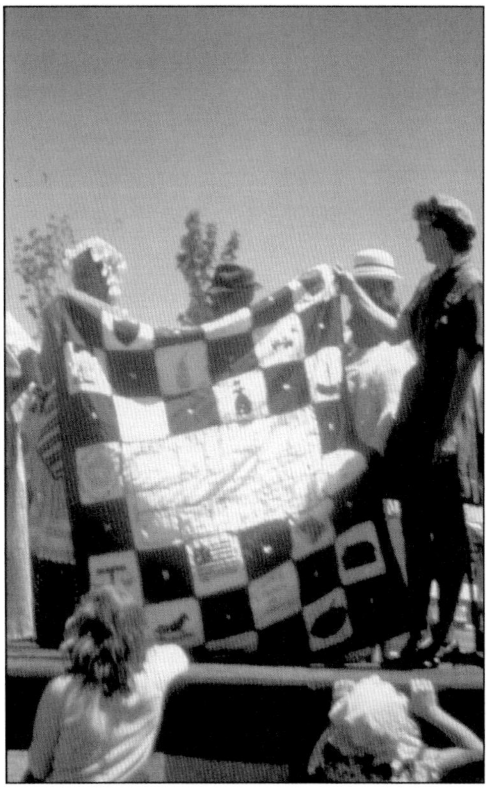

The quilt being held up was made by Girl Scouts who designed and donated it to the Ontario Historical Society. It is on display at the Warner House at Heritage Square.

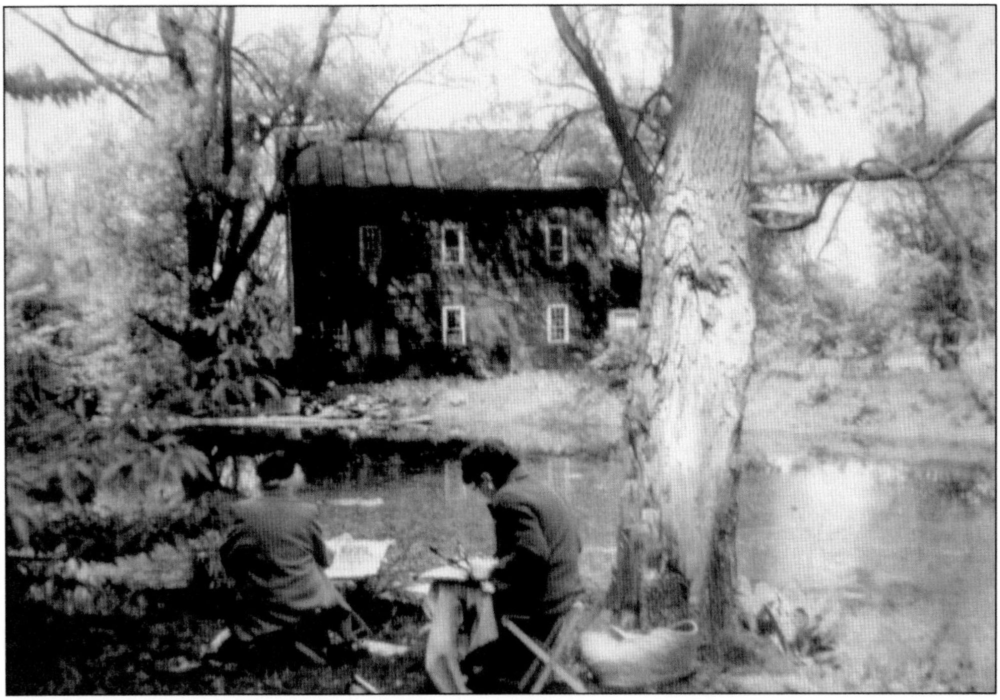

Artists from near and far gathered to paint the historic mill in Fruitland. Photographs and paintings are the only reminders of this mill, which was destroyed in a windstorm in 1972.

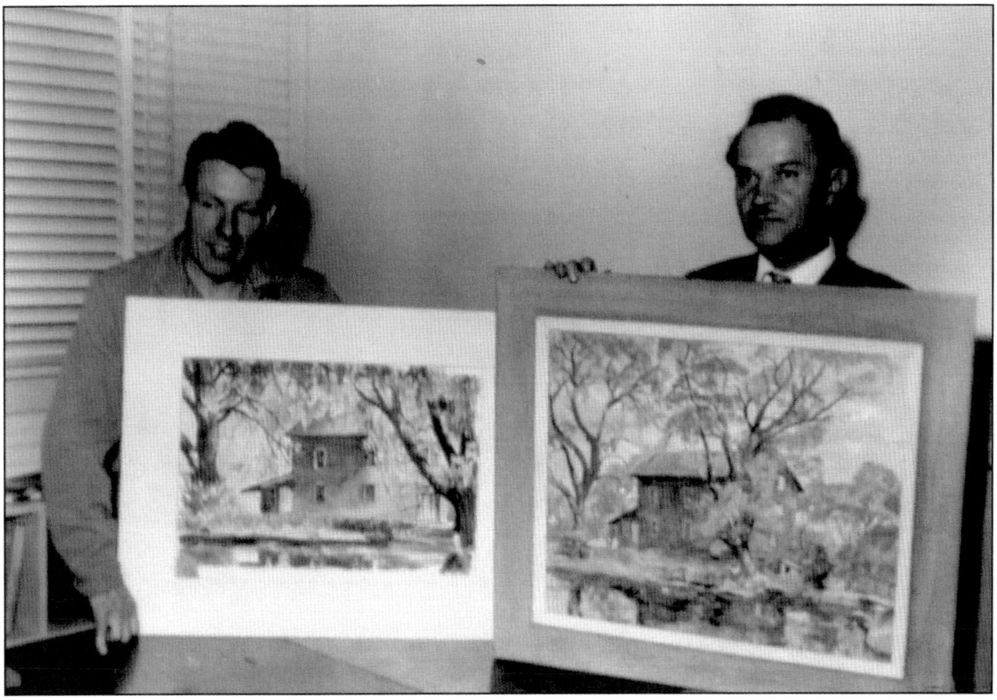

Here members of the Rochester Art Club show off two of the paintings done during the sesquicentennial celebration. The Ontario Art Club was organized in October 1973. It held its first art show on June 15, 1974, with 100 works of art done by 29 local artists.

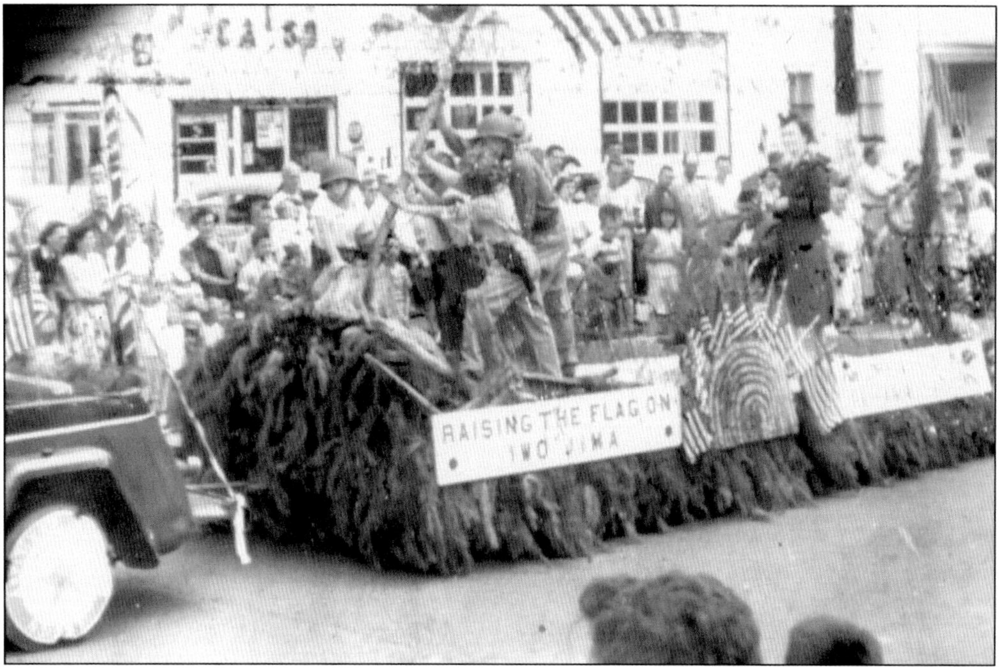

This float depicts the raising of the flag on Iwo Jima. It was created by the Myers-Ingraham Post No. 428 of the American Legion Auxiliary. The auxiliary was formed in 1948 with a membership of 19 people. Only wives, mothers, or sisters of the legionnaires are eligible for membership in the auxiliary.

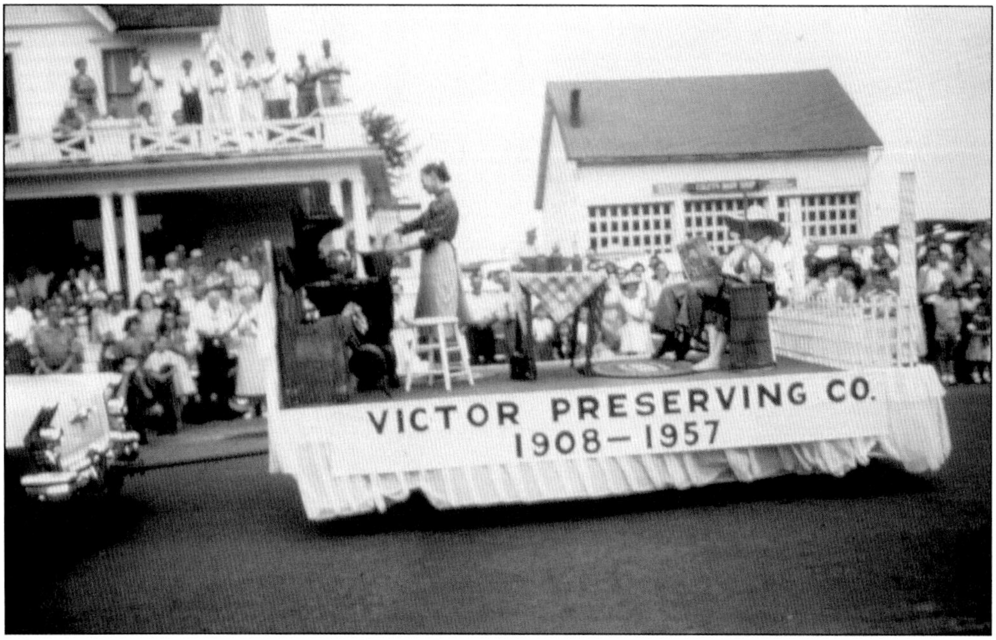

The Victor Preserving Company had a float that demonstrated the old-fashioned method of home canning. In 1920, after the death of her husband, Helen Tobin carried on the canning business and was the only woman president of a canning factory in the United States. The company continues to be run by the Tobin family.

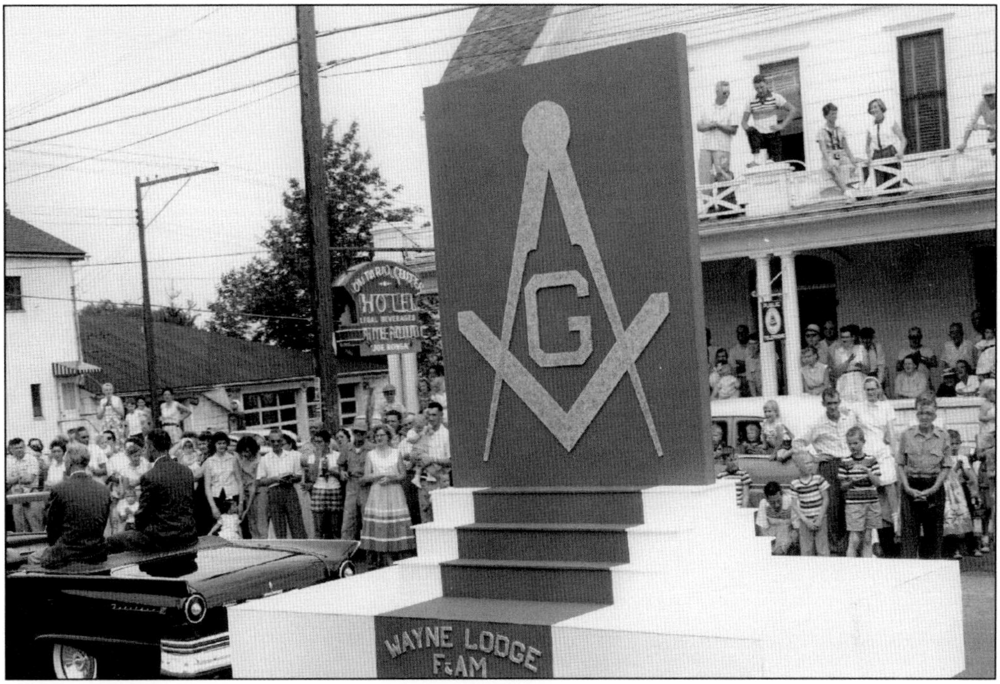

The Masonic lodge celebrated its centennial year in 1957 and participated in the parade with this float depicting the symbol of the Masons. In 2007, the group will again celebrate its founding with ceremonies during the summer.

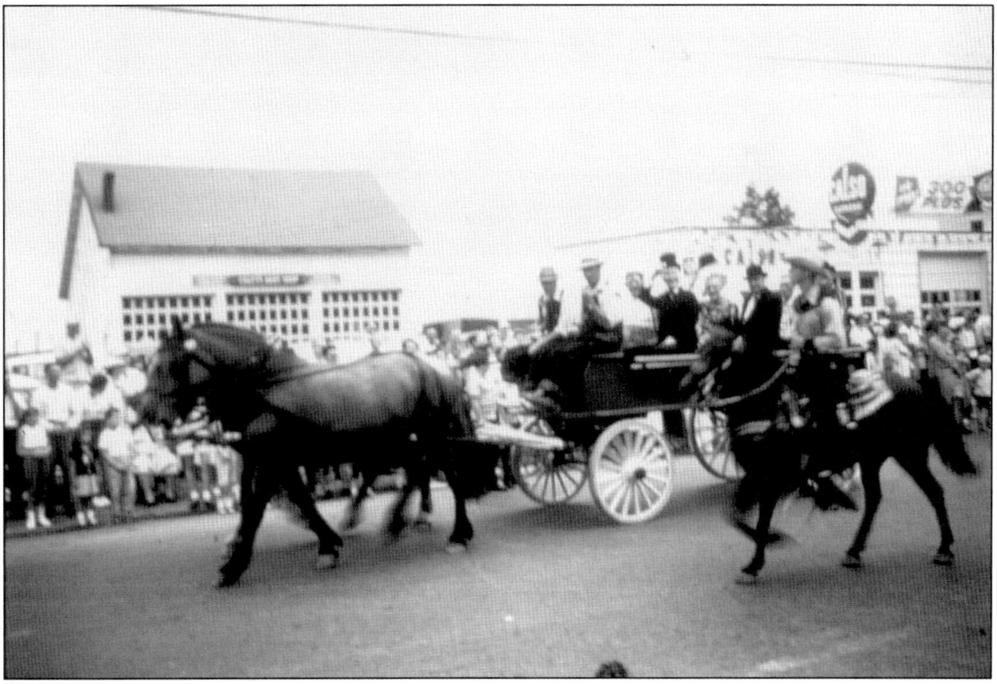
The Ontario town board members rode in a democrat wagon. Shown here, they are tipping their hats as they passed the reviewing stand. In 1957, the town supervisor was Francis T. Wallace and the clerk was Marion Biviano.

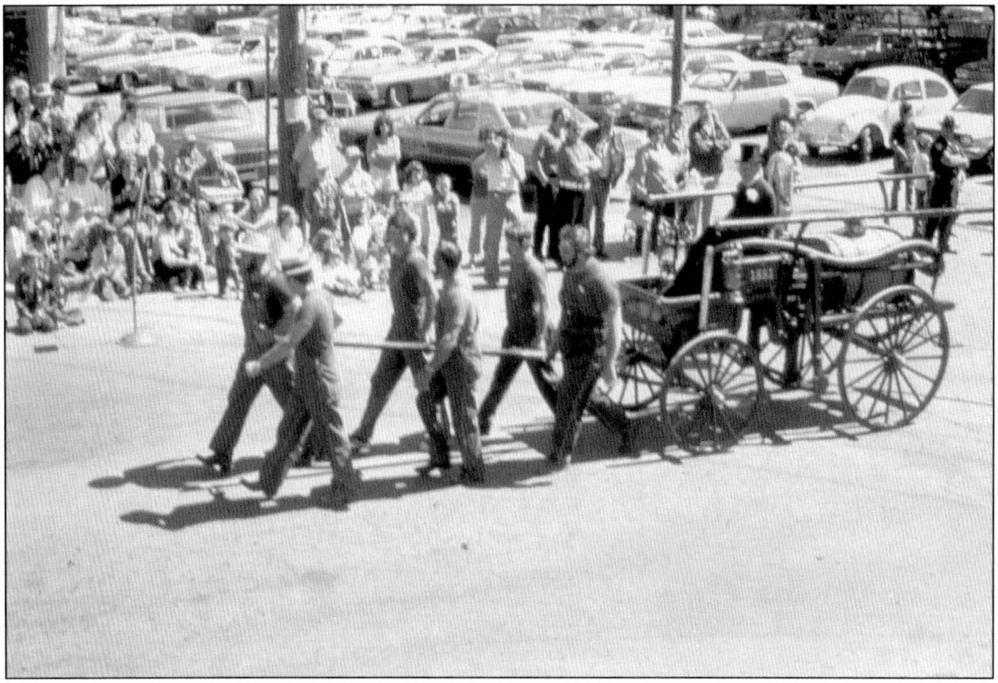

Firemen are shown here pulling a handcart demonstrating the way fires were once fought. The Ontario Fire Company was started in 1907 and purchased its first horse-drawn fire engine in 1909.

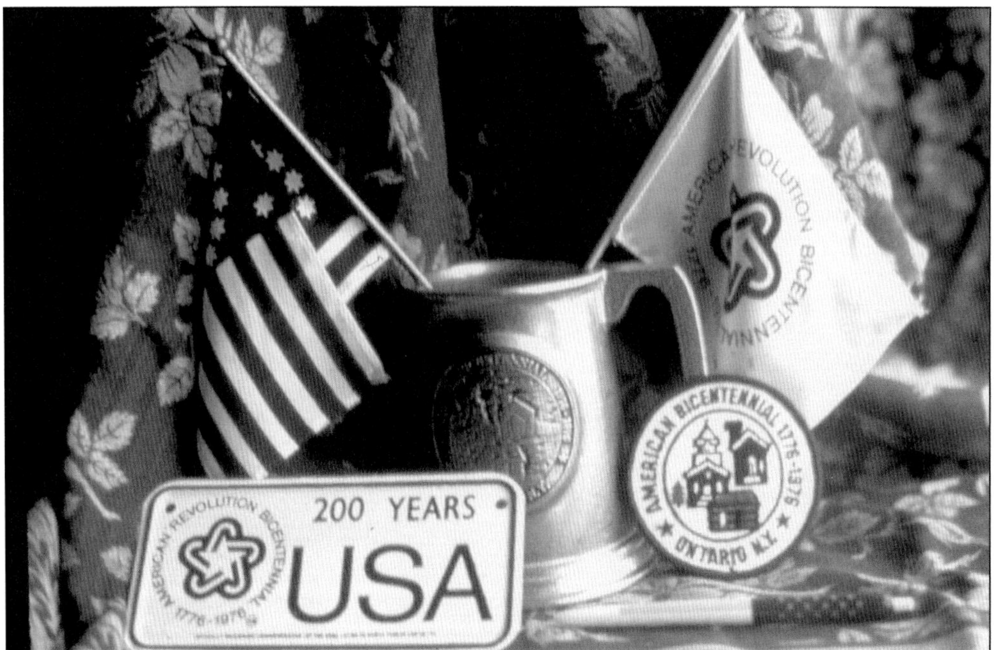

Not only did the people of Ontario celebrate their own history but the townspeople worked together to celebrate the country's bicentennial. In 1976, Ontario was given the designation of an official Bicentennial Town.

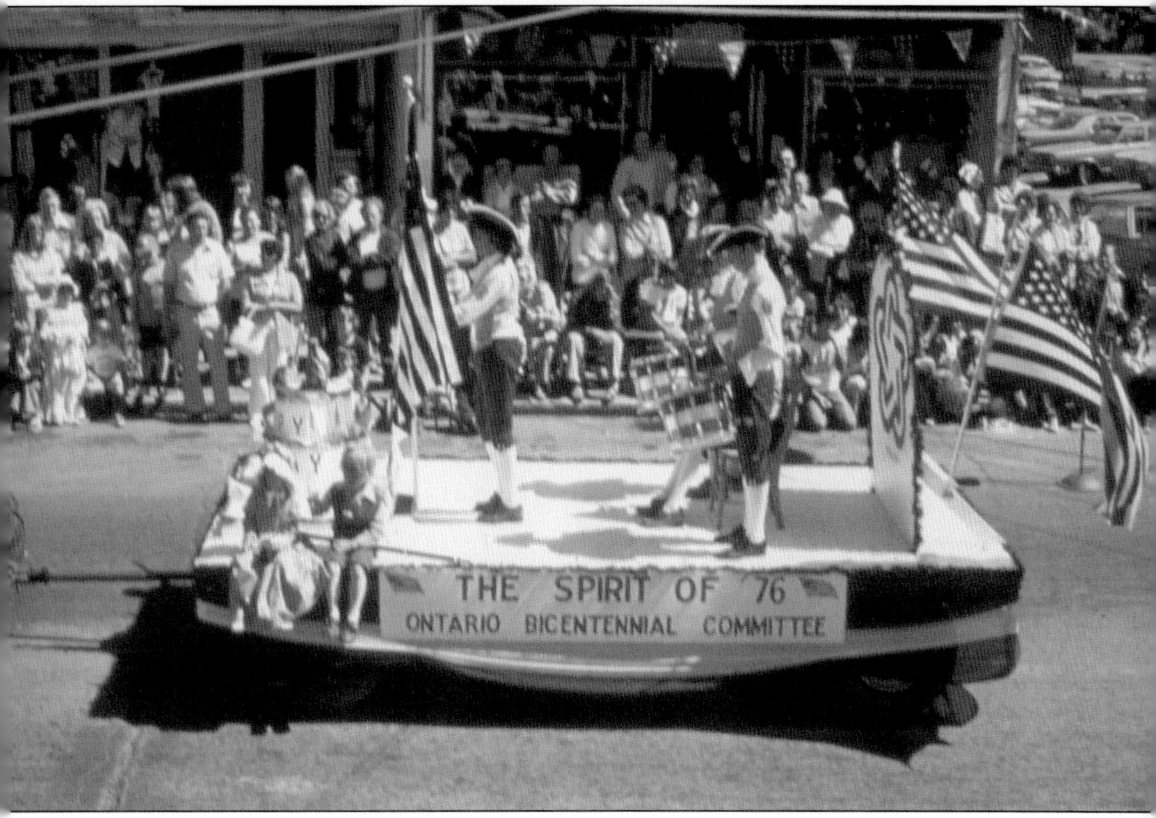

In July 1976, there was a parade to celebrate the event. Here is the float of the Ontario Bicentennial Committee. In 2007, Ontario celebrates its own bicentennial. Once again this community of good neighbors is gathering together to remember the town's 200-year-old history and will continue to work together to pave the way to the future.